HOLLYWOOD BOHEMIA

Also by Rob Leicester Wagner

Red Ink, White Lies: The Rise and Fall of Los Angeles Newspapers, 1920-1960

Witness to a Century (with Joe Blackstock)

Sleeping Giant: A Pictorial History of the Inland Empire

Firehouses

Style and Speed

Fabulous Fins of the Fifties

HOLLYWOOD BOHEMIA

The Roots of Progressive Politics
in
Rob Wagner's Script

ROB LEICESTER WAGNER

JANAWAY PUBLISHING
Santa Maria, California

Copyright © 2016, Rob Leicester Wagner

ALL RIGHTS RESERVED.
No part of this publication may be reproduced, stored in a retrieval system, or
transmitted in any form or by any
means whatsoever, whether electronic, mechanical,
magnetic recording, or photocopying, without the
prior written approval of the Copyright holder
or Publisher, excepting brief quotations
for inclusion in book reviews.

Published by:

Janaway Publishing, Inc.
732 Kelsey Ct.
Santa Maria, California 93454
(805) 925-1038
www.janawaygenealogy.com

2016

Library of Congress Control Number: 2016940290

ISBN: 978-1-59641-369-6

Cover photograph:
From left, Upton Sinclair, Charlie Chaplin and Rob Wagner. Taken on the set of
"Shoulder Arms," Chaplin Studios, Hollywood, California, in 1918.
Copyright © Roy Export Company Establishment

Made in the United States of America

To my wife, Sabria, and my daughter, Emily.

CONTENTS

	Introduction	1
Chapter One	*"Evils of Feudalism"*	9
Chapter Two	*In Search of a Voice*	21
Chapter Three	*"Bovine of Intellect"*	37
Chapter Four	*"Yours, for the Revolution!"*	52
Chapter Five	*"A Disastrous Adventure in Experimental Sociology"*	67
Chapter Six	*Ye Ed and Ye Real Ed*	77
Chapter Seven	*"Wagner is a dangerous man"*	87
Chapter Eight	*"Public censorship is killing bad pictures"*	107
Chapter Nine	*"Some little idiotic magazine"*	129
Chapter Ten	*"Beverly Hills Scratch Sheet"*	155
	Afterword	180
	Acknowledgments	183

Endnotes	187
Index	207
About the Author	219

INTRODUCTION

———•◆•———

Rob Wagner was in crisis. During the first week of December in 1919 he was the chief object of a Los Angeles County Grand Jury investigation into allegations of sedition. During the previous three years he had supported the antiwar effort before America's entry into the European conflict only to run afoul of Woodrow Wilson's Sedition Act of 1918. [1] [2]

Free artistic expression in movies dramatizing the horrors of war gave way to jingoistic patriotism. Film studios, under pressure from George Creel's Committee on Public Information in the Wilson administration, scrambled to turn out propaganda films in support of American policies. Only a year before his summons before the grand jury, Wagner had compiled a file on film censorship on local, state and federal levels. He found movies depicting "class struggle" and antiwar sentiments faced greater restrictions than films with crime, sex and violence. The Sedition Act had crushed dissent across the United States and Department of Justice raids swept up many leftists who were jailed on charges of subverting the war effort. [3] [4]

Wagner was furious, frustrated and apprehensive. His father was part of the Union forces during the Civil War. His uncle fought bravely for the Sixth Minnesota Volunteers in the Dakota Wars. His brother died while serving in the Navy during the Spanish-American War. His two cousins, Blake and Jack Wagner, were combat cinematographers in the Great

War. And although five generations removed from Germany, even his name, *Wagner,* was suspect.

Wagner, an avowed socialist, often had been labeled a "parlor Bolshevik" because of his sympathies for the Russian Revolution. Like many members of the Socialist Party in 1917 he was also a pacifist, but he generally kept his criticisms of the United States government low key. His downfall was his vocal defense of the men and women who were critical of the government and informants who reported his German sympathies. For Wagner was a constitutionalist and firm believer in the Bill of Rights. Freedom of expression and due process were the cornerstones of a fair and responsive government. Civil liberties should not be suspended because they were inconvenient during wartime.

His appearance before the grand jury and the prospect of jail and fines threatened to derail his career as a journalist and future as a motion picture director and writer. Since 1910, when unionist brothers John and James McNamara dealt the socialist movement a blow when they confessed to bombing the *Los Angeles Times* building, Wagner was careful to keep separate his interest in film as an art form and his political activities.

When he began writing about the film industry for the *Saturday Evening Post* and other national magazines in 1915 not once did he inject progressive issues into his coverage. While his socialist colleagues produced labor movement propaganda films, such as Frank E. Wolfe's seminal film *From Dusk to Dawn* (1913), he kept his participation at a minimum. Wagner, who began his career as an artist in Detroit, appreciated Wolfe's vision championing progressive causes by reaching millions of Americans through entertaining but message-driven films. But he also recognized that such films diluted the new art form. [5]

Wagner believed in the collectivism of socialism. He worked with socialist leader Job Harriman in 1913 and 1914 to create the Llano del Rio, the utopian community established in the Mojave Desert. He also was an associate editor for *The Western Comrade*. The magazine published numerous articles on Llano del Rio and other socialist projects, which all eventually came to naught.

However, his main interest was not collective socialism but its application to the individual, which stemmed from his experiences as an artist in his hometown of Detroit and later as an illustrator for the liberal literary magazine *The Criterion* in New York City. After studying art in Paris in 1903 and 1904, Wagner returned to Detroit to produce a series of portraits, many of them life-sized, for wealthy clients. He chafed at his subjects' insistence in putting a monetary value on his art. Their attitude dictated the size of the portrait and how he approached the subject in his painting, preventing him from establishing his own vision of the individual. He felt that his art was compromised even before he began a project. Wagner quickly realized the Victorian standards of the day victimized his art. As far as his clients were concerned, he, the artist, was answerable to them. There was no equal footing in commerce. The wealthy established the terms and conditions of individuals they employed. The upper class dictating the lives of the lower class that served them and consequently affecting the work of the lower class was a prevailing irritation for him throughout his career.

The nuts and bolts of collectivism in which every citizen had a stake in factories, farms and the mass production of goods was all well and good. But Wagner's belief in socialism was more visceral and personal. As naïve as it may sound today, many progressives in the first two decades of the twentieth century believed that uncompromised pursuit of art was a form of socialism. His commitment to this ideology coalesced when he joined *The Criterion* in 1898. The magazine's staff created *The Criterion* Independent Theater Group, a forerunner to the New Theater, which staged plays with progressive themes. Thus, the potential of filmmaking as a pure art form was tantalizing to Wagner. Yet he recognized that wearing socialism on his sleeve would in itself taint his own films during the 1920s. To the audience he would be either a socialist making movies or an unencumbered artist making movies. He chose the latter. [6]

By writing about motion pictures, and later directing and writing, without identifying himself as a socialist, Wagner kept his credibility as a participant in films. At the same time, he could work behind the scenes to further progressive causes inside the industry. Rather than writing about films as a socialist, which would limit his audience to a progressive readership, he could further liberal themes to reach a wider audience without the burdensome label.

He used this approach with great success when he founded his magazine, *Rob Wagner's Script*, in 1929 and established the publication on socialist principles. He did not pay his writers, believing that writing for monetary compensation would inhibit the truth of their writing. If the goal of a writer were to tell a story first and then receive a check second, then the content of the article would be compromised. *Script* provided authors with opportunities to express themselves freely not available in other publications beholden to big advertisers. This philosophy attracted nationally known writers like Edgar Rice Burroughs, William Saroyan, Dalton Trumbo, Rupert Hughes, Ray Bradbury and William C. deMille. [7]

Wagner was all too aware of the pitfalls of writers who wrote for national publications. From 1915 until his appearance before the grand jury at the end of 1919, he had a lucrative contract with the *Saturday Evening Post* to cover the film industry in a light and humorous manner. But his editors shut him down once he approached topics more seriously. When Los Angeles County investigators subpoenaed Wagner in their probe of radicals, the *Post* refused further story submissions except for one in 1926. [8]

This experience led Wagner to refuse advertising in *Script* from writers, directors, actors and film studios, any of which could mount pressure on the magazine to blue pencil articles or kill a story outright. Thus, *Script* was the only socialist publication in the United States in the 1930s without ever really identifying itself as such. Of course the magazine's profits were modest. Its circulation was regional, not national, and it never exceeded 50,000. In 1934 Wagner played with the idea to publish *Script* nationally, but ultimately rejected it because the magazine would lose control of its socialist foundation. National distribution meant big advertisers and attracting top-notch writers with big paychecks. Honest, undiluted writing would be the first casualty. [9]

Although limited in circulation, *Script* still managed a national reach. It was the first film magazine to address animal cruelty in motion pictures. It campaigned against the implementation of community standards established by amateurs to censor films. It championed the formation of actors, directors and writers unions to impose fair working conditions. Indeed, the magazine was an early – if not the sole – advocate in film media for organizing writers and directors guilds. Wagner also recognized that the formation of the Academy for Motion Picture Arts and Sciences was a transparent ploy by studio bosses to counter guild organizers by offering awards to film workers. Fellow socialist Upton Sinclair found fair coverage of his 1934 campaign for governor in *Script* when virtually every newspaper and magazine in the country demonized him. [10] [11]

Few mainstream American magazines in the 1930s wrote favorably about the Soviet Union, but *Script* covered the Russian education system among other aspects of Soviet life. Still, it was no sycophant, giving space to writers who found the Stalinist regime repugnant in its treatment of Jews and other minorities. However, the magazine's critics were justified in their complaints that *Script* loved Stalin a little too much, especially after the regime's murderous purges were well documented. This was particularly apparent when *Script* published an exclusive, but hagiographic, interview with Leon Trotsky while he was in exile in Mexico in 1938. After Wagner's death in 1942 his wife, Florence, assumed complete editorial control and published favorable articles on communist personalities. [12] [13] [14] [15]

To its credit, *Script* balanced its coverage of radicals with groundbreaking journalism rarely seen in California in the 1940s. It covered the plight of Japanese Americans uprooted from their homes and sent to relocation camps during World War II and wrote with empathy of the Mexican American community during the Zoot-Suit riots of 1943. *Script* was the only literary publication in the film industry to expose the resurgence of the Ku Klux Klan in Los Angeles and local government's housing discrimination policies against Native Americans.
16 17 18 19

Script got away with its leftist editorial policies in a highly anti-communist, anti-leftist climate fueled by the House on Un-American Activities Committee (HUAC) because it cloaked sensitive issues in humor. It poked fun at institutions, but was never mean-spirited. It never engaged in the gossipy blackmail employed by newspaper columnists Louella Parsons, Hedda Hopper and the notorious Jimmie Fidler to solicit a scoop. Wagner built his reputation on relationships, not promises and favors. Those relationships included an eclectic lineup of friends such as leftists William deMille, Upton Sinclair, Charlie Chaplin, Max Eastman and Sergei Eisenstein, but also the conservative or apolitical like Hughes, director Frank Capra and Universal Studios chief Carl Laemmle.

By straddling this fine line of radical politics and mass entertainment, Wagner managed to help infuse Hollywood with a liberal conscience. Although the film industry exemplified capitalism at its worst – or best depending on one's point of view – it still responded, albeit kicking and screaming all the way, to employee rights.

This book examines the origins of Wagner's political awakening and how he ultimately helped influence the Hollywood leftist intellectual community during the period after the collapse of the Socialist Party in the 1920s and before the rise of communist screenwriters in the 1930s and 1940s. Indeed, his campaigns for fairer treatment of studio employees and actors and other liberal causes during the silent era served as a bridge between the older progressive movement and the "message" films of class struggle produced by writers and directors sympathetic to communism. And with the founding of *Script*, Wagner had a wider audience to further those goals.

CHAPTER ONE

"Evils of Feudalism"

Detroit, Rob Wagner's birthplace, in the late nineteenth century was a provincial town with big city pretensions. It had the makings of a major metropolitan city, but it had no identity.

Shipping and lumber were the primary industries with the Detroit River an important transportation route after the Civil War. The construction of locks in 1855 at Sault Ste. Marie allowing ships to bring copper ore and iron to the city was a major boost to the city's economy. But it would be more than fifty years before that transportation access resulted in automobile production that made Detroit the epicenter of corporate America for more than three-quarters of a century.

In 1870 Detroit's potential remained unknown. It was a city of 79,577 souls, making it the eighteenth largest in the country, but it couldn't compete against the port cities on the East Coast. It also didn't have a meatpacking industry and railway terminus that Chicago possessed to attract thousands of workers to jobs each year. Chicago's population was more than three times larger than Detroit's. [1]

What Detroit did have was close proximity to Windsor, a border town just across the river in Canada, which served as a jumping off point for thousands of Canadians immigrating to the United States. By 1870 nearly forty-five percent of Detroit's population was foreign-born. As early as 1850 Canadians accounted for 5.5 percent of Michigan's population and made up eleven percent of all residents in Wayne County and Detroit. [2]

Rob Wagner's father, Robert, was one such Canadian, arriving in Detroit in February 1862 at the age of twenty-one to join the United States Military Telegraph as a civilian telegrapher to support the Union Army during the Civil War. Robert emigrated from Dickinson's Landing, a small village and once an important boat stop for St. Lawrence River traffic from Cornwall in Stormont County, Ontario. He left Canada for the same reasons many men of his age: the dearth of jobs and the severe, bone-crushing winters.

Robert was the fifth of six children born to Daniel Wagner and Rhoda Juliet Hawley. Following Rhoda's death in 1843, Daniel married her sister, Eliza, giving Robert five more brothers and sisters. Daniel, who possessed little ambition, owned one of five general stores operating at Dickinson's Landing. The Grand Trunk Railway opened in 1856 and established a station about one mile north of the village, making stagecoach and riverboat stops at Dickinson's Landing from Cornwall unnecessary and the village irrelevant.

Daniel shuttered his store and moved with Eliza to Blue Earth County, Minnesota, with their three sons, John Henry, twenty-one years old, eight-year-old Ira, who would die in 1862; two-year-old William Wallace, and two daughters, six-year-old Imogene, and four-year-old Arietta. Daniel first settled in the small town of Vernon Center, but during the Dakota wars in 1862 he moved to safety in Mankato where he established himself as an insurance agent.

The move for Daniel Wagner to Minnesota wasn't an easy decision. The Wagners had fallen on the wrong side of history and had seen their potential as American landowners crushed during the Revolutionary War. Originally from the Palatine region of Germany, Daniel's grandfather, Jacob Waggoner (spelled variously as Wagoner, Wegner and Wagner) immigrated to America at the age of fourteen in 1756 by way of Holland and England, with England sponsoring his journey.

The Wagners made their home at Stone Arabia in upstate New York. Jacob spoke Dutch, indicating his family had spent at least one generation in Holland before continuing to the New World. At the outbreak of the Revolutionary War, the Wagners remained loyal to the British, and by 1777 had been hounded from their home by rebels. Jacob, by then about thirty-five years old, had a farmed twenty acres, had a house and barn, five head of cattle, twenty sheep and two mares. He lost it all. The family found refuge in Canada with Jacob, as well as his sons Jacob Jr. and Henry, Daniel's father. The three men joined Sir John Johnson's King's Royal Regiment to fight against the rebels.

At the end of the war in 1784, the British government awarded each veteran 200 acres at Cornwall for his service. Their children also each received 200 acres once they reached maturity. Loyalist veterans were expected to farm the land, but many second generation Wagners opted to sell off their parcels and use the proceeds to operate their own businesses. Daniel had opened his store. A brother, Benjamin, owned and operated a successful hotel in Cornwall.[3]

Returning to America, even two generations removed, was a strange experience. For many Canadians who chose to make their home in the United States, particularly those returning to upstate New York, it seemed as though they were entering enemy territory. Daniel must have had the same misgivings in Minnesota, but his choices in 1856 were limited. Blue Earth County's population would grow from 4,803 people in 1860 to 17,302 in 1870, a staggering 260 percent increase. Prospects for employment there were much more realistic than remaining in a riverside village unable to draw enough traffic to sustain itself economically.[4]

Robert had worked for his father at Dickinson's Landing. Although barely weighing 150 pounds and standing about 5 feet, 5 inches tall, he was known, along with his brother, John Henry, as a "Wagner broadback" for his ability to carry two shoulders of large salt sacks while working at the store. When the family immigrated to Minnesota, fifteen-year-old Robert stayed behind to strike out on his own, eventually joining the Grand Trunk Railway as a telegrapher. Ten months after the outbreak of war he traveled with his friend, John Thomas, from London, Ontario, to Windsor, then across the river to Detroit to join the US Military Telegraph.

Initially under the command of General Don Carlos Buell, Robert laid telegraph wire in advance of Union lines and operated the telegraph at the battles of Shiloh and Perryville. At Shiloh, Robert recorded an urgent message, and after decoding it he left his tent and ran up to an officer to deliver it. At that moment a Confederate shell struck the officer in the head, decapitating him as the bloody stump fell into Robert's arms. The trauma remained with him, but he refused to discuss any of his experiences with his family after the war. Following Perryville, Robert telegraphed and laid wire at the Chattanooga Campaign, including the battles of Lookout Mountain and at Nashville.

At the end of 1864, Robert returned to Detroit. He took up residence at a boarding house at #18 Lafayette and resumed working for Grand Trunk out of the Detroit station. In 1868 he became a naturalized US citizen.

Although Rob Wagner was not close to his grandfather Daniel, he understood at an early age the fickleness of governments' treatment of property rights during unstable times and the consequences many families paid to remain true to their convictions. It must have seemed to the young boy growing up in Detroit and hearing of his grandfather's slide from business owner to an insurance agent that the family's economic progress while in Canada had been frozen for eighty-five years. The family had managed relative economic success only through the hard work of Robert and his recognition of the limitations of his own father.

Closer to Rob was his maternal grandfather, Matthew Belsaigne Hornibrook. Matthew's story was a mix of hard luck and sacrifice. It was also a cautionary tale of how Old European values had little relevance in the newly settled North America. Listening to Matthew's stories of his youth, Rob received his first exposure to a world where the working class and often the devoutly religious were at the mercy of the ruling class. He also learned from Matthew's own experiences in attempting to settle in Canada and carve out a living for himself, that the ruling class, as led by the "gentlemen" of the day, was not competent to ensure that one could lead a fulfilling and productive life.

The Hornibrooks fought in the Battle of Hastings in 1066 and the British rewarded their service with large tracts of land in County Cork, Ireland. Matthew's wife, Rob's maternal grandmother, was Charlotte Mannix Greaves, who came from a family with a long military tradition in Lancashire, England, and made their home Cork.

Charlotte had seven brothers and sisters. One brother, George Hudson Greaves, was a lieutenant colonel and commanding officer in the Sixty-fourth Liverpool Irish Rifle Volunteers and served nearly half of his thirty-year career in India. Another, John Henry Greaves, was a highly decorated paymaster and purser for the British Royal Navy. A third brother, Leycester Greaves, was a lace-maker in County Limerick employing 240 women at his factory at its peak of operation in 1845.

Matthew, born in 1805 in Duncareen, County Cork, was the son of Thomas Hornibrook and Mary Jane Belsaigne (Belesaigne is the more common spelling among the branches, but also occasionally spelled Bellesaigne), a Huguenot whose family originated in the villages of

Castrès and Albi, Tarn, France. Mary Jane's grandfather, Mathieu, was a merchant for a prosperous woolen cloth factory, but France in the mid-eighteenth century persecuted Huguenot Protestants. Several Belsaigne branches refused to renounce their religious faith following the Treaty of Nantes and faced two stark choices in fleeing the country: travel north to Amsterdam, an important shipping center where families could re-establish their commercial interests, or settle in Ireland where religious freedom was guaranteed. Mathieu saw Ireland as his salvation, helping organize the Irish Huguenot Settlement Plan of 1751-1753 to finance the journey to Ireland for refugees.

At Inishannon, County Cork, the Church of Ireland gave the Huguenots permission to have services and receive the sacrament at an annex of the church. Upon his death in 1761, Mathieu Belsaigne's headstone at the Inishannon Cemetery read, "Sacrificed his fortunes, country and all earthly considerations to his God and Religion." Mathieu's son, Jean Belsaigne, Mary Jane's father, attempted to recover the family's property in France after the Belsaignes had settled in County Cork, but he found strangers living in their home and no recourse for financial compensation.

If one were to sketch an extreme Irish stereotype, Rob's grandfather, Matthew Belsaigne Hornibrook, would be the perfect subject. In his later years he was balding with a long gray beard. He spoke with a heavy Irish brogue, was chivalrous, quick tempered and had a habit of challenging men, perceived to have insulted him, to gun duels. He once shot off the finger of his boyhood friend, Tom Gillman, and Gillman shot Matthew in the leg while practicing for a duel. When one young man failed to show up for another contest, Matthew Hornibrook denounced him as a "blackguard" and "scoundrel," no light allegations in early nineteenth century Ireland. When he was well into his eighties he attended a military parade in York (since renamed Toronto) with his daughter, Bessie Jane, and Bessie's sisters-in-law. While the women stood on a ladder to catch a better view of the soldiers, a young man attempted to look up their dresses. Enraged, Matthew landed a roundhouse punch to the side of the man's head, knocking him senseless.

Matthew and Charlotte married in 1834 in Bandon, County Cork, and had Thomas in 1835, Bessie Jane in 1836, and John "Jack" Henry Greaves in 1838. Given the Greaves' military background, Charlotte was a rigid disciplinarian with her children, who all escaped the Hornibrook household at the earliest possible moment once they came of age. Her martinet approach to child-rearing heavily influenced how Rob's mother, Mary, developed her relationship with her own children. She administered discipline on rare occasions and only with a light touch.

The Hornibrooks owned land and had tenants in Bandon, Kilbrough and Duncareen among other areas in County Cork. But by 1840, the British generated revenue through an oppressive tax system that included taxing the number of dogs individuals owned, the number of windows and doors constructed in dwellings and even water running through property they owned. Matthew and Charlotte decided to try their luck in Canada. They arrived in Toronto on July 1, 1840, and eight days later James Hudson Hornibrook was born.

Matthew, an accomplished horseman, never performed a hard day's labor in his life. He lived as gentleman in Ireland and he expected to do the same in Canada. He moved his family south of Toronto to Mississauga and bought enough acreage to have tenants work the land while he reaped an income from the rents. Matthew, however, had no grasp of frontier life. Land was so cheap that anybody could buy it. He could find no tenants to work his property. Rob described Matthew as "always ready to ride, but his business efforts were pathetic. He was the victim of a stupid system (in Ireland) that echoed the evils of feudalism. 'Gentleman' did not work in those days – and it was all right in Ireland, but it was disastrous in Canada in the early 40s."[5]

After a decade of failure and huge financial losses, Charlotte persuaded her husband to move to the larger, safer and far more sensible town of

Oakville. There, a decade after their arrival from Ireland, Rob's mother, Mary Leicester Hornibrook, was born on August 7, 1850. Although his ambitions as a gentlemen farmer were dashed by reality, Matthew received enough income from property he held in County Cork to allow him to pursue a leisurely life in Canada.

Like her brothers and sister, eighteen-year-old Mary wasted little time in escaping her mother's oppressive discipline, marrying Robert Wagner on October 1, 1868, at the Holy Trinity Church in Toronto. Children quickly followed, all of who were born in Detroit, with the eldest, Charlotte, arriving in 1869 and James Richard Hawley following in 1870. Rob was born on August 2, 1872. Clarence Rangley was an unplanned, but a very welcome addition, in 1880. [6]

Robert left telegraphy to open his own business as a railway ticket agent while Mary pursued a career as a ceramic artist and had a number of important art showings in Detroit, New York and later Paris. The couple first owned a residence at 105 Abbott Street, and then moved to 420 Second Avenue before finding a well-appointed residence at 2050 Woodward Avenue in 1888. While living on Abbott, the Wagners did better than most of their working-class neighbors of dressmakers, store clerks and plumbers. According to the 1870 federal census, their home was valued at about $3,000 (worth about $53,000 today), with about $2,000 in personal property (valued at about $35,000 today). By the time Rob was seven years old his father added tobacco sales to his business and moved his store to 112 Jefferson Avenue, and then to 155 Jefferson. [7]

Although the Wagner family generally lived within the strict societal mores of the late nineteenth century, they didn't always confine themselves to the Victorian standards. Robert was generous almost to a fault in how he raised his children and in his marriage to Mary.

Rob wrote of his father in 1903:

"Unorthodox, but deeply religious, (Robert) found expression for his noblest feelings in his home and secret societies. He was modest to the point of bashfulness, high-strung, nervous, and of exquisite feelings, could not administer punishment and would blush at even a risqué story, abhorred vulgarity and insincerity ... he never scolded but rarely corrected; as children we enjoyed the widest latitude and our house was a refuge for the fellows who for obvious reasons were afraid to go home." [8]

Mary and Charlotte traveled extensively in the late 1870s and for much of the 1880s, crisscrossing the country six months to a year at a time to visit relatives or take in tourist sites. Mary helped her brother, James Hudson Hornibrook, decorate the bedrooms of a mansion he was building in Little Rock, Arkansas, with intricately painted ceramic tiling. On another trip, she and her sister-in-law, Arietta Wagner, built a kiln to produce their ceramic art in a dark and filthy basement of the Mankato post office because it was the only building in town that had a gas line. She fruitlessly hunted in Canada and the American Northwest for her brother, Jack, who would disappear for years at time. Robert encouraged her trips, never protesting or complaining that his wife belonged at home. [9]

Unlike for Mary, the Woodward Avenue home was the center of Robert's life. He did not like to travel, having experienced deprivation far from home at the front during the war. He kept a huge butcher's meat refrigerator in the kitchen and his cellar fully stocked with food. Matthew and Mary's childhood nanny, Kate Champion, lived in the house after Robert's mother-in-law Charlotte Hornibrook's death in 1888. Their kitchen was the center of activity with Jim, Rob, Charlotte and Clarence's friends constantly coming and going. In the rear yard was a menagerie of animals: a cow, chickens, ducks, peacocks and pigeons.

There were few house rules and Robert rarely intervened in his children's affairs. He left the task of discipline to Mary, whose experiences with her own mother made her even less suitable than

Robert to punish her children for misbehavior. Robert abhorred betrayal and was offended when an adult felt compelled to report Jim or Rob's misbehavior. Once, when Rob was a freshman at the University of Michigan, a steward at Robert's club reported that he saw Rob drunk at a Fourth of July celebration. Robert looked at the steward and icily replied, "I don't think that is half so bad as for you to come and tell his father."

On another occasion, Jim came home drunk one night and passed out under a tree in the rear yard. Robert summoned Rob to help him drag Jim into his bedroom. After lying Jim on the bed and undressing him, Rob's father only said, "Please don't tell your mother."

Robert and Mary's *laissez faire* philosophy of child rearing allowed Rob free rein to roam Detroit at will. Rob once joined his friends at another boy's house *after* the boy's parents' party to drink the leftover alcohol. The boys drank themselves sick and sprawled under a table.

It was this experience as a twelve-year-old that formed Rob's attitude about alcohol for the remainder of his life. He indulged in alcohol considerably as a young man, especially while a member of the Sigma Phi fraternity at the University of Michigan. In 1930 he told *The Greek Review* that, "Fraternities were nothing more or less than saloons. I went to college and stayed drunk for four years." [10]

But early in his journalistic career and during his first marriage to Jessie Brodhead he was, for all intent and purposes, a light drinker. However, with his second wife, Florence Welch, Rob fancied himself a wine connoisseur. Like everyone else when the Volstead Act became law in 1920, Rob and Florence stocked up on alcohol. When their supply was exhausted, they chose not to drink again, at least not illegally. After repeal in 1933 they became occasional drinkers.

It was also at about twelve years old that Rob was awakened to the potential of a career in art, if not journalism. As a boy at the onset of puberty, Rob made it a habit to run down to the corner barbershop at Woodward and Jefferson to read the latest edition of the *National Police Gazette*, a forerunner to the tabloid newspapers. Ostensibly a publication devoted to law enforcement news, the *Police Gazette* was a heavily illustrated but lurid publication featuring prostitutes, scantily clad and debauched women, plenty of cleavage and stories reporting on the worst of humanity. And it was a weekly treat for Rob who reported many years later that the *Police Gazette* taught him that women "actually had legs" under those long skirts. Surreptitiously ripping out pages with the best illustrations, Rob posted them on the walls of the hideout he and his friends shared at the edge of downtown. The *Police Gazette* taught him the value of art complementing a story and the power of images in journalism. By this time Rob was sketching and the *Police Gazette* offered instruction on how to illustrate the female form. At twelve or thirteen Rob was too timid to copy the publication's racy illustrations, but it opened the door for him in his early career to use provocative art – not for the purpose of titillation but to sell magazines by using bold colors and female cover subjects.

By the time he reached sixteen years of age in 1888, Rob began to recognize there was a world beyond Detroit and that his hometown had limits in what it could offer a young man coming of age. This was no more apparent when he decided to travel by bicycle to visit his Aunt Bessie, now married to a businessman, Richard Tinning, in Toronto.

Shortly after his sixteenth birthday, Rob's friend, Arthur Hayes, left with his parents on holiday for the summer. He loaned Rob his nickel-plated forty-eight-inch-wheel Columbia Safety bicycle. The Columbia in 1888 was a luxury item for the wealthy that took to riding bicycles for recreation in the numerous parks scattered throughout Detroit. It was also a form of transportation for young men in the pre-automobile age. Women, given the restrictive fashions of the day, rarely had an opportunity to ride the high-wheeled bicycles. Since the price of a Columbia hovered around $130 (about $3,125 today), Rob had to be satisfied with his three-wheeled velocipede, which was more suitable for old men, young children and girls. But in the summer of 1888, he had the entire month to use the Columbia as he wished.

Although in adulthood Rob stood 5 feet, 5 inches tall and weighed between 150 and 160 pounds, at sixteen he was slight, only weighing eight-six pounds and barely reaching 5 feet, 3 inches. He was riding a fifty-pound bike and leg length meant everything on a forty-eight-inch wheeler. He decided to launch his 200-mile trip from Sarnia instead of Windsor because the roads were better. He stuffed $5 in Canadian money in his pocket, a lunch box under the seat and fastened a change of clothes to the handlebar.

Rob stopped at farmhouses along the way for his meals and accommodations. He became something of a celebrity among the young boys who marveled at the nickel-plated monster of bike and the pretty girls who asked him to sign their autograph books. He often added sketches of his journey to his autograph. When he wasn't charming the girls with his art, Scotch collies constantly terrorized him by chasing him down the road, nipping at his heals and determined to upend the machine. Rob initially defended himself with a slingshot and marbles, but realized it was easier, and perhaps more humane, if he just lifted his leg and rested it on the handlebar to avoid bites. Rob arrived at Aunt Bessie's house in three days. He was dirty and tired, but he still had four Canadian dollars in his pocket. [11]

Rob never looked at Detroit in the same way. His father's war experiences, the travel adventures of his mother and sister, Matthew's stories of his hardships in Ireland and Canada, and now Rob's pilgrimage, his journey of self-discovery, to Toronto, rendered Detroit too provincial. At the first opportunity, Rob would find a way out. As the decades passed, Detroit had become a city that stirred so few feelings of nostalgia for Rob Wagner that, after he left home for good in 1906, he returned only once after thirty-two years and stayed just one day.

CHAPTER TWO

In Search of a Voice

John Henry Wagner was something of a war hero to the Detroit Wagners. At the outbreak of the Sioux Uprising on August 17, 1862, in Blue Earth County, Minnesota, John, his father and stepmother, Eliza, and their three other surviving children, Imogene, Arietta and William, were living in Vernon Center.[1]

Vernon Center was a tiny hamlet vulnerable to Indian attacks and the Wagners moved within days to the relative safety of nearby Mankato. Just three days before the uprising, ignited by broken treaties, failed crops, famine, and settlers' excessive hunting of wild game, John Wagner joined the Union Army, Sixth Minnesota Volunteers, Company I, at Fort Snelling in Hennepin. For over two months, John participated in the battles of Yellow Medicine, Birch Coulee and Wood Lake. He was also with the Col. Henry Sibley Expedition that pursued bands of Indians into the Dakota Territory.[2]

After the Army quashed the uprising his company joined the fight against the Confederacy, engaging in dozens of minor skirmishes throughout Alabama and Arkansas, including the Battle of Fort Blakeley at Mobile, Alabama, on April 12, 1865. Immediately after the surrender of rebel forces, the Sixth Minnesota Volunteers served as part of the occupational forces in Mobile, Vicksburg and New Orleans. The regiment suffered 177 fatalities, mostly due to disease after joining the fight against the South. [3]

Following the war, John settled in Chicago to establish an architectural and engineering business as its sole owner and operator. He married late in life, at age fifty-one, to ceramic artist Ann Frances Brown of Chicago, but had no children. By 1890, at the age of fifty-five, John was thinking of retirement. Rob Wagner had finished high school and John approached him and his parents about taking over the business. The plan was to send Rob to the University of Michigan to earn a degree in mechanical engineering, and then move to Chicago to take over. [4]

Like many working class families in the 1890s it was often decided that only one child would attend college. The question for Robert and Mary was whether to give Jim or Rob a university education. The natural choice would be the eldest son, but Jim had displayed a strong interest in business and had been working since he was sixteen years old, first as a messenger for the American Exchange National Bank of Detroit, then teller and bookkeeper for Peninsular Savings Bank. In 1890 he joined a Detroit tobacco firm as a traveling salesman with an eye towards taking over his father's wholesale tobacco house, R. Wagner & Co., when Robert retired. Rob, on the other hand, had demonstrated since childhood that he had a flair for design, making him more suitable as an architect. On a bright, warm September morning in 1891, Rob stepped off the train at the Ann Arbor station as a freshman at the University of Michigan. He also became a member of the Alpha Sigma Phi fraternity.
[5] [6] [7]

Rob was an indifferent student at best. By his sophomore year he had abandoned any pretense of having an interest in mechanical engineering and spent most of his time in the Literary Department where he found likeminded thinkers and his first taste of the bohemian lifestyle. He was a perfect fit in his new environment: outgoing and social with the ability to consume copious amounts of beer. Rob's education didn't come from the classroom, but from the many hours sitting on the back porch of the Sigma Phi two-story Victorian fraternity house on campus surrounded by kegs of beer arguing politics, the pros and cons of the Progressive movement, and whether Benjamin Harrison had any business being president of the United States. Studies took a backseat to two important aspects of university life: publishing *The Palladium*, the university's yearbook, and the far more interesting literary magazine, *The Wrinkle.*

The Palladium was a sophisticated annual published since 1858. Students originally conceived *The Palladium* as a book for fraternities, which at their peak numbered fifteen on the University of Michigan campus. As the student body grew, the number of students belonging to fraternities dropped from about two-thirds of the population to one-third, giving those named in the book significant status. Sigma Phi had a pivotal role in *The Palladium's* production and Wagner joined as a staff member. He rose to vice editor before his resignation in his senior year in December 1894 to make way for the new wave of editorial managers.[8][9][10][11]

The book was primarily a showpiece for the senior literary class and since 1884 had rivaled any professionally produced book in production quality and content. Many editions after 1889 were bound in leather. *The Palladium* was heavily illustrated and featured comic and serious poetry.

Over the years, and by the time Wagner arrived at the Michigan campus in 1891, prominence in coverage was still given to fraternities. *The Palladium* remained without question an elitist publication. University of Michigan administrators, like most universities across the United States in the nineteenth century, took a hands-off approach to student publications, allowing complete freedom in editorial content. Editors could exclude from the book any segment of the student population they wished. And they did so with impunity.

Non-fraternity members, or independents, took exception to their treatment in *The Palladium* and a group founded *The Castalian* in 1890. *The Castalian* had superior literary content to *The Palladium* and was far more daring. It prompted *The Palladium* editors to develop their own literary section to compete. A rivalry was born with each publication stealing ideas from the other. The primary difference between the two was *The Castalian* was principally a literary publication while *The Palladium* featured more general editorial content with a literary section. As expected the rivalry resulted in two superb yearly books between 1890 and 1896.

The competition also prompted pranks between the two competitors. In the spring of 1893, Wagner, then a principal artist for *The Palladium*, slipped into *The Castalian* editorial offices and stole the publication's illustrations. Soon after, *The Castalian* editors announced that a fire had destroyed its cuts and it would not publish an 1893 edition. It's unknown whether Wagner destroyed the illustrations, which seems unnecessarily malicious, or an unrelated fire was to blame.

It's difficult to reconcile Wagner's antipathy towards elitists later in his life, when he often wrote with disdain of communities establishing censorship boards, with his fraternity membership and his snobbish attitude toward independents. The independents were typically poorer than fraternity members and could not afford membership dues much less purchase expensive tickets to campus social gatherings and dances.

Although he appears not to have written about his theft of *The Castalian* illustrations, he did provide a mea culpa of sorts thirty-seven years later to *The Greek Review*. In an interview, he noted that, "The danger lies in grouping together of the wrong type of men, and this was the misfortune of a majority of the fraternities in the nineties."

He added: "In my day, independents were so much cattle according to fraternity standards. Men like Hoover, Wilbur and Lindbergh were dirt. We had a Negro who shined our boots to earn his way through the University, who later became Assistant District Attorney of the City of Chicago. A man who shined our boots was the mental superior of us all." [11]

The Palladium taught Wagner the mechanics of publishing, but the very nature of the yearbook was confining. His first love, above all else at the University of Michigan, was publishing *The Wrinkle*.

The impact *The Wrinkle* had on Wagner's path to a career as an artist and journalist and even his socialism can't be underestimated. Similar to the New Journalism movement in the 1960s and 1970s pioneered by Truman Capote and Hunter S. Thompson who employed literary techniques to tell a story, *The Wrinkle* adopted a bohemian attitude with comic, if not nonsensical, poetry, jokes, high-quality illustrations that in some cases came close to photography, and a smart-alecky, but not offensive, tone. [12] [13]

Wagner was an original staff member when the twice-monthly publication debuted on October 13, 1893. Conceived by William Edward Bolles and Hal Horace Smith, who, with Wagner, were members of the Class of '95, *The Wrinkle* initially had twelve pages, which grew to about twenty after its first year. Bolles served as managing editor during its first year while Smith was the business manager. Single copies sold for ten cents. Wagner even convinced his father, Robert, to sign an advertising contract with *The Wrinkle* for his retail tobacco business. Above the staff box on the title page was the publication's editorial philosophy: "Enjoy life while you live for you will be a long time dead."

Wagner shared the duties of illustrator with Melancthon Woolsey Campau, producing hundreds of images between the two of them over three years.

Humor and thumbing its nose at convention were *The Wrinkle's* chief attractions to readers. And although Wagner was primarily an artist in 1893, *The Wrinkle* and the even more radical *Clack Book* influenced the way he later approached his journalism by using a mixture of fact and humor to tell a story. It was a literary style he used not only to report on the infant motion picture industry in the 1910s, but also to sell socialism and defend extremists who had run afoul of the Department of Justice. It was this type of humor that characterized *Script* magazine.

Wagner maintained a relationship with *The Wrinkle* long after he graduated in 1895, serving as an advisory editor through 1900. He continued illustrating and had implemented a cover redesign beginning with the October 20, 1898, issue that modernized its presentation. His output between 1895 and 1900 was extraordinary given that he was also illustrating in equal measure for the *Detroit Free-Press*, the *Clack Book* in Lansing and *The Criterion* in New York.

* * *

On December 4, 1894, Robert Wagner died of heart disease at his home. He had been ill for some time. He was unconscious on December 1, a Saturday, rallied a bit on Sunday and Monday, but died at about 1 a.m. on Tuesday. His family was with him. He was just fifty-four years old. [14]

Rob Wagner wrote years later without rancor that his father left the family "penniless." Mary was bitter towards her husband's business partner, John T. Woodhouse, for not giving the family their share of the proceeds from Wagner & Woodhouse Co. Jim Wagner was not so sure that the family was entitled to anything. He worked for his father and Woodhouse for two years as a tobacco salesman and was certain that whatever assets were left belonged rightfully to Woodhouse.

But to say that Robert Wagner left his family nothing was inaccurate. Robert had established a reputation in the Detroit business community as an astute businessman. Following his stint as a telegrapher with the Grand Trunk Railway he partnered with H.D. Edwards in the rubber business, and then dissolved that company to establish a ticket agency and broker's office at the corner of Woodbridge and First streets. He then opened an office at the Michigan Exchange Hotel where he later leased another office next door in order to open a retail tobacco and cigar shop with Ross Holmes. He dissolved that partnership in 1878 and was going it alone as a tobacco agent until he took in Woodhouse as a partner in 1887.

Mary's contention was that her husband had invested $10,000 (valued today at $245,000) in Wagner & Woodhouse Co. while Woodhouse had only put up $2,000 (about $49,000 today). Should not the family have seen the initial investment returned? While the company's books have been long lost to history, whether Woodhouse hoodwinked the Wagners out of their share of the company will never be known. [15] [16]

Notwithstanding Mary's concern for her "reduced circumstances," Robert Wagner had always earned a handsome salary at $200 a month (about $4,900 in today's dollars), while Woodhouse earned $150 monthly (about $3,675). Moreover, the Wagners lived in a well-appointed large six-bedroom home at 2050 Woodward Avenue in one of the most desirable neighborhoods of Detroit. Behind and adjacent to the Woodward house was a forty-acre plot of land. In 1891 Robert had purchased a 7 ½-foot-by-280-foot strip for $562 (about $14,320 in today's dollars) that considerably enlarged the Wagner property. When Mary and Charlotte sold the house in 1901 to move to Santa Barbara, CA, the residence was likely valued in excess of $200,000 in today's dollars. The Wagners were hardly destitute. [17]

* * *

Following Rob Wagner's graduation from the University of Michigan in the spring of 1895 with a meaningless bachelor's of science degree in mechanical engineering, he returned to the Woodward home to help support the family while studying art at the Detroit Fine Arts Academy. Jim was traveling extensively as a salesman for the American Tobacco Co. and was rarely home. Charlotte took up dressmaking and Clarence, at fourteen years of age, assisted Charlotte as a pattern maker. Rob joined the *Detroit Free-Press*, which more or less served as a day job at $12 a week while he in indulged in his passion as illustrator for the fledgling *Clack Book*. At the *Free-Press* he illustrated news articles and features, including creating images for Charles Bertrand Lewis, who wrote under the pen name "M. Quad." [18] [19]

When not submitting his work to the *Free-Press*, Wagner spent most of his time with the *Clack Book*. The *Clack Book* may be considered an extension of Wagner's devotion to *The Wrinkle*; both shared similarities. But the *Clack Book* attracted some of the best writers of the day and was far more daring in its editorial content for its audience was not limited to an eighteen- to twenty-four-year-old demographic but now included free-thinking, progressive adults with an appreciation for the fantastic.

The *Clack Book* was part of a trend of "Chapbooks" that originated in England and often referred to as Bibelots, Ephemerals, Brownie magazines or Freak magazines. The original *Chap-Book* was a semi-monthly that debuted on May 15, 1894, in Cambridge, MA. The presentation of the *Chap-Book* was unorthodox. Publishers produced it in an odd size and featured wide margins, unusual typeface and uncut pages. As one critic described it, the *Chap-Book* was an exercise in "decadence." It broke every rule in conventional magazine publishing. [20] [21]

The British chapbook *Yellow Book*, notorious for its reverence for the Decadent movement of the 1890s and its illicit French fiction, served as the model for the *Clack Book*, which focused on bohemian fiction and poetry under editor Frank G. Wells. The thin booklet debuted April 1896 and featured mild fantasy and quasi-science fiction stories from a wide range of writers. The first three issues measured 10 ½ inches by 3 inches and afterwards 9 ¾ inches by 4 inches. Single issues sold for a nickel and fifteen cents for double issues, which averaged about forty-eight pages.[22]

It billed itself "a burlesque on the popular little magazines of the day." Following its debut issue, the *Indiana State Journal* wrote, "The *Clack Book* is the latest venture in miniature magazines. It offers weird art and fragments or, as its editors would doubtless say, gems of literature of a kind that is undoubtedly pleasing to the public, else so much of it would not be printed." In its April 8, 1897, edition, the *Scranton Tribune* observed, "Very gorgeous in outward garb and unexpectedly interesting internally is the Easter *Clack Book*, a 'decadent' magazinelet that is almost good enough to know better."[23]

The editorial content was revolutionary, at least to American reading tastes, with some poems and stories bordering on the nonsensical that emphasized a turn of a phrase, verse and rhythm rather than plotting. An anonymous poem, "Afternoon," in the April 1897 edition typified the *Clack Book's* freestyle writing by smashing the conventional rules of grammar and punctuation:[24]

> Lookin' at the sunshine
> Slant'n' on the wall, 'Druther watch the sunshine
> Slant'n' on the wall.
> Watchin' where the shadders
> Uv the maples fall.
>
> Jest a lazy swayin',
> Wavin' to an' fro,
> Where the sun 'n' shadders
> Kinder come 'a' go.

> Ain't a-thinkin' nuthin',
> Jest a-layin' here,
> Soakin' in the gladness,
> Soak'n up the cheer.
>
> What's the use o' doin'
> Anythin' at all?

This style often punctuated Wagner's writing throughout his journalism career albeit on a much more modest scale primarily because he was more influenced in his professional career, still a decade away, by the higher caliber of writers contributing to the *Clack Book*.

Contributing to the *Clack Book* was Karl Edward Harriman, a University of Michigan alumnus and Wagner's colleague at *The Wrinkle*. Harriman went on to become editor of the *Blue Book*, a pulp magazine specializing in fiction, crime and science fiction. Among the *Clack Book* contributors were fantasy writer John Kendrick Bangs, whose "Bangsian Fantasies" were set in the afterlife, and novelists George Washington Cable and Percival Pollard. Another regular was Elia W. Peattie, an irreverent if not dissident writer who specialized in progressive causes. Her writings of the Wounded Knee Massacre, lynchings, prostitution, unwed mothers and capital punishment were often sprinkled with sarcasm, witticisms and humor that made her an exceptional voice for the publication. And either to make it appear the publication had a large staff, or perhaps as an inside joke, Wagner signed some of his illustrations as "Leicester Belsaigne." [25] [26]

Perhaps the most important member of the *Clack Book* group to Wagner was Rupert Hughes. Although only six months older than Wagner, Hughes became his journalism mentor. The uncle of billionaire Howard Hughes, Rupert was a short story writer and playwright. He published his first book, *The Lakerim Athletic Club*, at twenty-six years of age. He went on to become a successful screenwriter and music composer. Although polar opposites in their political leanings – Hughes was fiercely anti-communist – they maintained a warm friendship over five decades and even collaborated on a biography of Father Neal Dodd, the so-called priest to the stars, in 1936.[27]

In fact, Wagner's journalistic fortunes were tied to Hughes over the next six years. In 1898, Hughes was working as an assistant editor for *The Criterion*, a left-leaning literary magazine and forerunner to *The New Yorker*. After the *Clack Book* ceased publication with the June 1897 issue and bored with newspaper work, Wagner began scouting around for assignments outside Detroit. Restless, he hoped that New York had something to offer.

Percival Pollard and Hughes, well acquainted with Wagner's art, recommended to editor Joseph I. C. Clarke that he hire Wagner to illustrate *The Criterion's* covers. *The Criterion* actually was born in St. Louis when Grace Davidson, a retired schoolteacher, acquired *St. Louis Life* in 1896. *St. Louis Life* was a sister publication of *New York Life* that carried much of the New York publication's editorial content. Davidson soon changed the name to *The Criterion* and began publishing original material. Her editor, Frenchman Henry Dumay, recommended the magazine relocate to New York to reach a wider, more sophisticated audience.[28]

Like the *Yellow Book* and to a lesser degree the *Clack Book*, The *Criterion* embraced the Decadent movement and counted Oscar Wilde, George Bernard Shaw and Henrik Ibsen as its influences. The new magazine turned the arts and letters community upside down with its opinionated and saucy criticisms and satire. Writers Pollard, James Gibbons Huneker and James L. Ford, the Austrian poet Arthur Guitermann, and the drama and literary critic Vance Thompson were among the contributors.

It was all too much for Davidson, who fired Dumay in January 1898 after he published a story on the "little sanitary stops of a French dancer's dog." She replaced him with Hughes until she found a permanent editor. Clarke came aboard in March 1898. To Clarke's credit, he kept most of Dumay's editorial policies in place. Clarke also broke design rules by having art emerge from the margins. With Wagner now the chief artist, the magazine's covers featured bold two-color images. Bright reds, heavy blacks and deep yellows and blues dominated the artwork. [29] [30]

In 1898, Clarke decided to boost Theodore Roosevelt's campaign for governor of New York. Wagner was already familiar with Roosevelt and his theatrics, particularly Roosevelt the Rough Rider during the Spanish-American War. Wagner's brush with Roosevelt, or at least the Roosevelt mystique, occurred in the summer of that year. Wagner enlisted as a private in the New York Seventh Regiment Infantry, probably at the urging of Hughes who already was an officer there. Hughes later became a captain with the Sixty-Ninth New York Infantry. Wagner went to Cuba with his regiment, but he did no fighting. Instead he sketched artwork of scenes for *The Criterion*. He saw enough fighting to cement his commitment to pacifism as it later became his overriding political philosophy during the Great War. [31] [32] [33]

His disgust with war was further solidified by the death of his younger brother Clarence. At seventeen years of age, Clarence was a draughtsman for the Frontier Iron Works in Detroit. Against his mother's better judgment Clarence persuaded her to allow him to join the Detroit Naval Militia, which was scheduled to leave Norfolk, VA, on the USS *Yosemite* for Cuba in mid-May 1898. Mary reluctantly consented. The Naval Militia traveled by train to Norfolk to the waiting *Yosemite*. On May 19, Clarence came down with an earache and was hospitalized for two days before returning to duty aboard the ship. But he suffered a relapse and was hospitalized at the Norfolk Marine Hospital. For ten days, Clarence lapsed in and out of consciousness. Both his mother and brother, Jim, raced to Norfolk to be by his side. But Rob was closer, arriving by train from New York on May 29 in time to be at the boy's bedside. Clarence died the next morning at 3:15 from complications of spinal meningitis with Rob there to hold his hand. [34]

Although Dr. Delos L. Parker, the *Yosemite*'s ship's surgeon, believed that the illness could have occurred anywhere and may have originated while Clarence was living at home, it was small consolation to the family. The only evidence that family had of Clarence's service in the Navy was a City of Detroit service medal commemorating the Spanish-American War. Rob Wagner would occasionally write about his brother's death, noting that he was "killed" or died in the war while serving his country. Perhaps Rob felt he would diminish his brother's sacrifice by acknowledging that Clarence died of illness and not in combat. Only twenty-three Navy men were killed in the war and sixty-six wounded. Clarence was among the seventy-four Navy personnel who died of illness or disease. To Rob, indeed the entire family, Clarence's death was no different than those killed in action. [35]

Rob Wagner's bitterness over the destruction he witnessed in Cuba and his brother's death shaped his attitudes about war in general. When the Socialist Party announced its opposition to America's entry into World War I, Wagner didn't waver from his antiwar stance despite the capitulation of many of his socialist peers under government pressure. [36]

Yet to examine Wagner's illustrations of the war, the reader would never know his political leanings. Like most professionals working for newspapers and magazines in the late nineteenth and most of the twentieth century, reporters, editors and artists supported their publishers' editorial policies regardless of their own personal convictions. Obligations and loyalties were solely to their employer. Wagner's illustrations celebrated America's military might in the war.

And like many journalists who had personal contact with Teddy Roosevelt, Wagner succumbed to the future president's charms. During the summer, Clarke assigned Wagner to provide a portrait of Roosevelt for the cover. It received considerable attention in New York and several other publications re-produced it. Roosevelt was thrilled with the illustration and visited *The Criterion's* editorial offices to personally thank Wagner, who seized the opportunity to ask permission to make some character sketches of Roosevelt at work. Roosevelt agreed.

On a Monday morning, armed with a pencil and sketchpad, Wagner found Roosevelt's office at the Republican headquarters at the Fifth Avenue Hotel in Manhattan. While Roosevelt went about his day, Wagner sat in the corner and sketched furiously.

Wagner recalled later: "The politicians began to arrive – big fellows with high hats, little fellows with keen eyes. The colonel talked to each in turn, briefly and crisply, and got them out one at a time with utmost dispatch. His dynamic energy was amazing."

About an hour later, Wagner attempted to slip out of the office unnoticed, but Roosevelt caught him. "Oh, Mr. Wagner! May I see your sketches." Roosevelt examined each one closely, and then made one suggestion: Substitute nose glasses for "these awful tennis spectacles. They make me look like a school teacher."

Wagner acquiesced to the request and another set of illustrations graced the magazine in its insistent positive portrayal of the candidate for governor.

An offshoot of magazine was *The Criterion* Independent Theater group, a forerunner of the Century Theater, in which virtually the entire editorial staff staged matinees with radical themes at the Madison Square and the Berkeley Lyceum theaters. Among the themes explored by *The Criterion* Independent Theater were Ibsen's commentary on the conventional marital roles of men and women in society and the groupthink of the masses. Closer to Wagner's heart were German dramatist Herman Sudermann's plays on the right of an artist to lead a freer moral life. These plays challenged the moral conventions of society with frank treatment of sex, gender inequality and even sexually transmitted diseases rarely seen on the New York stage. Wagner's work both with the theater group and his poster-style covers for the magazine attracted the attention of New York theatrical producer Augustin Daly, who commissioned the young artist to produce posters for his attractions. [37] [38]

New York exposed Wagner to opportunities that were not possible in Detroit. Although he would return to Detroit for short periods through 1906, Wagner understood that artistic stimulation and the exploration of ideas considered taboo in Middle America would not be found in his hometown, but in New York and Europe. California, which would be his home for nearly forty years, did not even enter his consciousness at the turn of twentieth century. Instead, the immediate future held something entirely different and it was not necessarily of his making, but that of his new friend and mentor, Rupert Hughes.

CHAPTER THREE

"Bovine of Intellect"

As passionate as Grace Davidson was for *The Criterion*, the magazine was hemorrhaging cash by 1901. Davidson had a wealthy St. Louis benefactor who had been funding the magazine since its inception, but she had an independent streak that proved fatal to the magazine. She refused to use the American News Company, which was virtually the only distribution outlet in the country for American magazines. Her own distribution methods were woefully inadequate and expensive. When it became apparent that the magazine would never be in the black, funding ceased and Davidson was on her own. [1]

Rupert Hughes recognized *The Criterion* had lost momentum and was past its glory. By 1902, he signed on as an editor with London-based *The Historians' History of the World*, a multi-volume encyclopedic set that charted the rise and development of nations. His first task was to hire Wagner as an illustrator. In September 1900 Wagner boarded the *S.S. Deutschland* passenger liner for England. He settled at 28 Bedford Place on Russell Square in London. [2]

His job was the mass production of illustrations that required extensive research of military clothing and arms and scenes ranging over several centuries. In all, Wagner produced more than 2,000 illustrations over nineteen months. Working with him was a much older British artist whose work, at least to Rob, was severely dated if not rudimentary. Hughes routinely rejected the old man's art but he never considered firing him. Wagner, sensing the artist was desperate for help, began picking up the illustrations from his co-worker's table after he had gone home for the evening and toiled late into the night reworking them. In the morning, a revised batch of illustrations was at the old man's table. Wagner and his partner never discussed the arrangement and the routine continued until Rob's departure for the United States in April 1902. Perhaps more satisfying creatively for Wagner was his relationship with Robert Barr, once an editor at the *Detroit Free-Press* and who had founded London literary magazine *The Idler* in 1892. Barr hired Wagner to pen many cover illustrations during his stay. [3]

When Wagner returned to New York he followed Hughes to the *Encyclopedia Britannica* where he continued illustrating much like he did in England. By late spring 1902, Wagner was back in Detroit. His first stop was 597 Jefferson Avenue.

Jefferson Avenue in 1902 was a fashionable section of Detroit just six blocks from downtown. While working for the *Detroit Free-Press* he had met Jessie Willis Brodhead while boarding a trolley near Woodward and Jefferson. They struck up a conversation and met occasionally afterwards. Jessie had hazel eyes and light brown hair, often worn in a bun and always tucked under a narrow-brimmed hat. She barely topped 5 feet and weighed a scant ninety-nine pounds. She was quiet and soft-spoken, but possessed a quick wit. She was also staunchly Catholic, attending the Jesuit Church of Sts. Peter and Paul several times during the week and frequently receiving communion. She attended Sacred Heart Academy Catholic School and was a member of church's Rosebud Charitable Society. She also was an amateur actor as a member of the Detroit Comedy Club. [4]

Her father was John Thornton Brodhead, son of Michigan Civil War hero Colonel Thornton Fleming Brodhead who was mortally wounded at the Second Battle of Bull Run while covering a retreat of Union forces. The colonel was brevetted a general before he died of his wounds on September 2, 1862. His son, John Brodhead, who once rode with his father to watch first-hand the Battle of Harpers Ferry when he was twelve years old, had been a second lieutenant in the Marine Corps and based for most of his military career in Washington, D.C. Attached to the Mediterranean Fleet in 1876 he escorted the infamous Tammany chief William "Boss" Tweed from Spain to New York aboard a Naval warship. A year later he commanded a twelve-man unit to break up a mob at a Baltimore rail yard during the Great Railway Strike by plowing a locomotive through hundreds of rioters. [5]

Jessie's mother, Jessie Mary Willis Brodhead, was the youngest daughter of composer and writer Richard Storrs Willis, whose brother was the poet Nathaniel Parker Willis and whose sister was writer Sarah Payson Willis (aka Fanny Fern). Jessie Brodhead's mother, Jessie Cairns of Roslyn, New York, had died while her daughter was still an infant in 1858, and her father re-married in 1861 to the Detroit socialite and widow Alexandrine Macomb Sheldon Campau. At the urging of his new wife, Willis converted to Catholicism. Alexandrine, a philanthropist who donated to numerous Catholic projects and charities, wielded considerable influence in Catholic circles, garnering audiences with Pope Pius IX and Pope Pius X. Jessie, as a young woman, had followed in her father's footsteps, writing for the Catholic publications *Catholic World*, *Sacred Heart Review*, *Catholic Truth* and *The Musical Times*. She was also active in the parish of the Jesuit Church of Sts. Peter & Paul. But it was her stepmother who had had a profound influence on Jessie's religious upbringing. [6] [7]

Despite Jessie Willis' strong religious beliefs, she had no reservations marrying John Thornton Brodhead, whose family were Methodists to the core. John Thornton Brodhead's grandfather, John, was a minister supervising Methodist societies in New Hampshire and was a state senator who also served as the senate's chaplain. The younger John Brodhead converted to Catholicism, although it's not known whether he became a Catholic before or after his marriage to Jessie.[8] [9]

The couple's daughter, Jessie, the eldest of six children, was born on March 2, 1878, at their home at 1311 Fourteenth NW in Washington, D.C. In 1881, John was ordered to China for a three-year stint. When the Marine Corps would not permit his family to accompany him to his new posting, Brodhead resigned his commission and returned to Detroit where he opened a real estate business.[10]

Given her mother's liberal attitude about her own marriage into a Methodist family, Jessie probably didn't expect the vehement response to her announcement to the family that she accepted Rob Wagner's proposal for marriage. The couple had been meeting regularly on Grosse Ile, an island across the river a short distance south of Detroit where the Brodheads had a second home. Rob had little experience in romance. A neighbor girl, Alice Ives, was his sweetheart while attending Cass School and Detroit High School, but he could not boast that he had a handle on courting a young woman. Nevertheless, he was holding Jessie's hand on the Brodhead's boathouse dock under a half moon on late Sunday, August 10, 1902, when he proposed to Jessie.[11]

While John Brodhead was largely silent about the pending nuptials, Mrs. Brodhead could barely contain her fury, directing her anger not so much at her daughter, but at Rob. To Mrs. Brodhead, Rob Wagner was the antithesis of everything she wanted in a son-in-law. He was a bohemian artist with progressive ideas and no solid employment prospects. His plan was to whisk her daughter to Paris so he could study art. Worse, he was not religious and made it no secret that he had no use for religion. He respected his fiancée and would not hurt her, but when pressed about his religious beliefs he could not hide his ambivalence.[12]

The engagement soon became a battle of wills between the mother and future son-in-law over who would win Jessie. In his 1902-1903 diary Wagner framed the episode with Mrs. Brodhead as a contest in which there would be a winner and a loser. He was the "winner" and the "loser" felt nothing but deep anger and resentment that she had "lost" her daughter to what she perceived as a ne'er do well. Rob and Jessie should have anticipated Mrs. Brodhead's stormy opposition. Young Jessie, at twenty-four years old, was a member of the "Jefferson Avenue set." Her family wasn't just part of Detroit society, it was Detroit society and listed annually in Dau's Blue Book. Wagner, on the other hand, had no such position. For the first time in his life he personally experienced the deep divide between Detroit's wealthiest families and his own modest background.

Mrs. Brodhead's rejection stung and fueled his own resentment over what he perceived as a ruling class in a provincial city lording over the working class. Although Wagner and Mrs. Brodhead reconciled after the birth of her grandson, Leicester, in 1904, Rob never forgot how he was marginalized during his first year of marriage. The battle raged through the summer and fall of 1902. It wasn't until December that the Brodheads announced the engagement in the *Detroit Free-Press*. On May 15, 1903, the couple was married at the Jesuit Church of Sts. Peter and Paul in Detroit in a rare occasion where Rob participated in a religious ceremony as an adult. [13] [14]

During the late spring and early summer Rob and Jessie prepared to sail to Paris where Wagner planned to study art at the Académie Julian, the famed art school founded by Rodophe Julian in 1868 and favored by American artists. The Brodheads, including a sulking Mrs. Brodhead, saw the newlyweds off at the Cleveland boat in Detroit, opting not to bid them farewell in New York.

At 5 a.m. on Saturday, August 22, 1903, the Wagners set sail aboard the *S.S. Minnetonka* from the Hudson Street dock for Southampton, England. The night before, family members and friends gathered at the dock, including Rob's mother, Mary Leicester Wagner, his Aunt Bessie Hornibrook Tinning, and close friend Elsie Reasoner, a newspaper war correspondent during the Spanish-American War and fiancée of Lester Ralph, a New York illustrator and son of journalist Julian Ralph.

On August 31, the couple arrived at Southampton and took the train to London where they were soon ensconced at Rob's old apartment on Russell Square. Two weeks later, they arrived in Paris. Wagner withdrew 600 francs from his line of credit and rented for 800 francs a year, paid quarterly, a third-floor walkup apartment at 25 Rue Boissonade at the corner of Boulevard Raspail. It had no studio, but it had working plumbing.

Wagner arrived at Académie Julian on October 2. He paid twenty-five francs for the first month of instruction, plus six francs for an easel and chair. As he entered the studio he was met with boisterous, but good-natured jeers from ill-disciplined students already working on the day's project. It was a cosmopolitan bunch: French, British, Portuguese, German, Greek, Japanese, Russian and American. Wagner's first day was nerve-wracking as many artists were singing and yelling. Few students apparently took baths and most ignored basic grooming. [15]

To his dismay, Wagner quickly discovered the school forbade pencils and paints to newcomers. His instructor forced him to work in charcoal, with which he was completely unfamiliar. He found charcoal difficult to master, and to add to his stress he found that the Académie Julian was less about instruction and more about competition between artists.

Each day Wagner arrived at the studio, he found about forty naked women in a queue, each taking a turn on the rotating pedestal to audition as models. Some models were hard and brazen, practically challenging the students with their sexuality, while others were embarrassed and shy. Students selected the day's models with a vote of raised hands. This process was repeated each day. [16]

The new student found nothing sensual about naked models, and even expressed some discomfort in sketching them, preferring instead to illustrate men. Perhaps naively he was skeptical that an artist would consider taking a model as a lover. "No serious artist has a model for a mistress," he wrote dismissively in his diary.

For nearly a decade, Wagner had immersed himself in a bohemian lifestyle that included exposure to writers who stretched the boundaries of literature by mixing fact and fiction, and explored the supernatural and science fiction. While attending university he spent four years in the company of young men who lived for drinking and skirt-chasing. But deep in his heart he was prim in the matters of the opposite sex. He also was conflicted about his attitude toward women. He supported the suffrage movement and insisted that women be treated on the same level as men in the workplace and that they should be granted the right to vote.

He believed strongly that women should be taken seriously in the professional and political arena. He knew far too many women who were handicapped by the rules of Victorian society. His new wife was a perfect example. He blamed Jessie's parents for raising her as a "helpless doll" who was told "she would never be happy without a maid." To Wagner, his new wife was "ill-prepared for married life" and unable to take responsibility for her own life. To Jessie's credit, and to Rob's delight, she overcame her privileged upbringing to become resourceful and self-sufficient without any significant input from him. [17]

Yet for all of his expressed disgust over class divide and society's treatment of women, he could be remarkably elitist, if not cruel, in his assessment of female intellect. He revisited the relationship between artist and model in 1911 when Robert W. Chambers published his best-selling romance novel, *The Common Law*, which tells the story of a model who preferred to live with her artist paramour without the benefit of marriage. In an interview with fellow socialist Estelle Lawson

Lindsey for the *Los Angeles Record*, Wagner dismissed *The Common Law* as a complete lie of an artist's life.

"The plain facts are simply that there is nothing less romantic, more uninteresting, cheaper and more commonplace than the life of the artist's model," he said. "Artists who do serious work have wives in the perfectly proper and conventional manner of the plain citizen: we bathe and shave at least as often as the bank clerk; some of us pay our bills – when we can get the money – and we do not fall in love with, entertain, fraternize with or make confidants of our models.

"This is not because the artist is very good, but because models as a class are ignorant, bovine of intellect, cheap of view – mental as well as physical – and occupy the same niche in the life of the artist as the monkey wrench in the life of the plumber."

Given the eight-year span between Wagner's first assessment of artists' models in Paris and his interview with Lindsey, his attitudes toward women can't be dismissed as a single instance of venting. As if he wanted to make his position on models clear he bluntly and gracelessly insisted to Lindsey that, in his experience, Paris models were "stupid."

"Do you suppose any woman would make her living by gazing day in and day out at a knot hole for twenty-five cents an hour – forty cents if she poses in the altogether – unless she were too stupid to earn a living any other way?" [18]

By 1911, Wagner had fully embraced socialism and the suffrage movement, but, like many freethinking men of the era, he also demonstrated intellectual dishonesty. His cynical view of women taking undesirable employment to feed themselves and their families exposed him as a hypocrite. Try as he might to shed the shackles of the rules of Victorian society, he couldn't help but cling to the archaic sensibility that a female model who posed in the nude must have the intellect of a cow.

Wagner struggled in the chaotic environment at Julian, but he finally received some attention from his instructor, Jean-Paul Laurens, a kindred spirit who shared Rob's anti-clerical views. Laurens, a tough taskmaster and blunt critic, dismissed Rob's art because he was "choking himself" with a "wooden technique." He cannily determined that his new student had been a magazine illustrator because "his work was not thorough." [19]

Wagner wrote little of his political thinking in his diary during his seven-month stay in London and Paris. Most of his time outside art school was consumed with visiting tourist sites and entertaining American friends, mostly Jessie's circle of acquaintances, and new friends from Académies Julian and Delecluse. While Wagner attended school, Jessie spent her days wandering Paris, meeting with American expatriates, and visiting the city's numerous Catholic churches. Each week, if not more often, she received communion. Wagner was skeptical of his new wife's religious practices and was particularly suspicious of French Catholic priests, describing them as mean in temperament and filthy in their grooming habits. Yet he never complained and dutifully escorted her to church whenever he was available.

Among the friends the couple entertained was John Donovan, a marine landscape artist from Detroit who grew up four blocks from the Wagners' Second Avenue home. They had never met in Detroit, but they became acquainted at Delecluse. Donovan would become a devoted friend for many decades.

One such visitor to the Wagners' apartment, however, helps provide a glimpse into Rob's early interest in Russia and his hope for new government there. On Sunday, December 27, 1903, Bertha Cristy Smith of Detroit, and her fiancée, Baron Alexandre De Freedericksz, a Russian diplomat to the United States, stopped by for an evening visit. Smith was the granddaughter of Henry Howland Crapo, a governor of

Michigan. Serious-minded with little sense of humor, but well versed in international politics, Bertha had married Martin Smith, whose family were prominent entrepreneurs in Detroit. Smith died in July 1901 and about a year later she became engaged to Freedericksz. [20]

To Wagner, Freedericksz behaved more like an American than a Russian and had an obvious affection for American culture. Five years older than Wagner, Freedericksz was charming and intellectual, but spoke in a courtly fashion influenced by his years in European diplomatic circles. It often took him a while to get to the point in a conversation. With Wagner, Freedericksz was unusually frank about Russia's central government that had done nothing to improve the literacy rate for its people. At least eighty-five percent of the Russian population could not read or write and lived in extreme poverty. Freedericksz wanted to see his country establish free institutions to improve education, develop natural resources and control trade in Asia. The diplomat believed that Russia was capable of feeding Asia because Russia "is the only one capable of understanding the Asiatic mind," while the United States could feed the rest of the world. [21]

Wagner agreed, noting that Russia should extend its railway with the construction of the Trans-Siberian Railroad into Manchuria as an eventual means to tame it, but Freedericksz's homeland's primitive and autocratic political system would only serve to worsen the living conditions of Asians. Without an adequate education system Russia was in no position to govern other people. To Wagner, the "effete monarchies of southern Europe were over civilized" while Russia languished far behind in developing its huge agricultural resources and mining potential.

Russia in 1903 had a population of 128 million people with three-quarters of its twenty-three million square kilometers in Asia. The task of feeding its population was overwhelming. "I sympathize with Russia. She is a vast conglomerate of varied races, struggling up from the soil and its government has a fearful task on their hands," Wagner wrote in his diary. [22]

Wagner's encounter with Freedericksz and with the Russian students at Académies Julian and Delecluse exposed him to a world in which millions of people needlessly lived in darkness with little hope of rising above poverty and illiteracy because their government lacked the will to provide for its people. When Bolsheviks overthrew Czar Nicholas II and implemented communism fourteen years later, Wagner saw vast opportunities to provide a successful model for educating its population. At the height of Joseph Stalin's power in the 1930s, *Script* touched on these themes. Wagner recognized by the mid-1930s that Stalin was not the Soviet Union's savior. Yet he believed the communists' education system was far superior and much more sincere in eradicating illiteracy than the American school system, although *Script* made little mention of the heavy influence of Bolshevik ideology and the militarization of students in the classroom.

At Julian, Wagner believed his art was not progressing and felt particularly ill-suited working in charcoal. In February 1904 he left the noisy Julian for Académie Delecluse a smaller, quieter school, but with a reactionary reputation for its cutting-edge approach to art. Equally important to Wagner was that instruction was given in English. But even Delecluse was too restrictive. Just a few weeks later he moved into a studio operated by the Chicago-born artist Robert Lee MacCameron, who studied under William Merritt Chase, James McNeill Whistler and Jean-Leon Gerome, and was a member of the Paris Society of American Painters. [23]

MacCameron gave Wagner one-on-one instruction and allowed him the freedom to explore his art in pencil and paints. He thrived during this brief period and his work matured rapidly. This is not to say that the Académie Julian failed him. On the contrary, charcoal forced Wagner to break the conventions of illustrative journalism. His work transformed from two-dimensional depictions of scenes and individuals to a more three-dimensional look. His switched from the posterish art of bright reds and yellows to earth tones and muted colors. He worked in deeper reds, browns. His representation of flesh tones was deep, rich and accurate. [24]

When Cristy and Freedericksz had visited the Wagners, Rob was three weeks deep into his first oil painting that was not a class assignment at Julian. He chose Jessie as his first subject, sketching her during much of December before tackling the oils in March in MacCameron's studio.

Neither Rob nor Jessie realized that their time in Paris was nearing an end. In early February, Wagner's mother, Mary, suffered a stroke. On February 27, Jessie learned that her father was gravely ill. More bad news arrived a day later when her brother, Richard, cabled that their father was "sinking rapidly." On March 1, 1904 John Brodhead was dead. To add to the urgency of returning home, Jessie was five months pregnant.

Following a brief stopover in Antwerp, the Wagners boarded the *S.S. Kroonland* on May 1 for New York. Arriving a week later, they remained in New York long enough to attend the wedding of Elsie Reasoner and Lester Ralph on May 15, which was also their first wedding anniversary.

Arriving in Detroit, the Wagners left by boat for the Brodhead home at Grosse Ile on June 23 where Jessie would rest until the birth of the baby. Mrs. Brodhead, still in mourning, remained frosty with Rob, as did Jessie's spinster aunts, Katherine and Eleanor Brodhead. But Jessie's brothers and sisters – Richard, Jack, Willis, Archange and Alexandrine – were indifferent to the drama. [25]

Jessie spent her days lounging in a hammock with Queenie, the family dog, usually at her feet. Wagner spent his days sketching and painting, taking on about eight portrait assignments from a number of wealthy patrons, almost all of whom were friends of the Brodheads. Later that year the Detroit Museum of Art, in a joint exhibition with John

Donovan's seascapes, displayed Wagner's paintings of Teddy Delano, son of Fred M. Delano, Etta Keena, wife of James T. Keena, Frederick S. Stearns, John Donovan, Richard Storrs Willis, Jessie, her brother, Richard, as well as a self-portrait.

On July 19, Jessie went into labor and Wagner rushed his wife to Detroit on the 4 p.m. boat. Reaching 597 Jefferson Avenue at about 5 p.m. they waited for Dr. Herbert Rich to deliver the baby. At 11:30 p.m., Dr. Rich delivered Leicester Wagner. Rob recorded in his diary that his son's full name would be John Leicester Wagner after John Brodhead and his mother, Mary. And although the boy would always be known as Leicester, it appears that "John" was dropped by the time the birth was registered and he was renamed Robert Leicester Wagner. [26]

On August 20, a local parish Catholic priest baptized Leicester in a small chapel on Grosse Ile. The Wagners chose Mrs. Brodhead as godmother and Jessie's brother Richard as godfather. At about 4:45 the next morning Rob awoke to the smell of smoke and saw flames rising over the end of the bed. He and Jessie were in the same bed with Leicester at their side in a bassinette. A window had been left open and a breeze carried the sheets at the end of the bed over a low-burning lamp on the floor. Rob jumped up and batted down the flames with his hands. He suffered second and third degree burns, but Jessie and Leicester were unhurt.

Unfortunately, that same day, Rob was scheduled to take the train to New York for a job interview arranged by Rupert Hughes. With his hands painfully swollen and heavily bandaged he took the 4:25 p.m. train for New York. Arriving the next morning, he found Hughes had unexpectedly left for Toronto and his prospective employer was nowhere to be found. Rather than waste a trip, he visited Elsie and Lester Ralph and his cousin, Jack Tinning, before returning to Detroit the next day.

Through 1905 Wagner continued working on commissions. In October the Detroit Museum of Art exhibited his portrait of J.B. Ford, president of the Michigan Alkali Company, in a special showing of Michigan artists. [27]

In late 1905 Jessie, who was always in fragile health, came down with tuberculosis and had a severe throat infection. She was pregnant with her second child, and although she was eight months along, Rob felt that the Detroit winter would be too much for her. In early January, Rob, Jessie and Leicester boarded the train for Los Angeles, and from there traveled to Santa Barbara.

Rob's mother, Mary, and his sister Charlotte, had already moved to Santa Barbara in 1901 at the urging of his brother James R. H. Wagner. Jim, as he was known, had chosen to leave the New York winters and live in California permanently with his wife, Mabel, and two young daughters, Arline and Harriet. He had become enamored with Southern California after several visits, enjoying the mild climate during the winters. After many years in the tobacco business, he joined the advertising staff at the financial newspaper New York *Commercial* in 1901. In April, he was back in Los Angeles on business and decided to stay.

Jim joined the William R. Staats Company in Pasadena. On October 23 he was elected president of the Pasadena Tournament of Roses Association. A week later he organized the first Rose Bowl football game by inviting the University of Michigan to play Stanford. A year later he bought a home in Santa Barbara after joining the Santa Barbara Realty Company. [28]

Rob and Jessie found a small Spanish-style residence at 10 East Sola Street following their arrival. On January 22, 1906, their second son, John Thornton Wagner, was born. Jessie's condition did not improve through the spring and early summer. Her throat infection was persistent and it prevented her from speaking. But in August she felt well enough for an automobile trip to Los Angeles. [29]

The couple arrived on August 15 and stayed at the home of Mr. and Mrs. William H. Schweppe at 2722 La Salle Avenue. Wagner had completed a life-sized portrait of his friend, the novelist Stewart Edward White, and the couple attended its exhibition at George Steckel's studio at 220 South Spring Street. Two days later, on a Friday, they returned to Santa Barbara. [30]

On Sunday afternoon, Rob took Jessie for an automobile drive around Santa Barbara and that evening they pushed Leicester and Thornton in a carriage for a walk in the neighborhood. The Wagners' full-time nurse noted that Jessie was breathing easily and did not appear, at least outwardly, in distress. But after going to bed early, she died without warning in her sleep. [31] [32]

As was his habit, Wagner never wrote and rarely spoke of the circumstances surrounding the deaths of family members. While he wrote of his love for his father and his regret over his brother Clarence's death, he rarely revealed his emotions. He wrote nothing of Jessie and only rarely over the decades did he mention her by name in his letters. To Wagner, his three-and-a-half-year marriage was a closed book and left to the past.

CHAPTER FOUR

---·◆·---

"Yours, for the Revolution!"

West of downtown Los Angeles just over the hill on South Figueroa Street and a block south of Sixth Street stood expansive two-story Victorian homes and Colonial-style family apartments. At Sixth and Figueroa was the Bellevue Terrace Hotel that catered to families. Behind a mansion on sweeping grassy grounds at 625 South Figueroa Street of this upscale mixed residential-commercial neighborhood was an empty coach house previously occupied and used as a studio by the sculptor Alexander Stirling Calder.

In the fall of 1909, Rob Wagner found the coach house perfect for his own studio and residence, which would also serve as a salon for artists, writers as well as parlor socialists and Bolsheviks. On November 1, Wagner moved in and opened the studio's doors to advanced art students and models. [1]

The coach house featured high ceilings and an airy large room. It also had full exposure to natural light for most of the day. In the evenings the studio filled with the smell of incense and subdued with soft light from Japanese lanterns hanging from the ceiling. Benches, stools and chairs were scattered about for the frequent informal roundtables held by Wagner. [2]

It was a far cry from the woodshed-cum-studio Wagner shared with fellow artist John M. Gamble on State Street in Santa Barbara. Regardless of the cramped quarters at the State Street studio and the tendency of Leicester and Thornton to run willy-nilly around the paints and furniture, it served as a refuge for Wagner to focus on his art. Since Jessie's death in 1906, he worked furiously to establish his reputation as one of the top portrait painters on the West Coast. His most notable accomplishment was his portrait of novelist Stewart Edward White. He also received good notices for his painting of Father Thomas Sherman, son of Civil War hero General William Tecumseh Sherman, of San Francisco. In less than two years, Wagner produced at least a dozen large portraits, including paintings of the city's society leaders, Acacia Orena and Earl Graham. [3] [4] [5]

Santa Barbara artists were a competitive bunch in the first decade of the twentieth century. Wagner easily cornered the portrait genre and his output was strong, yet money was always an issue. He relied on students to provide a steady income, but he found the pool of paying pupils shallow in a town of less than 12,000 residents. He looked south to expand his search for a more reliable income.

He left his two boys in the care of his mother, Mary. It was not unusual in 1909 for single fathers to leave their children in the hands of female relatives while they pursued their careers. Mary, though, must have been frustrated with the added burden. She was busy in her own ceramic art studio and had worked as a correspondent for *Keramic Studio* magazine. She represented the National League of Mineral Painters at the Paris Art Exposition in 1900 and frequently traveled to Los Angeles to work with her sister-in-law Arietta Wagner, who was also a ceramic artist. Although she had recovered from her stroke in 1904, Mary's illness slowed her down. Just a year shy of sixty years old, she was not prepared to handle two boys ages six and three. [6] [7] [8]

The boys more or less ran amok under their grandmother's care, but Wagner never felt the need to bring them to Los Angeles. Rather, he focused on his painting, teaching and hosting Friday afternoon roundtables with his students and visitors to his studio.

He was also a member of the Severance Club, a cultural conversation group founded in 1906 by Caroline M. Severance, a suffragist and socialist. She held meetings for an intimate group on the second and fourth Fridays of each month to discuss progressive issues. Its members included guest speakers Upton Sinclair, artist Edward Weston and Max Eastman. Charlie Chaplin and Douglas Fairbanks later became occasional guests. The club was private, left leaning and literate. [9]

By the time of Wagner's arrival in Los Angeles, he had become president of the local chapter of the Intercollegiate Socialist Society, founded by Sinclair with the enthusiastic backing of Clarence Darrow and novelist Jack London among other left-leaning figures. Chapter meetings were held at the studio. Sinclair founded the ISS to recruit college students for the socialist cause, but more importantly it operated outside the party and more or less was a means to further intellectual discussion on how to apply socialist principles to issues of the day, particularly labor. Wagner applied the same principles of discussion at the Severance Club to his ISS meetings. Wagner was no activist. He gave no fiery soapbox speeches. He preferred friendly persuasion, which the Severance Club and the ISS offered. Wagner's own modest group were progressives and radicals, including a large number of high school teachers. But his greatest pleasure was shaping the minds of his young students by instilling a sense of duty to their community. [10]

The ISS suited his needs. In contrast to the aggressive, if not anarchist, activists in Northern California and Washington, the ISS since its inception in 1905 was a moderate reform organization that advocated progressive policies, municipal ownership of public utilities, the suffrage movement and corruption-free government. Wagner, agreeing with Job Harriman, also believed that for the Socialist Party of Los Angeles to succeed it needed to align itself with labor unions. This was a contentious issue within the party with many hardliners demanding the party stand on its own and not compromise with some of the goals labor unions sought. The split severely damaged the party. Still, Wagner saw the party and the ISS as a voice for workers and an antidote to the *Los Angeles Times* publisher Harrison Gray Otis' anti-labor campaigns. Steering clear of incendiary rhetoric, Wagner frequently wrote on the suffrage campaign in the labor-friendly *Los Angeles Citizen*. [11] [12] [13]

Later, as World War I raged, Wagner eschewed organized socialist causes to work outside mainstream groups with the exception of the ISS. He believed he was more effective by influencing decision-makers in one-on-one conversations and intimate roundtables. It would become his hallmark as a socialist, influencing and then building a coalition of intellectuals that included Charlie Chaplin, William C. deMille and actor Charles Ray, among others, to address the common man in their films.

These early years in California proved a prolific artistic period for Wagner. Before leaving Santa Barbara, he exhibited his work (as did Mary and Aunt Arietta) at the 1909 Alaska-Yukon-Pacific Exhibition in Seattle. By February 1910, he had joined the California Art Club, and the following July exhibited oil paintings with other Southern California artists at the Carnegie Library in Long Beach. Among his paintings and sketches completed by mid-1910 were studies of dramatist and teacher Alfred Allen, artist Elmer Wachtel and the Union Labor Party's Arthur M. Lewis. In October 1913, he joined Franz Bischoff as a member of the jury at the Los Angeles County Museum of Art for that year's exhibition. [14] [15] [16] [17]

* * *

Wagner arrived in Los Angeles just as the local socialist movement was gaining momentum, particularly in the immigrant community and with union members. But two events shook progressives to the core. On

October 1, 1910, a bomb exploded at the *Los Angeles Times* building killing twenty-two people. On Christmas Day, the non-union Llewellyn Iron Works sustained heavy damage in a bombing. In April 1911 police arrested labor activists and brothers John J. and James B. McNamara. However, their arrests didn't immediately affect labor organizations and the local Socialist Party.

If anything, the pending trial served to galvanize progressives and labor organizers. Clarence Darrow headed the defense team and Job Harriman assisted in courtroom defense strategy. Harriman had run as a socialist in 1898 for California governor and as a vice-presidential candidate with Eugene V. Debs, the presidential nominee on the 1900 socialist ticket. The defense, funded largely by the American Federation of Labor (AFL), argued that the McNamara brothers were framed for the attack. And in speeches up and down the California coast, the fiery radical Emma Goldman argued that the McNamaras needed public support. [18]

Harriman had won the Los Angeles mayoral primary in 1911 and was poised to win the seat in the December runoff election. But on December 1, just five days before the election, the McNamara brothers shocked their supporters by pleading guilty. James admitted to bombing the *Times* building and John acknowledged he was responsible for the Llewellyn Iron Works attack. To labor organizers and progressives, the guilty pleas were an act of betrayal and a critical blow to the movement. Harriman lost the mayoral election on December 5 by 7,000 votes. He would run for mayor again in 1913, but failed in his attempt. [19] [20]

Wagner supported the local socialist ticket, particularly in 1913 when his friends and dyed-in-the-wool socialists H.A. Hart, Frederick C. Wheeler, Mila Tupper Maynard and Frank E. Wolfe ran for Los Angeles City Council. Only Wheeler would win a council seat. He served two terms through 1917. [21]

But Wagner had a cool relationship with Harriman. In *Script,* eighteen years after the 1913 council election, Wagner wrote:

"Strange man, Job. Terrific energy and an intense idealism. He cared nothing for individuals, not even his intimates. But he loved ideas and people in the mass. The injustice of the world irked his spirit and he was all for the socialist state. Impatient, he would bring in the Brotherhood of Man at once. On Thursday!" [22]

It does not appear that Wagner actively campaigned for the socialist ticket in 1911 or in 1913. He undoubtedly spoke of his support at his studio roundtables. By this time he was also speaking before civic groups – often women's clubs and literary groups – mindful that discussing "socialism" was a sure way never to be invited back. Rather, he discussed the benefits of the progressive movement, particularly woman's suffrage, to receptive audiences.

While Wagner would bristle at the suggestion that he was a propagandist, he took great care in laying out what he deemed to be the facts of the socialist movement. He saw his job within socialist circles was to expose the myths of socialism perpetrated by the mainstream media. One of the biggest lies, he believed, was the portrayal of Emma Goldman. The diminutive forty-one-year-old feminist and anarchist had been a thorn in the side of law enforcement since her arrival from Russia in 1885. She inspired her lover Alexander Berkman to assassinate industrialist Henry Clay Frick in 1892 for the deaths of nine striking steelworkers at the hands of Pinkerton detectives hired by the financier. Berkman's attempt on Frick's life failed and he was imprisoned. Meanwhile, Goldman toured the country disseminating information about birth control and advocating for education reform and women rights. Her speeches often resulted in her arrest and imprisonment for allegedly inciting riots. [23] [24] [25]

On May 6, 1911, Wagner attended a social event to honor Goldman at the Burbank Hall at 542 South Main Street near downtown Los Angeles.

Burbank Hall was formerly the home of an evangelical Christian organization, but had since become a meeting place rented out to various groups for large-scale events.

Meeting Goldman for the first time, Wagner witnessed a profound independent thinker who reflected his own deep concerns about the abuses of government authority and the dangers of the herd mentality of public opinion. Writing in the *Los Angeles Graphic* newspaper, Wagner observed of Goldman:

"Believing as she does, in individualism, her whole propaganda is devoted to a protest against economics, religions and political authority. Hating war and all forms of militarism, her creed is opposed to violence. It is a tenant which holds that all government rests on violence and that ninety percent of crime are crimes of property that authority is designed to protect." [25]

He was struck by the large number of schoolteachers attending the speech and her emphasis on promoting the individual in education. Anarchy to Wagner was not a philosophy to be feared but to be embraced.

"Of course, she is talking 'anarchy,' " Wagner wrote in *The Graphic*, "but after you hear her expound her doctrines and cite such anarchistic successes like the Red Cross … the medical and scientific societies, YMCAs and all the many purely voluntary organizations that thrive without government assistance of authority, you begin to realize that you are much more of an anarchist than you thought you were." [26]

In advocating individualism, the core of Wagner's socialist and artistic beliefs, Goldman found a devoted acolyte. Goldman further charmed Wagner by dancing with him during the post-speech social, which led him to write a portrait that depicted her as a human being rather than a raging dragon that was portrayed in the press.

A year later, Wagner was put in a potentially dangerous situation involving Goldman and her manager Ben Reitman who were chased out of San Diego by a mob. Goldman's predicament offered Wagner an opportunity to provide her with safety and privacy to repay a debt he believed he owed to her for spending an evening with him at the Burbank Hall event.

Goldman and Reitman had arrived by train from Los Angeles to San Diego for a speech on May 14, 1912. A crowd of about 1,000 people showed up at the train depot demanding that she not be allowed into the city. Goldman ignored warnings from the police that her safety could not be guaranteed, but law enforcement offered no protection. Goldman insisted on going ahead as planned. She arrived at the U.S. Grant Hotel where the crowd swelled to about 2,000. During the trip to the hotel, Reitman and Goldman had traveled separately from the depot because of the unwieldy crowds. [27] [28]

Under police protection a small group of men, numbering about four, kidnapped Reitman from the hotel and drove him to La Penasquitos Ranch twenty miles north of the city. There, he was stripped naked, tarred and had desert sand rubbed on his body. The vigilantes branded the letters IWW – the acronym for the radical Industrial Workers of the World – into his back, forced him to sing the "Star Spangled Banner" and kiss the American flag. [29] [30]

Goldman, thinking that Reitman had already left for Los Angeles, fled San Diego on the train in the middle of the night. Early the next morning she arrived at the Santa Fe depot in Los Angeles where IWW members greeted her. From there, they drove her to Wagner's South Figueroa Street studio. The vigilantes released Reitman, who walked several miles naked until he found some clothes. He finally boarded a train for Los Angeles where he was taken to Wagner's residence to join Goldman. Goldman and Reitman remained with Wagner for two days before leaving for San Francisco. [31]

The fallout for Wagner providing hospice to the two radicals was surprisingly minimal. *L.A. Times*' publisher, Otis, banned Wagner's name from its columns. Wagner, long the go-to socialist for newspaper reporters seeking comment on progressive issues, still maintained a cordial relationship with the city's other, less vindictive newspapers.

* * *

Wagner continued his Friday afternoon roundtables at the studio. One such meeting in early 1910 would forever change his life and how he viewed his art. Among his guests was Hobart Bosworth, a stage actor, who had turned to films. Bosworth signed with Selig Polyscope Company, a Chicago studio founded there by William Selig in 1908. A year later Selig relocated to Edendale not far from downtown Los Angeles with Bosworth as his star. [32]

Bosworth told Wagner of his brief history with Selig and urged him to watch the filming of a movie. The actor was embarrassed that he was slumming for motion pictures following a distinguished career on the stage. "But they're really doing things," Bosworth whispered to Wagner one Friday afternoon. "These movies are going to be great things someday. You should come over and see what we are doing." [33]

Wagner spent the day on the set with Bosworth and by the end of filming was thoroughly hooked on movies. Wagner saw it as a revolutionary art medium that made painting and still photography seem quaint by comparison. Bosworth introduced Wagner to Selig and his top director, Francis Boggs. Rob returned often to the studio, sometimes daily, to watch filming and pick Boggs' brains about the new craft.

In 1911, he asked Boggs to direct a scenario he had written. The film, *The Artist's Sons*, gave audiences a glimpse into the bohemian lifestyle and "sweet home story" of a Los Angeles artist that charted the progress of a portrait he was painting. The two-reeler featured Sydney Ayers as the artist and Rob's sons, Leicester and Thornton, playing themselves. Selig released it on October 6.[34][35]

The Artist's Sons was Wagner's effort at dipping his toe in the waters of filmmaking to determine whether his vision of artistic excellence was compatible with movies. While Wagner would come to rely on several Hollywood directors and writers to teach him this new art – most notably Hal Roach, Charlie Chaplin, Rupert Hughes, Charles Ray and William deMille – Boggs was his first mentor in films. Boggs was the director of Wagner's little film, but he gave Wagner wide latitude to tell his own story with the director providing a guiding hand.[36]

Wagner was certain that Boggs was poised to become D.W. Griffith's rival in epic filmmaking. They would have made a good team, but future collaborations never came to be. Three weeks after *The Artist's Sons* opened in Los Angeles, on October 27, Boggs was dead.[37]

Now a regular visitor at the Edendale studio, Wagner had jumped off a streetcar near the front gate on the afternoon of the 27th when he heard a gunshot from inside the main building. At the same time, he saw Tom Santschi, a Selig stuntman and actor known for his film roles as villains, also near the gate. Both men ran inside the building with Santschi leading. In the conference room they found Boggs dead from a bullet wound to the chest and Selig shot in the arm. Santschi subdued the gunman, who apparently had had a mental breakdown before shooting Boggs and his employer.[38][39]

The Artist's Sons was Wagner's only movie for Selig. It was another three years before he again tackled filmmaking, when, in late 1914 he wrote a scenario for Mack Sennett that became a Fatty Arbuckle and Mabel Normand vehicle entitled *Fatty, Mabel and the Law*. Still, his films almost seemed like a diversion as he pursued commissions, new pupils and kept his Friday afternoon meetings on schedule.

Maintaining a steady income continued to be his main concern. That meant that portrait commissions and finding new students was his priority since filmmaking could only be a hobby. When an opportunity to become a credentialed teacher and to have a steady job presented itself, he leaped at the chance. In the spring of 1913 he joined Manual Arts High School as an art and Greek history teacher. The state Board of Education formally issued him a teaching credential the following September.[40]

Wagner was in his element. He not only had his paying art students at his South Figueroa Street studio, but he was also now getting a regular salary at Manual Arts. The high school was less than three years old when Wagner joined the faculty. About 2,000 students crowded the campus on South Vermont Avenue, which had once been a bean field. The faculty included liberal thinkers Ethel Percy Andrus, who had been a social worker at the Hull House in Chicago, socialist and feminist Mila Tupper Maynard and Anne Edwards, who taught Latin, and would later write for *Script* on the Russian education system.[41]

Wagner never hid his socialist background. His leftist leanings suited the Los Angeles School Board, which, in 1913, had adopted progressive policies and had expanded funding of its industrial arts curriculum. Wagner was impressed that Manual Arts had purchased enough equipment to create an inviting environment for shop work. Manual Arts, according to Wagner, provided industrial courses to its students that offered "dignity in labor."

Unorthodox in his teaching methods, Wagner taught socialist philosophy to his students with fervor by emphasizing individualism. He credited Los Angeles educators for "blazing" trails to become the "world's greatest martyrs" while public opinion was "almost invariably wrong" about their approach to teaching. The school board's broad-minded approach to encourage individuality in its students and teachers also impressed Wagner. He probably felt differently when in 1917 his antiwar stance and very public friendship with Prynce Hopkins got him fired. But for four glorious years he had young and impressionable teenagers eating out of his hand.[42]

His classroom was in the basement away from prying eyes of visitors and administrators. He loathed interruptions by administrators who came by to observe his teaching. He often had his students line up against the wall and sing Broadway songs at the top of their lungs until the embarrassed school district staff left. His students considered themselves the school's intellectual elite. According to Frank Capra's biographer, Joseph McBride, in his book, *Frank Capra: The Catastrophe of Success*, Wagner greeted his students at the beginning of each class with a quote from Gilbert and Sullivan's *HMS Pinafore*.[43]

> "My gallant crew, good morning!"
> "Sir, good morning," his students replied in unison.
> "I hope you're all quite well!"
> "Quite well; and you, sir?"

It was a daily ritual that inspired an *esprit de corps* and loyalty. Students accepted without question that progressive thinking was part of the curriculum. According to McBride, when one student, asked Wagner to sign his yearbook, he wrote, "Yours, for the revolution!"[44]

By promoting individualism, he played on his students' strengths to shore up their weaknesses. He never saw a classroom full of students, but each young man and woman with a potential to do great things. One morning he arrived at class to find that all the girls had identical hairstyles. Wagner, who worked briefly for Florenz Ziegfeld during his days of staging plays for *The Criterion Independent Theater*, pointed out that no two Ziegfeld dancers looked the same. He suggested that his students express themselves as individuals instead of "goddamn sheep."[45]

His students included film actress Phyllis Haver, opera singer Lawrence Tibbett, Broadway actress Ruth Hammond and aviation pioneer and future World War II hero General Jimmy Doolittle. Frank Capra typified the student who credited Wagner as a major influence. Wagner's breezy and slightly subversive teaching style captivated the future film director, who was often an indifferent student. He described Wagner as a "delightful, enterprising" personality who believes that art provides "more to human happiness than all the other professions combined." [46] [47]

Wagner quickly became Capra's mentor. He assigned the teenager to paint scenery for the school plays directed by his teacher. It was Capra's first taste of the performing arts and he was soon a regular backstage. [48]

In early 1915 Wagner was fresh off his writing assignment on the Fatty Arbuckle comedy when he approached the school board for permission to make a documentary film on the Los Angeles School District for the upcoming Panama-Pacific International Exposition in San Francisco. The film, *Our Wonderful Schools*, would cover the progress of the schools with an emphasis on Manual Arts High. The film featured numerous segments showcasing school programs and classes, including scene painting, stagecraft and even wrestling matches coached by Wagner. Hugh McClung served as Wagner's cameraman. [49]

Reliance-Majestic Studios, a short-lived company owned by D.W. Griffith before it became Fine Arts Studio, released the documentary on June 11. Although likely acquainted with Griffith, it was probably Wagner's cousin, Blake Wagner, who helped get the studio to back the documentary. Blake Wagner was a staff director for the studio and had worked for Griffith as a furniture painter, cameraman and second-unit director since the legendary director had moved his studio operations from New Jersey to Hollywood in 1910. [50]

Blake and his brothers – Jack, Bob and Max – were fun-loving, hard-drinking, undisciplined men who saw Hollywood movie lots as their own personal playground. They worked hard, but played harder, and had been part of motion pictures since its earliest days. Their father, William Wallace Wagner, a half-brother of Rob Wagner's father, Robert, was a train conductor. Their mother, Edith Gilfillan Wagner, was a writer. William and Edith were a bohemian couple ill equipped to raise their four boys. Jack, Blake and Bob were born in California. Max, the baby, was born in Mexico. [51]

When William was fired from the railroad for unspecified reasons he relocated the family to Torreon, Mexico. There, he was paid well as a conductor and the boys learned to speak fluent Spanish. Jack and Blake frequently made trips between Torreon and Los Angeles and, at times, lived with their aunt Arietta. Jack could be particularly troublesome. At the age of fifteen, Los Angeles police arrested Jack and another boy on burglary charges. The pair had burglarized hardware stores of enough merchandise to provide sufficient equipment to set up their own repair shop. Luckily for Jack, he only received probation for his crimes. [52] [53] [54]

At the outbreak of the Mexican Revolution in 1910, Jack, then nineteen years old, and Blake, at eighteen, returned to Los Angeles. Blake's twin brother, Bob, left for New Orleans, finding work in the infamous Storyville red light district. Max remained with his mother and father in Torreon where Edith, who had been a contributor to *The Smart Set*, *The Gray Goose* and *The Bellman* magazines, wrote dispatches on the revolution for *The Christian Science Monitor*. [55] [56]

In late 1912, Mexican rebels hijacked William Wagner's train outside Torreon. The rebels attacked Wagner with machetes when he refused to give up the locomotive. He was fatally injured, and died in November of his wounds in Los Angeles. With nothing left in Mexico, Edith took Max to live in Salinas, California. By 1924, Edith and her son had moved to DeLongpre Avenue in Los Angeles. Max took on acting and joined his brothers in Hollywood. He would ultimately appear in more than 400 movies and nearly 200 television episodes. Bob followed in 1926 to work for First National Pictures as a second-unit cameraman. Until Edith's death in 1944, the Wagner boys – with the exception of Bob who lived with his wife and two sons in North Hollywood – lived under the wing of their mother in a little enclave at the top of DeLongpre. [57]

Blake and Jack worked first for Griffith and later joined Mack Sennett and William Fox's studio. During World War I the brothers were combat photographers for the first motion picture unit in France. Jack filmed the Meuse-Argonne offensive and the Battle of Saint-Mihiel. For Fox, the brothers filmed the *Hallroom Boys* comedies. Jack also performed camera duties for director Rex Ingram and served as an assistant director for Allan Dwan and Lewis Milestone. By the early 1920s, Jack quit camera work to write scenarios and gags for Sennett and Hal Roach. With the advent of sound, Fox established a department to film movies in Spanish and hired Jack as a director. [58] [59]

In 1915 Rob was, at best, a fringe player in the movie industry. Blake and Jack introduced their cousin to the right people and the three often exchanged information on film projects through the 1910s and 1920s. Long established at the Sennett and Roach studios, it's likely that Blake and Jack occasionally got Rob jobs on the comedy lot. Blake was on the *Our Gang* camera crew when Rob joined him as an assistant director for *It's a Bear*. Blake also filmed Ben Turpin's *The Dare-Devil* that was co-written by Sennett and Rob. When Blake botched an interview for a cameraman slot on the Monty Banks film, *Atta Boy*, Rob's appeal to the studio execs got him his job back. [60]

Rob and Reliance-Majestic delivered *Our Wonderful Schools* on time. Several of the sixty cinemas screening Pan-Pacific Expo entries in San Francisco played the film, which received good reviews. The effort garnered Wagner and the school district a silver medal in competition. Even more than *The Artist's Sons*, *Our Wonderful Schools* served as Rob's entrée into the motion picture business.

Maternal grandfather Matthew Hornibrook influenced Rob Wagner's early outlook on economic upheaval and the sometimes precarious nature of land ownership. *(Author's Collection)*

Robert Wagner preferred the comforts of home and encouraged his wife, Mary, to travel extensively throughout the United States. *(Author's Collection)*

Mary Leicester Hornibrook Wagner studied art in Detroit and was an influential ceramic artist in her own right. *(Author's Collection)*

University of Michigan's *The Wrinkle* staff in 1896. Bottom row from left are Charles B. Parsons, Arthur M. Smith, George R. Barker, Edward Ferry, John E. Lawless and Julian H. Harris. Top row from left are Norman Flowers, Edwin H. Humphrey, Rob Wagner and Harold M. Bowman. *(Courtesy University of Michigan)*

Rob Wagner was drawn to the *Clack Book's* liberal and free-thinking attitudes and contributed numerous cover illustrations. *(Author's Collection)*

Clarence Wagner's death at the age of 17 during the Spanish-American War solidified Rob Wagner's antiwar position. *(Author's Collection)*

For most of 1898 and 1899 Rob Wagner was the principal cover artist for *The Criterion*. *(Author's Collection)*

Jessie and Rob Wagner on their honeymoon in Paris in 1903. *(Author's Collection)*

Right: Rob was skeptical of organized religion and was sometimes impatient with Jessie's desire to frequently visit Catholic churches on their honeymoon in Paris. Here, she sits in solitude in a Catholic church in a photograph by Rob in 1904. *(Author's Collection)*

On their return to the United States, Jessie and Rob attended the wedding of their friends Elsie Reasoner, the journalist and war correspondent, and newspaper illustrator Lester Ralph. Elsie Reasoner Ralph, left, with Jessie, was married on the Wagners' first wedding anniversary, May 15, 1904. *(Author's Collection)*

Left: Wagner struggled with drawing in charcoal at the Académie Julian while attending the Paris art school in 1903. *(Author's Collection)*

Jessie Willis Brodhead Wagner in a 1906 photograph presumably for a portrait that was never painted. *(Author's Collection)*

Rob's brother, James R.H. Wagner, brought his mother, sister and Aunt Bess to Santa Barbara in 1901. *(Author's Collection).*

The fiery Emma Goldman sought solitude in Wagner's art studio following her harrowing experience with an angry mob in San Diego. *(Library of Congress)*

Rob Wagner in his Figueroa Street studio in Los Angeles in 1910. He held roundtable discussions in the studio on progressive politics with his art students and fellow writers. *(Author's Collection)*.

Movie poster for the 1911 film *The Artist's Sons*. *(Author's Collection)*.

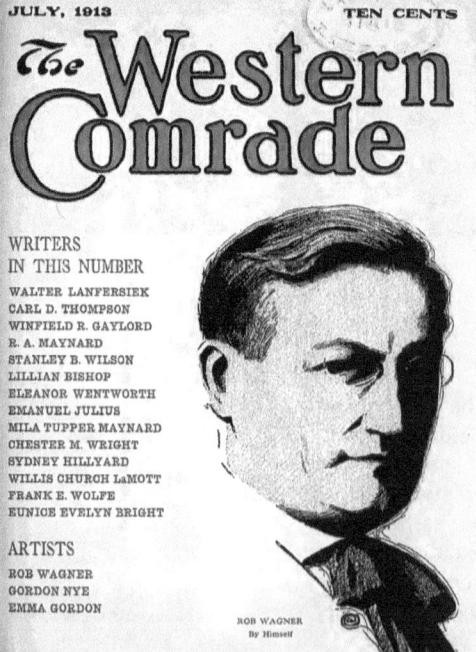

Wagner was the art director and staff writer at *The Western Comrade*, a socialist magazine, before it devoted most of its editorial content to the Llano del Rio project. *(Courtesy Marxists Internet Archive)*.

This self-portrait was likely Rob Wagner's last oil painting before turning to writing in 1915. *(Carol Wagner Mills-Nichol Collection)*

The Kansas-born Florence Welch in about 1911 before her marriage to Rob Wagner. *(Author's Collection)*

Jack Wagner on the set of *The Sea Beast* in 1926. He introduced Rob to important film people during his early years in Hollywood. *(Kathleen Wagner Starrett Collection)*

Blake Wagner occasionally collaborated with Rob on films at Mack Sennett and Hal Roach studios. *(Kathleen Wagner Starrett Collection)*

Actor Max Wagner appeared in more than 500 films and television shows. *(Kathleen Wagner Starrett Collection)*

Above: Above: Bob Wagner, second from right and brother of Jack, Blake and Max, with his second unit camera crew for *The Dawn Patrol* in 1927. *(Kathleen Wagner Starrett Collection)*

Left: Opera singer and actor Lawrence Tibbitt, left, was a student of Rob's at Manual Arts High School. *(Carol Wagner Mills-Nichol Collection)*

CHAPTER FIVE

———•◆•———

"*A Disastrous Adventure in Experimental Sociology*"

On a sweltering June morning in 1914, three automobiles full of men wound their way along a dusty unpaved road deep in the Mojave Desert twenty-five miles east of Palmdale and about one hundred miles north of Los Angeles. In the lead car was former preacher Job Harriman, the West Coast's leading socialist, failed Los Angeles mayoral candidate and a man eager to leave a legacy.

Following a four-hour drive, the caravan stopped at the base of a mountain near Big Rock Creek. The spot was desolate, unforgiving and absolutely no one's idea of a future community. Yet Harriman explained to his weary travel companions the site that was nothing more than sagebrush and Joshua trees would be Llano del Rio, a cooperative community that promised to demonstrate that socialism was more than political agitation. The community would be the "gateway to the future."[1]

To some members of Harriman's entourage it came as no surprise that he chose the desert to establish his utopia. The land was cheap. Harriman found five partners to invest $80,000 in 2,000 acres. It also suited his needs to breathe clean air to ease his tuberculosis. Harriman was a desert rat by nature. The future farmers of Llano del Rio? They would just have to deal with it.

Rob Wagner was among the group of men sweating under the desert sun. If he was skeptical about the project, he kept his reservations to himself. Never a devoted follower to Harriman, Wagner nonetheless agreed with him that for socialism to succeed it must cooperate with labor unions. It also must prove itself as a practical solution to solving economic disparity between workers and employers and to provide a cooperative that allows colonists to share the wealth of producing their own goods. As Harriman learned the hard way, the existing political system in a democratic society was not kind to socialists.

Wagner embraced the Llano del Rio project with the fervor of religious convert, joining attorney Clarence Darrow and Dr. John Randolph Haynes, a government reformer, in promoting the plan. It was an enticing opportunity to put into action what he had preached in his articles and at all those meetings at the Severance Club and at his studio. [2]

Ten months before his trip into the desert, Wagner had joined a hearty band of socialists to establish *The Western Comrade*, a monthly magazine published by the Citizen Publishing Company at 203 New High Street in Los Angeles. It initially focused on the socialist ideology and practical coverage of labor relations with business, the suffrage movement and featured profiles of leading leftists. Only later, and without Wagner, did it become a propaganda sheet for Llano del Rio.

The masthead read like a who's who of Los Angeles progressives. Stanley B. Wilson, a labor activist and head of the Los Angeles Teachers' Union, and Chester M. Wright, a former editor at the *New York Call* and police commissioner in Milwaukee, served as editors. Its associate editors were Wagner, who also served as art director; suffragists Eleanor Wentworth and Mila Tupper Maynard, her husband, attorney Rezin A. Maynard, and Emanuel Julius, who later took his wife's name to become Emanuel Haldeman-Julius. He would later become publisher of the socialist tracts *Little Blue Book* series. Frank E. Wolfe, a former editor at the *Los Angeles Herald* and director of the labor propaganda film *From Dusk to Dawn*, joined the staff later. Fred C. Wheeler, the only socialist on the Los Angeles City Council, rounded out the staff. [3]

The Western Comrade and Llano del Rio were inextricable. Harriman set up Llano del Rio while working out of the Citizen Publishing offices on Hope Street and later the Higgins Building when the magazine moved there in July 1914.

Through 1913 and the first half of 1914, Harriman and his team persuaded about 1,000 people to join Llano del Rio. He required each person signing up to contribute $500 that would fund equipment and tools. The group also raised money for a dairy, bakery, cannery, offices, residences, a printing plant, a lime kiln, a sawmill and barns. [4] [5]

Harriman obtained the water rights to Big Rock Creek and purchased stock in the Mescal Water and Land Company. Eventually the cooperative planted over four hundred acres of alfalfa and two hundred acres of corn. There was a nursery and truck garden, but laborers struggled with inconsistent climate and soil conditions. Water was not always available as the creek was often dry. About forty percent of the residents were experienced farmers, and some had worked on other cooperatives. They were a weary, hard-bitten group, but firm believers in Harriman's vision.

The radical idealistic fringe took the administrative positions. W.A. Engle, who headed the Central Labor Council, and *The Western Comrade's* associate editor Wolfe, were among the leaders. However, the majority of the members were mainly interested in a system that provided them with the necessities of life that equaled or was better than the average wage. [6]

In 1914, the average skilled laborer's wage was $4 a day. Bricklayers were the most highly paid at about $7 a day while bakers and blacksmiths were at the other end of the spectrum at about $3.50 per day. Harriman's offer was reasonable with colony residents hoping they could do better by sharing their income. Harriman promised $4 a day with $1 applied to purchasing stock in the cooperative and the remaining $3 to be paid when the cooperative distributed its profits. However, there were no significant profits and workers received scrip, which was worthless outside the community. [7]

Wagner was tasked with soliciting money from his artist and literary friends. In October 1913 he asked novelist Jack London to purchase a $2,000 stake in the project. "You will always have a home here and you could rent it too all the time you're not," Wagner wrote London on October 7. "Even as an investment it would be far from rotten – but as a domestic and social asset." [8]

There is no record of a response from London, but it's unlikely that he agreed to invest any money in Llano del Rio. London was suffering from acute alcoholism at this point in his life. Although he was a champion of socialist causes for many years and had run for Oakland mayor as a socialist in 1901 and 1905, he had become disenchanted with the progressive movement. Focusing on his writing to earn a living, he was more interested in maintaining his home in Glen Ellen, CA, and keeping his landscapers and builders in line and productive. By 1911 he had more or less given up on socialism.

It certainly didn't help Wagner that the author of *Call of the Wild* had previously feuded with Emanuel Julius over a friendly profile Julius had written on him in the June 1913 issue of *The Western Comrade*. [9]

In a May 21 letter London, having read an advance copy of the article, berated Julius for being careless with facts, misquoting him and failing to provide context to his comments. He accused Julius of being "provincial and insular." Worse, according to London, Julius misidentified the hat London was wearing as a "sombrero" when it was another style. London was further incensed when Julius failed to reply promptly to his scolding. He wrote a second letter on June 11 accusing Julius of being stupid. [10] [11]

Julius replied to London, claiming he was an inexperienced writer. "Only four years ago, I was a factory hand," he wrote in his defense. He failed to mention that he had worked for several years on socialist and labor-friendly newspapers, such as the *Philadelphia Daily*, *Milwaukee Leader*, *Chicago Daily World*, *Los Angeles Citizen* and the *New York Call*. [12]

To further deflect responsibility, he laid the blame on his colleagues. According to his autobiography, he wrote London in a June 13 letter, that, "I asked Rob Wagner what he thought of the story, and he said it was a jim dandy. I pointed out the things you objected to, and he didn't think them very serious." [13]

Serious or not, Julius discovered that well-intentioned laudatory profiles of socialists with deep pockets didn't necessarily translate into investments in Llano del Rio.

In the spring of 1913, while Wagner continued to drum up support for Llano del Rio as well as write articles and illustrate the magazine, Wolfe was preparing to film *From Dusk to Dawn*. Before joining *The Western Comrade* and Llano del Rio, Wolfe had been a union organizer for telegraph and railroad workers. By 1909, he was a journalist managing the *Los Angeles Daily Herald*. He had given the newspaper a socialist voice and was fired as a result.

As *The Western Comrade* was about to release its first issue, Wolfe began production of *From Dusk to Dawn*. In the magazine's July issue Wolfe wrote that socialism was only reaching a fraction of its intended audience through printed literature and meeting hall speeches. He saw labor films as the answer to swaying millions of workers to the socialist cause. By exploiting this new entertainment form, he promised to take "socialist propaganda into the motion picture show ... and the motion picture show into the socialist meeting halls." [14] [15]

From Dusk to Dawn tells the story of the rise of a young iron works employee fired from his job because he is perceived as a union agitator. When his friend dies in a plant explosion he is inspired to aid oppressed workers by joining the labor ticket to run for governor. The film featured Clarence Darrow with cameos of Harriman and *The Western Comrade* staffers Wheeler and Wilson. Shot at the Occidental Motion Picture studio in Hollywood, it was a film of epic proportions: 5,000 feet of celluloid, which ran one and one-half hours. Occidental released it in September 1913 on the East Coast followed by a preview for Los Angeles labor leaders at the Mozart Theater on Grand Street. [16]

Wagner made no appearance in front of the camera, but he worked as part of the production set decoration crew. He also provided a portrait he painted of his sixteen-year-old niece, Harriet Wagner, as a principal set piece in the film.

Wolfe's film posed a dilemma for Wagner. He had more experience in filmmaking than any other staff on *The Western Comrade*, although he had only one film credit. He had the resources at Selig Studios and he could easily assemble a production crew. If there was any time to seize an opportunity to bring socialism to a limitless audience, it was in Hollywood while the industry was still in its infancy. There was no class division, no unions and film studios did not wield the power they would gain in the 1920s. Anybody with the modest backing of a small number of investors could produce films. Wolfe was correct in his belief that movies could fire the imagination of millions of struggling workers.

Audiences not only bought into political causes portrayed on the screen, but considered such topics as part and parcel of all types of movies, from the love story, to the crime thriller and even the western. Depictions on film of class struggles excited audiences as much as heated romances. [17]

Wolfe was following the example of other pro-labor films that strived to portray trade unionism as the answer to earning a living wage and leading a respectable life without having to answer to capitalists. The AFL, for example, had spent $2,577 to produce *A Martyr to His Cause* in 1911 to answer the wave of antiunion films and to defend the McNamara brothers. [18]

Such films could be commercially successful as well as entertaining while at the same time get their message across to workers. "If I had ten different big features depicting the class struggle, I could keep them all working," Wolfe said in 1914. In 1915 he was so confidant that labor films were the new propaganda tool that he announced that a film studio would be built at Llano del Rio. [19]

Wolfe's dreams never materialized. When the United States declared war on Germany in April 1917, filmmakers turned to patriotic messages in their movies. There was little room for pro-labor films. Depicting the class struggle and resistance to capitalism was perceived as un-American.

But even before America's entry into the war, Wagner saw what Wolfe could not. Wagner shied away from making a career producing labor films because he doubted he could earn an income. He knew enough wealthy socialists to understand that spouting socialist ideology in the comfort of one's own home did not translate into parting with one's money to finance a film.

Perhaps the best example of Wagner's experience with wealthy leftists was the Parnassus cooperative apartment project in Pasadena. He championed the scheme in the October 1913 edition of *The Western Comrade*, signed on as an investor, and then watched it fall apart. The organizers of the project hoped to involve about sixty well-to-do professionals to invest in building a luxury apartment complex on Pasadena Avenue opposite Mt. Washington on a ten-acre parcel. Sitting on a hill eight hundred feet above sea level, the proposed project would provide a stunning panorama of the San Gabriel Mountains to the north and Los Angeles to the southwest.

It would feature two hundred apartment units at a total cost of about $600,000. Each apartment would sell between $2,000 and $8,000 depending on the size and location. Forty percent of the apartments would be sold and the remaining sixty percent would be luxury rentals. [20]

The Parnassus would also feature a common dining room, ball and assembly rooms, a theater with cinema equipment, playrooms for children, smoking and dining rooms, and a billiards room. Contracts drawn up by Harriman's law firm stipulated that building would not begin until forty percent of the apartments had been sold. Among the investors with Wagner were Severance Club president Dr. T. Perceval Gerson, the Christian socialist Dr. J.E. Wilson and Richmond Plant, an advocate for the single tax movement.

Parnassus failed to materialize when the original investors could not sell the required forty percent of the apartments. Given his experience with Parnassus, Wagner was skeptical that Wolfe could continue to finance his films. Producing such movies might even be too risky. But what was more important, Wagner still saw socialist-themed films as propaganda and not a true artistic vision.

The Parnassus debacle should also have served as a warning of what the future held for Llano del Rio. Harriman's name attracted about 1,000 colonists to the cooperative. Settlers didn't mind the hard work it took to dig irrigation ditches and clear hundreds of acres to plant crops. The community's education system rivaled, if not surpassed, the state school system with a Montessori program. The elementary school received tax money and followed the County Superintendent of School's educational policies and regulations. Much to the delight of Wagner, Llano del Rio established an industrial school to teach students a trade. [21]

But infighting among settlers and administrators, so often a problem that plagued utopian communities, cropped up. Harriman established the community as an incorporated business subject to California state law, which in and of itself was contrary to its participants' desire for a socialist community. Colony administrators wanted no board of directors nor managers, another utopian ideal, yet it made managing the enterprise almost impossible. Worse, settlers accused Harriman of becoming too authoritarian, refusing to listen to the general membership. But the fatal flaw in the operation was an insufficient water supply. Harriman believed he could irrigate 20,000 acres with the Mescal Water and Land Company, but the supply never met the heavy demand. When the settlers could no longer sustain Llano del Rio, they pulled up stakes in 1917 and moved the colony to Vernon Parish, Louisiana. However, only one hundred settlers made the move. [22]

Wagner observed with hindsight and the distance of seventeen years: "I was not one of the colonists but how I worked with Job on his plans, never realizing then that the scheme had no more chance of success than would Bullock if he attempted to inaugurate a free-trade policy in the midst of a high protective system of government. Llano proved to be a disastrous adventure in experimental sociology." [23]

The Western Comrade didn't fare any better. In December 1913, the Union Labor News Company, which had purchased the magazine from the Citizen Publishing Company, sold the publication to Chester Wright and Emanuel Julius. The new owners reduced the page count from 36 to 32, but enlarged the size for better reading. Eleanor Wentworth, who had been with the magazine since its inception, took on a larger role with more coverage of women's rights issues. Not unexpectedly, its coverage of Llano del Rio increased. But in June 1914 the magazine was sold again. Harriman and Frank Wolfe took over as co-owners with Harriman serving as managing editor. The new owners did not publish a July issue, but resumed in August. [24] [25]

By May 1914 the core of the original editorial staff of *The Western Comrade* was gone. Wagner resigned in May. Julius left after producing the June issue. Perhaps a bigger blow to the quality of the magazine's editorial content was the departure of the underutilized drama critic Mila Tupper Maynard, who left after the October 1913 edition. While Eleanor Wentworth covered the suffrage movement, Maynard had more experience. She had been writing on women's rights issues since 1895 and had given a speech on a women's suffrage bill before the Nevada State Assembly the same year. The magazine's ever-changing editorial staff, its focus on Llano del Rio beginning in late 1914 and moving its editorial offices to Llano del Rio in 1916 led to its instability and inconsistency in editorial quality. Its circulation averaged only about 4,800. [26] [27]

Wagner characterized this period in his life as "I deserted my class" to promote socialism. It was typical Wagner humor, but he said it to Upton Sinclair in 1919 when he had become a target during the infamous US Justice Department's Palmer raids on leftist radicals. Perhaps to deflect the mounting pressure on his involvement in socialist causes, he attempted to distance himself from his prewar activities. But it was far from a phase. With war on the horizon he indeed wrote less about the leftist movement, but his influence did not come in the form of leaflets and magazine articles, but in his association with Charlie Chaplin and members of the film industry. Often working as a liaison, Wagner introduced key movie players to leading radicals. However, he also became more vocal during his private roundtable discussions of his pacifism and sympathies for Germany, which would lead to a federal investigation and surveillance of his activities as an alleged German agent. [28]

CHAPTER SIX

─•◆•─

Ye Ed and Ye Real Ed

If there was any indication that Rob Wagner was contemplating changing the direction of his career in 1914 he kept it to himself. He had a comfortable life at his Figueroa Street studio. Although drawn to motion pictures, it was portrait painting and his involvement in the art community to promote Southern California artists that consumed his life. Films were a distraction, an avocation much like his indulgence in his other newfound hobbies of photography and woodworking.

At forty-one years old, he was at the peak his art career. And for nearly twenty years he had garnered excellent notices for his work. Yet he scrambled for assignments, which were not particularly plentiful given his involvement in socialist publications that paid little if anything for his time. Soliciting commissions was a full-time job, and for every twenty prospective clients he approached, he might only elicit a single assignment. He also wasn't particularly adept at managing his time. He neglected his sons and his daily routine seemed to go from one roundtable political discussion to another. Food for the brain, but it was hardly a recipe for money in his pocket or an answer to what do with his boys. Financial pressure was building as he struggled to help his brother,

Jim, support their mother in Santa Barbara and pay for the boys' education.[1] [2]

The answer, perhaps the one he wasn't looking for, but certainly an option that delighted him, arrived in the summer of 1913 when one of his endless political social engagements resulted in the chance encounter with a Kansas woman who thought of the world much as he did.

Florence Mason Welch was born on January 23, 1883, in WaKeeney, Kansas. She was raised in Topeka as the second youngest of eight children born to James Miller Welch, a Civil War veteran, farmer and later a boarding house owner, and Mary Ellen Mason. At thirty years old she was much older than most Kansas girls readying themselves for marriage. She put finding a husband on the back burner as she sought first to establish a career in journalism and work on the suffrage movement.[3] [4] [5] [6] [7]

The Welches had an artistic and literary streak. Florence's older sister, Ruth, was an artist, and another sister, Grace, was a musician. Florence preferred the works of Ralph Waldo Emerson and William Wordsworth. When she graduated from Washburn College in 1905 with a bachelor's degree in literature, she chose "The Human Element in Wordsworth" for her senior thesis.[8] [9]

Following her graduation, she joined the *Topeka Daily Herald* as a society reporter. She then moved to the *Topeka Daily Capital* where she earned a reputation as an aggressive reporter, and later as the society editor, covering social causes with an emphasis on the suffrage movement. She joined the suffrage lecture circuit in Kansas on her own time to drum up support for women's voting rights. In 1911, she toured Europe, writing dispatches for the *Capital* on European culture and architecture. Written in the form of a personal diary, she recorded her tour group's experiences from Munich and London to Venice and Florence. Her writing was languid and absent of insight into European culture. Topeka readers didn't seem to mind, lapping up the experiences of a local girl abroad. The newspaper often sent her to high schools and universities to discuss journalism careers for women. [10] [11] [12] [13]

Although not considered a beauty, Florence was tall, handsome and confident in her journalistic abilities and her political convictions. It wasn't until much later that she revealed her leftist political leanings beyond her circle of friends, by publishing articles sympathetic to communism and socialism in *Script* following Rob's death. She was aggressive and direct, particularly while managing Rob's career, and often displayed a ruthless streak in her personal relationships. She could be intimidating and did not suffer fools gladly. She allowed her brown hair to turn gray as she got older but occasionally dyed it platinum blonde, as was the fashion in the 1930s. She defied the stereotype of a corn-fed, marriage-minded Kansas girl. [14] [15]

In her summer visit to Los Angeles, she stayed with her sister, Grace, and her husband, Joseph Blondin, also a musician, at their home on Westminster Avenue just south of Santa Monica. It's likely that Florence met with a number of reformists on her trip and perhaps fell in with Rob Wagner's roundtables at his studio since both traveled in the same political circles. At the end of the summer when Florence was scheduled to return to Topeka, she stayed with her sister instead and took a teaching job. [16] [17] [18]

Her romance with Wagner blossomed through the fall and on January 14, 1914, they formally announced her engagement in the Topeka press. Four days later at noon on Sunday they were married in a private ceremony at Wagner's studio. Grace and her husband were the only Welch family members to attend. Rob's mother, Mary, and sister, Charlotte, drove down from Santa Barbara. His nieces, Harriet and Arline Wagner and Imogene Lidgerwood, also attended. If Wagner's sons, Leicester and Thornton, were present no newspapers mentioned it. [19] [20]

Following the wedding Florence hoped to open a Montessori school that emphasized teaching to children ranging from two to six years old in the same classroom and allowing students to choose their own activities. But by 1913, many school boards were becoming hostile to what they perceived as a foreign technique in education. Instead, Florence taught journalism at Polytechnic High School while her new husband continued teaching at Manual Arts during the day and working at *The Western Comrade* in the evenings. [21] [22]

Neither their engagement nor wedding announcements mentioned that Wagner was a widower with two small sons. Leicester and Thornton were expected to call their stepmother "mom" but in return they received none of the benefits of a mother.

Rather than have the boys join their parents in Los Angeles, Rob and Florence decided they should remain in Santa Barbara. Rob had already enrolled his sons at Boyland, a boys' private boarding school perched atop thirteen acres on Mission Ridge in Santa Barbara. Rob's friend, the eccentric Prynce Hopkins, whose family made their fortune as major stockholders in the Singer Sewing Machine Company, owned and operated the school.

Educated at Columbia, Yale and London universities and holding a doctorate in psychology, Hopkins, a co-founder of the ACLU, wrote several books on social reform and religion. He was an early advocate of psychoanalysis and had traveled extensively throughout Asia where he acquired an appreciation for Eastern philosophies. He was somewhat prim in his mannerism and affected a high British accent much to the bemusement of his friends and acquaintances. A socialist and ardent opponent of America's entry into World War I, the press called him the "socialist millionaire" for contributing vast sums of money to leftist causes.

Hopkins' based Boyland's curriculum on the Montessori method, which appealed to Florence. Her husband approved of Hopkins' methods because it allowed the boys plenty of time outdoors. He appreciated that the boys studied from 6 to 11 a.m. and then had the rest of the day to play under the sun, ride the school's miniature locomotive and work in the school's vegetable garden. [23]

Leicester and Thornton proved to be indifferent students with a tendency to take shortcuts in studying and physical education despite Hopkins' liberal attitude towards teaching. Letters to his father indicated that Leicester was an unhappy child. He usually reported the events of his day without much enthusiasm and as if it were a requirement. He signed off as "Leicester Wagner, manager of The Boyland Views," which was the school's newsletter. Thornton appears to have not written to his father at all. [24] [25] [26] [27] [28]

During the summers the boys didn't stay in Los Angeles with their parents, but instead Rob and Florence sent them to work. As young teenagers they took part-time jobs in the state forestry service or similar employment requiring hard labor. Leicester also spent a summer on a dairy farm while Thornton worked in the chalk mines in Lompoc. When the boys were in Los Angeles, Florence often sent them to stand in the breadlines in Mexican communities to get a sense of how the fringes of society lived, although the extended family believed that she just didn't want to spend money on them. In an interview many years later, Rob claimed he learned little from a university education and instead wanted his sons to discover life on the streets and through labor to encourage them to stand on their own. It was far from the truth. Privately, Rob had wanted to send the boys to college because his experience at the University of Michigan had been an important part of his life. He acquiesced to Florence, who didn't want to pay the tuition. [29] [30] [31] [32] [33]

Florence demonstrated a deep jealousy of Rob's relationships with his family and his outgoing, social demeanor. Later, when Leicester reached adulthood, Florence repeatedly prevented Leicester's children from seeing their grandfather. Florence claimed the visits would take too much time away from Rob's work. She also could be unforgiving. Florence froze Rob's niece, seventeen-year-old Harriet Wagner, out of the family when Harriet made an innocent but sarcastic remark about her on the telephone. [34] [35]

Florence was also a harsh disciplinarian, often beating — by her own admission — the boys on the backside with a hairbrush for infractions. Only Rob's intervention prevented the spankings from getting out of hand. Whatever attempts by Rob to encourage independence in the boys failed. They were homesick for a home they never lived in. Florence never gave ground to her stepsons who remained under Prynce Hopkins' care until about 1922. Only when Boyland closed and the boys were too old to remain with Hopkins did Florence allow them to come to Los Angeles where they attended Franklin High School. [36] [37]

The boys, according to Florence, would also take anything that "wasn't nailed down." Hopkins corroborated Florence's assertion, noting that Florence found a pocketbook stolen by Thornton from a woman on a Boyland field trip. Hopkins wanted to keep the theft a secret, but to Thornton's credit he told Hopkins that he was willing to accept responsibility and public humiliation if Hopkins thought it a necessary consequence. In 1920 at the age of sixteen, Leicester spent a year at the Boys Republic of Chino, a reform school that helped troubled teenagers without jailing them as adult criminals. While the boys were considered wild under their grandmother Mary's care, they were clearly deeply troubled as they reached their teen years due in large part to Florence and Rob's neglect. [38]

It would be unfair to pin treatment of the boys entirely on Florence's insecurities. Certainly corporal punishment of children was more or less the standard in the early twentieth century although Rob had veto power over any decision Florence made about his sons' upbringing. Yet it appears he rarely intervened on his children's behalf. It was a matter of Florence willing to sacrifice the happiness of her stepsons, and later of her step-grandchildren to further her husband's career. The result was Leicester and Thornton rarely displayed physical affection with their own children.

Yet the boys flourished after finishing high school. They took different career and political paths. Leicester followed his father into journalism and carved out a notable newspaper career in Los Angeles. Although not a socialist, he embraced the same values as his father and championed the causes of the working class and ethnic minorities. Thornton, however, distanced himself from his father's profession and progressive causes. He rarely wrote letters home. He embraced his mother Jessie's family, the Brodheads, as his own. He worked for his uncles, Willis and Jack, at their East St. Louis automobile dealership, selling, as he wrote in a rare letter to his father, "fast cars to bootleggers." His first love was flying. He started in 1928 with lessons he paid for himself at Carpinteria, CA. He subsequently became a commercial airline and test pilot and flew aircraft for the Air Transport Command during World War II. His politics were decidedly conservative.

Throughout their lives Leicester and Thornton often expressed devotion for their stepmother, much to the consternation of Leicester's wife, Lucy, and Sarah, Thornton's wife. Both daughters-in-law were dismayed that their husbands' displayed affection for a woman who emotionally abused them and prevented access to their father for most of their lives. [39]

Thornton sent flowers to his stepmother every Mother's Day for the rest of her life. He even named his daughter after her, much to the fury of Sarah. It's telling that Florence Carol Wagner never went by the name of Florence, but instead Carol, thanks to Sarah's determination. Still, Thornton often expressed indifference – or perhaps his priorities – to his parents with silence. In January 1934, Rob's brother Jim complained of the financial burden of supporting their mother and his expectations that neither Leicester nor Thornton would contribute further monetary support. He noted that during the previous year Leicester performed reasonably well, contributing $105 ($1,870 today) over twelve months while Thornton paid just $40 ($712 today) over four months. [40] [41] [42]

Rob's casual approach to parenting extended to his career. He was perfectly happy to continue as an artist and further the socialist cause, but Florence would have none of it. Not only did she take control of the parenting responsibilities she also envisioned a different career for her husband. She had no desire to be the wife of a starving artist. Four months after the wedding, Rob resigned from *The Western Comrade*. Florence also put an end to Rob's financial participation in what she viewed as hare-brained schemes such as Llano del Rio and the disastrous Parnassus cooperative apartment venture.

One of his last painting projects, a self-portrait, was completed in April 1914. His last art award was a bronze medal from the 1915 Panama-Pacific International Exposition for painting in oil. He kept his memberships in various art organizations, but his participation in art-related events began to dwindle. [43] [44]

Rob's studio and residence, the converted coach house, would also not do as a home for the newlyweds. By November 1914, Rob and Florence – using Florence's money – completed construction on a two-bedroom, one-bath home at 226 Isabel Street off of North Figueroa Street between West Avenue 37 and Ulysses Street in Los Angeles. The Wagners had the existing house on the lot, previously owned by a British army officer, demolished and based their new home on the original residence's floor plan. The house stood on a terrace about thirty feet above the street and was surrounded by trees. They remained there until a fire destroyed it in December 1922.[45][46]

Although Rob Wagner worked on only a handful of films, his circle of friends widened to include many actors, directors and writers in the film colony. He usually brought his new wife to his speaking engagements, mostly sponsored by women's groups, to discuss movies as an art form. One night in 1915 on the way home from such an event, Florence suggested that Rob start making money off his knowledge of filmmaking by writing about it for national publications. Rob agreed and wrote an article on spec for the *Saturday Evening Post*. The *Post* editors not only liked the article, but they asked for more. They paid $100 ($2,200 today) for each feature with the expectation that he would become a regular contributor. His first contribution, the two-part "A Film Favorite," was published on October 9 and October 16, 1915. Over a four-year period he contributed twenty-five film-related articles to the *Post* until he was fired after the November 15, 1919, issue for his antiwar activities and pending appearance before the county grand jury. He wrote only one other article for the *Post*, "The Quickie," for the November 20, 1926, issue. However, his collection of *Post* stories resulted in his first book, *Film Folk*, published in 1918. [47] [48]

Wagner displayed remarkable loyalty to the *Post*, writing almost exclusively for the magazine throughout the teens. By the time his relationship ended with the magazine, he had attracted attention as an authority on filmmaking. He immediately received assignments beginning in 1920 for the *Woman's Home Companion*, *Red Book* and *Blue Book* magazines, thanks to his old Michigan University chum Karl Harriman, as well as for *Liberty*, *Collier's* and *Screenland*. He wrote only a few articles for socialist publications, but kept up with the Severance Club and other roundtable groups. He also continued his duties as president of the Intercollegiate Socialist Society and furthered the group's mandate to work outside the Socialist Party. [49]

The financial incentives of writing far outweighed his devotion to painting. He saw the future of art in motion pictures. He wasn't abandoning his art but simply changing direction.

Florence became Rob's *de facto* editor, which had a profound influence on his writing. She blue-penciled his attempts to write about abstract ideas and his penchant for satire, which worked well when writing about socialism, but which would never work with a mass audience that wanted a behind-the-scenes look at the movie world. Her experience as a newspaper reporter kept Rob's own reporting simple, direct and without literary adornments. She allowed him to create composites of individuals and compose quotes from multiple sources to attribute to a single person. This was an acceptable journalistic practice of the day, but she pounced on any digressions from the topic and any attempts at fiction. Rob was also not used to writing 4,000-word articles that required extensive reporting. Florence helped him write lengthy pieces by showing him how to break down his topic into a beginning, middle and end. She created a marketable writer.

Florence refused to take credit for her contributions to Rob's work. She told her hometown newspaper, *The Capital*, in 1917 that, "I merely suggested to my husband that he could write stories, and I edited and helped shape the first one or two. We have never collaborated so far as the creative part of the work is concerned." [50]

Nonetheless, whatever collaborative agreement the couple had, lasted throughout the rest of Rob's journalism career whether Florence admitted to it or not. Florence and later Leicester were the only members of *Script's* editorial team trained in journalism. Rob had no such writing and reporting training. When Rob referred to himself in *Script* as "Ye Ed" and Florence as "Ye Real Ed," he wasn't joking. He was giving credit to Florence for teaching him the craft of journalism. Rob's editorial voice was the hallmark of *Script*. It was a voice shaped by Florence.

CHAPTER SEVEN

"Wagner is a dangerous man"

The two most important friendships Rob Wagner had as the United States inched closer to the war in Europe were with Prynce Hopkins and Charlie Chaplin.

Hopkins was largely responsible for raising Wagner's boys, Leicester and Thornton, in Santa Barbara. He also had become increasingly engaged in antiwar efforts, which Wagner felt duty-bound to defend even if it meant jeopardizing his fledgling career in motion pictures.

Wagner's relationship with Chaplin was much more complex. Seventeen years Chaplin's senior, Wagner was the young comedian's mentor if not father figure during Chaplin's early years in Hollywood. Wagner exposed Chaplin to people whose interests were intellectual and political. For a man who grew up in extreme poverty in east London and experienced classism at its cruelest, the people Chaplin met through Wagner raised his consciousness and whetted his appetite to film stories depicting class struggles through the eyes of the humble, but subversive, tramp.

These relationships proved controversial throughout the duration of World War I and the Red Scare in the late teens and early 1920s. Hopkins would pay the heaviest price for his antiwar activities with a conviction and steep fine. Chaplin's punishment for his leftist leanings didn't come for another three decades, but it, too, carried a price when the US government barred his re-entry into the country in 1952.

Wagner survived by maintaining a split personality. He took his radicalism underground while writing and directing innocuous movies. In a sense he rehabilitated himself, at least in the eyes of the conservative studio bosses following the Roscoe "Fatty" Arbuckle scandal in which the comedian was accused of raping and contributing to the death of starlet Virginia Rappe in 1921. In an effort to take away the taint of scandal, studio bosses asked Wagner to wage a publicity campaign portraying the positive contributions to the community by Hollywood's hard-working professionals. [1] [2]

Wagner would remain committed to further enhancing Hollywood's reputation with favorable coverage for the rest of his life. But he also managed to pull off what so many socialist magazines – *The Masses* and *The Liberator* to name just two – failed to accomplish: Produce a successful publication based on socialist principles and turn a modest profit. *Rob Wagner's Script* may have appeared as the so-called *New Yorker* of the West Coast, and it certainly emulated the East Coast magazine's literary style. But no other periodical in the late 1920s through the 1940s actually operated with an editorial policy that didn't pay its writers or accept national advertising to guarantee that its coverage of the motion picture industry would be uncompromised. This allowed him to champion movies, directors and actors without being beholden to them. It also allowed him to be an advocate for their causes such as working conditions and collective bargaining.

Wagner often liked to tell his friends that the idea for *Script* came about on Christmas Day 1928 while he and Florence were lamenting the state of film journalism, and then six weeks later produced their first edition.

Rather, the birth of the magazine took root in part from his experiences with Chaplin, Hopkins and Max Eastman during the war years. When the *Saturday Evening Post* dumped Wagner in 1919 he turned to screenwriting and freelancing for other mainstream magazines, including the frothy *Screenland*, to earn a living. He chafed that editorial independence eluded him and it took a full decade to achieve that independence. This provided the basis for going solo with *Script* in 1929.

Regardless of his friendship with Wagner, Chaplin was already exploring the economic struggles of the poor. A stage performer since the age of five, Chaplin had a rough education starting with his work in English music halls, and then later in comedy and burlesque roles. He toured America's vaudeville circuit for twenty-one months beginning in 1910, which led to a contract with Mack Sennett's Keystone Studios. He arrived in Los Angeles in December 1913 at the age of twenty-four and shot his first film, *Making a Living*, which was released on February 2, 1914. As he studied filmmaking techniques, he developed his beloved Tramp character. The Tramp was a bundle of contradictions, wearing baggy pants, a too-tight coat, a bowler hat too small for his head, oversized shoes and a square patch under his nose for a mustache. His Tramp debuted in *Kid Auto Races at Venice* a week after the release of *Making a Living*.[3]

Chaplin soon tired of the crude humor of the Keystone comedies. When his contract with Sennett expired at the end of 1914, he sought to renew it at $1,000 a month, which Sennett refused. In January 1915, Chaplin signed a contract with Essanay Film Manufacturing Company in Chicago for $1,250 a week, plus a $10,000 signing bonus. He had virtually complete freedom to produce the kinds of films he envisioned. Unhappy working in Chicago, Chaplin moved his film production unit to Niles, CA, where Essanay had a facility. By the spring, he had convinced Essanay to open an office in Los Angeles.[4]

Sometime in mid-1915, Chaplin and Wagner had become friends, although the two men most likely met the previous year while both worked at the Keystone lot. The two men were also frequent patrons at Harlow's Café in downtown Los Angeles so it was inevitable that they would run into each other. At Keystone in late 1914, Wagner was developing a script for the Fatty Arbuckle comedy short *Fatty and Mabel and the Law*, which featured Mabel Normand in the female lead. Chaplin was finishing his contract at Keystone before leaving the studio in December. Arbuckle and Wagner's short was filmed January 8 through 13, 1915, at Hollenbeck Park in Boyle Heights and the Keystone lot. Sennett released it on January 28. The Arbuckle picture was Wagner's only film for Mack Sennett's Keystone during this period, although he would return to the film producer for brief periods in 1923 and 1925 at the Mack Sennett Comedies lot. [5]

As Chaplin began to expand his range, spending more time on each film and becoming more focused on a narrative instead of relying solely on visual gags, Wagner gave him a copy of Upton Sinclair's *The Jungle*. The 1906 sensational novel exposing Chicago's gruesome meatpacking industry and the harsh working and living conditions of immigrant workers had deeply affected the comedian. Wagner, along with Florence, suggested that Chaplin meet Sinclair and arranged to have a dinner for him with Sinclair and his wife, Mary Craig, at the Sinclairs' Pasadena home. Soon, Chaplin was screening his unfinished films for the Sinclairs and seeking their opinions about his work. [6] [7] [8] [9]

Chaplin became a regular dinner guest at the Wagner and Sinclair homes, and Wagner brought him to Severance Club meetings. It was a fertile period for the club with Bolshevism, the European war, government censorship of the private press, education and art often the topics discussed throughout the teens and 1920s. [10]

The club's membership records through 1940 offered a glimpse at an eclectic group. Socialists John Randolph Haynes and Kate Crane Gartz, who would be subpoenaed with Wagner before the Los Angeles County Grand Jury in 1919, were regulars. Artists Edward Weston and William Wendt joined them. The future Los Angeles County supervisor John

Anson Ford became a member along with architect Irving Gill, a supporter of progressive causes and who focused on the social impact of architecture in the community. [11]

Job Harriman and the anarchist and artist Bertha Fiske comprised the more radical element of the Severance Club. Whiskey manufacturing magnate Chauncey Clarke, perhaps more conservative than a majority of the members, was a frequent guest along with his wife, the staunch anti-colonialist Marie Rankin Clarke. Poet and publisher Jacob Zeitlin, Paul Jordan-Smith, later a literary critic for the *Los Angeles Times*, and Dr. Perceval Gerson, founder of the Hollywood Bowl Association and director of the Southern California branch of the American Civil Liberties Union, were also on the roster. [12]

John Bovingdon, an interpretive dancer and Harvard-educated economic analyst, was also a member in the late 1920s. He would fall victim to the anti-communist hysteria when he was fired in 1943 from the Office of Economic Warfare for his connection to the theater arts and alleged links to communist organizations. [13] [14] [15]

The Severance Club's meetings were never secret, and its membership had a liberal attitude toward members bringing any guest they wanted. Eventually the club came to the attention of the Justice Department, which was increasing its scrutiny of subversives. It wasn't long before Chaplin was linked to the radical element of the West Coast.

America's entry into World War I, the Russian Revolution, and the struggles of immigrant workers sparked Chaplin's political awakening. He wasn't much of a speaker in groups and preferred to listen rather to participate, but the discussions at the Severance Club articulated how he felt about the world and crystalized his thoughts about the working class. One evening as the socialist and author Upton Sinclair was driving back to his Pasadena home to host a dinner party, he turned to Chaplin and casually asked him whether he believed in the "profit system." As their discussion progressed Chaplin realized that he would never look at economics in a historical context but as a living and breathing system that profoundly affected the common man. [16]

Yet Chaplin never embraced radicalism. He was too much a free-thinker and artist to get caught up in politics. He confounded the press and his friends by rarely answering questions directly about his political leanings, giving the impression that his thinking was muddled. He generally declined to give money to leftist causes when his radical friends approached him hat in hand asking for donations. But there was nothing muddled about his films, especially *Modern Times* and *The Great Dictator*, which both displayed a keen sense of justice for the common man and exposing the hypocrisy of fascist governments. He fooled his critics with his independence.

It helped that by 1916, Chaplin had become a star with his films universally loved by the public. The movie-going public never abandoned him even through his darkest times of broken marriages, the scandals involving romancing very young women and public suspicions about his leftist leanings.

He took chances with his films, but the United States was still a year away from joining the war when he began producing comedies depicting the class divide. In *The Floorwalker*, Chaplin's first film for Mutual in 1916, he attacked consumer capitalism with an examination of class differences. In *The Rink*, he again addressed the issue of class with the story of an obese older wealthy man's many attempts to romance a lower class young woman. *The Rink* is a blunt commentary on the wealthy's bourgeois tendency to commit adultery as well as their power over the weak.[17] [18]

His rise to stardom gave him the economic independence to say what was on his mind. While on a European tour in 1921, he was shaken by the ravages of war in Berlin and Germany's economic woes. He wanted to do big things to lift people out of poverty, but felt helpless as an actor. As he expressed his feelings the press pounced on him, frequently asking his opinions on the new Soviet Union and whether he was a Bolshevik or socialist. He would grow wary of these questions, but he had only himself to blame. Typically, he couldn't keep his mouth shut, which often got him in trouble. On his return from Europe to the United States in 1921, for example, he stopped at the New York branch headquarters of the Socialist Party. He told reporters that, "It is a pity that the socialist forces of the world were not united, because if they were not split up and quarreling with each other they could accomplish big things." Not surprisingly, this only fueled the insistence of the press that Chaplin was "red." [19]

Often tongue-tied and lacking confidence when engaging the press and intellectuals in discussions about politics, he enlisted Wagner as his part-time secretary to help him articulate his political views in conversation and on paper. Wagner frequently coached him on how to respond to the press although he found that it was a job more or less like herding cats. Chaplin being Chaplin said what he pleased. When Chaplin wrote articles about filmmaking, he usually turned to Wagner for help. Wagner authored such articles as "What People Laugh At" for *American* magazine under the Charlie Chaplin byline in November 1918. [20]

By the end of the summer in 1917, Chaplin had completed his final film for Mutual, *The Adventurer*, which he had shot at his studio and at Santa Monica beach. Wagner was often on the set and even brought his sons for visits. After wrapping up editing the film, Chaplin sent it off for release on October 17. Although regarded today as his best comedy for Mutual, Chaplin wouldn't be present for *The Adventurer's* release.

Exhausted, he hoped to get some rest with a three-week vacation in Hawaii before returning to begin working for First National and to complete construction on his own film studio on North La Brea Avenue. Accompanied by his aide Tom Harrington, leading lady Edna Purviance, and Wagner, Chaplin boarded the *S.S. Mauna Kea*. The party arrived in Honolulu on October 16. If Chaplin had hoped for rest and relaxation he was mistaken. His celebrity status, especially among Hawaii's children, made it almost impossible to have time to himself and his small entourage. "Taking a rest with Charlie Chaplin is a joke," Wagner later complained to a reporter. "All the kids in the world seem to know him as soon as he comes in sight. The result is that walking down a street is just like heading a triumphal procession of the juvenile population." [21] [22] [23]

Wagner hoped that he could have time alone with Chaplin to develop a biography of the comedian. While he didn't get the depth he needed from Chaplin because of the demands on the actor's time, he managed to obtain enough material to write the biography. Once the Chaplin party returned from Honolulu to San Francisco on November 6, Wagner began writing. By January he had a working manuscript. Written in longhand on yellow paper, he had about 50,000 words. He pitched the biography to publishers as the definitive portrait of Chaplin, who had been plagued by unauthorized biographies mostly from newspapermen who collected news clips and conducted one or two interviews with Chaplin. In one instance Chaplin had obtained a permanent injunction to prevent the sale of an unauthorized biography. [24]

But Wagner had Chaplin's cooperation. He focused on the actor's early years in London's music halls and with Karno's vaudeville troupe. The book would also feature "an analysis of his humor, methods of workmanship, intimate glimpses of his acting and of the technical contribution he made to this newest of art forms." It was a sanitized version of Chaplin's life with no references to his politics. [25]

He submitted the manuscript to Chaplin in early 1918. In a letter to Wagner on May 15, the actor implied that he approved. "I am returning your manuscript, and I only wish I could picturize my art on the screen as sympathetically as you have written of mine." Privately, though, Chaplin told Wagner that he was too young to have a biography written about him and that his best work lay ahead of him. Wagner shelved the manuscript and settled for a few magazine articles, including his analysis for *American* magazine and a profile for the August 1918 edition of the *Ladies' Home Journal*. [26] [27]

Chaplin's first film for First National was *A Dog's Life* in which he gave Wagner a bit part as a man in several dance hall scenes. The film was one of Chaplin's finest for First National about the homeless tramp outwitting the police after stealing sausages with his canine friend and ultimately winning the affection of a dance hall singer played by Edna Purviance. Chaplin cemented his skills in social commentary by making use of material covering poverty, hunger, hostility of police towards the poor and the victimization of women by their reduced circumstances.

The film was released on April 18, 1918, to positive reviews, but Chaplin was not ready to begin his next project. He faced immense criticism from the British press for failing to enlist in the army during the war. While with Mutual he was contractually obligated to remain in the United States, which the British press objected to since Chaplin was only twenty-seven years old in 1917 and fit for military service. When the United States entered the war in April 1917, he faced similar criticism from the American media. To his credit, Chaplin attempted to enlist in the US Army only to be rejected for being underweight. [28]

His next film, *Shoulder Arms*, which would be released in October 1918, was a deliberate effort to produce a patriotic film to boost the morale of the common doughboy. Actor Douglas Fairbanks advised Chaplin against releasing the film because it made fun of war in a time when the media questioned his loyalty. But *Shoulder Arms* proved to be a hit and allowed Chaplin to join the ranks of Fox, Paramount, Vitagraph and Universal studios in providing the US government with pro-war propaganda. Even D.W. Griffith, who produced the pacifist *Intolerance* in 1916, came up with the aggressive pro-war film *Hearts of the World*. [29]

To further mitigate the hostility of the press, Chaplin, at the urging of Wagner, joined the third Liberty Bond tour. Fairbanks and his future wife, the actress Mary Pickford, toured the Northeast United States while Chaplin traveled through the Southern region. Accompanying Chaplin on the trip were Wagner, his publicity man, Carlyle Robinson, and Charles Lapworth, an ardent socialist and journalist who served as a consultant on *A Dog's Life*. [30] [31]

Wagner had problems of his own and his inclusion in the Liberty Bond tour provided the perfect opportunity to help silence allegations that he, too, was disloyal to the United States in a time of war. Certainly Wagner's relationship with Chaplin drew scrutiny from the Justice Department's Bureau of Investigation, but it was Wagner's emerging pro-German position, pacifism and friendship with Prynce Hopkins that would cause him the most trouble.

Hopkins at thirty-three years old in 1918 was a strident antiwar activist. He was a socialist but unlike Upton Sinclair, who broke with the Socialist Party to support the war effort, Hopkins remained committed to his opposition to America sending troops to France. He worked closely with Emma Goldman and Alexander Berkman in organizing antiwar speeches and took over as chairman of the League for Amnesty of Political Prisoners when Goldman was jailed for her antiwar activities. [32]

In early 1918 Hopkins continued his efforts. In April, he vehemently announced his opposition to the war before a large audience at an International Workers of the World (IWW or Wobblies) meeting in Los Angeles. The IWW was a radical labor union with ties to the socialist and anarchist movements. Hopkins was arrested on suspicion of violating the Espionage Act, which the Bureau of Investigation liberally applied to all manner of perceived anti-government activities. Prosecutors alleged that he was interfering with army recruitment, which Hopkins did not deny. Federal agents raided his beloved Santa Barbara school, Boyland, and confiscated antiwar literature and the facility was shuttered. He pleaded guilty to violating the Espionage Act and was fined $25,000. [33] [34]

Wagner rushed to the defense of his friend, including addressing rumors of his sexual orientation, by writing to the Justice Department:

"Prince started out in life with a silver spoon, a million dollars and a chance to dedicate his life to polo and highballs, but as a mere youngster surprised and shocked his friends by showing an amazing intellectual appetite. Yes, Prince is a 'nut,' according to country club standards, but it always seemed to me he was simply a good healthy protest against his own bunch …

"When I was in Santa Barbara last, everybody was telling me that they were going to 'get' Prince, and they all seemed most happy about it. They whispered about mysterious doings at Boyland, sex degeneracies, and whatnot! It was dear old sex-sick Santa Barbara. I lived there six years and I know how the idle parasites love to play in the mud. But my answer to all that stuff is that I sent my own two boys to Boyland and I regard Prince Hopkins as one of the finest influences that ever came into their lives … If Prince holds any 'liberal' sex ideas, they are purely intellectual; his own life has been as disciplined as a monk's."

Wagner didn't help himself or Hopkins with his frank letter. Instead, he succeeded in piquing the government's interest in his own activities during the war. While Hopkins was being tracked for subversive activities, Wagner received a visit from federal agents. He had rented a room at an abandoned winery at the end of Avenue 39 in Los Angeles to have some quiet time to write. On July 18, 1918, agents Frank Turner and Edwin Van Wirt interrogated Wagner. They asked why he worked in an abandoned structure and wanted details about his comings and goings. They were particularly interested in why he hung a colored flag in a nearby eucalyptus tree and why he climbed another eucalyptus tree to hang a large sheet of canvas. The agent implied he was sending signals to spies. Wagner said the canvas sheet was hung to block the light from an annoying street lamp in the evenings and the flag was to signal a vegetable seller he was ready to buy from his cart.

The agents also asked about Chaplin's visit to the winery and they told Wagner that they knew his brother, James. In typical Wagner fashion, he joked about the encounter in *Script* twelve years later, but the interrogation must have shaken him. He had already lost his teaching job at Manual Arts High School for his support of the antiwar activists and his friendships with Hopkins and Chaplin were bringing further unwanted attention from the Bureau of Investigation. [35] [36]

Wagner needed to be involved in the Liberty Tour as much as Chaplin. The tour proved to be a tremendous success for both men, albeit only temporary for Wagner.

Chaplin, Wagner, Robinson and Lapworth soon discovered on their trip that Fairbanks and Pickford probably got the better deal in touring the Northeast, finding that their hosts in the South were a little rough around the edges. To their amusement, small Southern towns appeared woefully unprepared to deal with the magnitude of Chaplin's celebrity. As the entourage traveled from town to town Chaplin did his part to stand on small stages and rally crowds to buy war bonds. Local committees organized to welcome Chaplin viewed him like most rural communities did throughout country: an actor of questionable moral character.

As Chaplin stopped in each town community leaders greeted him as if he was a visiting drunken fraternity brother. Unshaven, unwashed and slightly drunk, they would take the time to tell the comedian and his group dirty stories. Somewhere along the tour word spread that perhaps they should clean up a bit. After all, Chaplin was about as close to royalty that they would ever get. Soon, small towns caught on and were better prepared for the visit.

A lesson in real Southern hospitality occurred in one Tennessee city when Chaplin shared the stage with Secretary of Treasury William G. McAdoo in front of crowd of about 10,000 people. At a dinner party that evening after McAdoo had long since departed, Chaplin, Wagner, Robinson and Lapworth were guests of honor at a restaurant. The group soon discovered that each of them was "assigned" a "date" for the evening.

As the entertainment and meal drew to a close, the host leaned over to Chaplin and nodded toward the women putting on their wraps and whispered, "Mr. Chaplin, they all have their own cars and – well, we hope that you will all have a pleasant time. Everything is paid for."

Chaplin, well aware that all eyes were on him, replied, "Thank you so much. Hospitality could go no further than this, but I regret that our rather rigid schedule makes it necessary for us to return to our hotel and catch a few hours' sleep before we leave. Please explain this to the ladies. I'm sure *they* will understand." [37]

Chaplin's leg of the tour ended in New York City in front of the United States Sub-Treasury Building with Chaplin, Fairbanks and Pickford entertaining tens of thousands of people. In all, the Bond Tour program helped raise $17 billion. Six months later, Chaplin released *The Bond*, a half-reel film for the Liberty Loan Committee, to further encourage film audiences to purchase bonds.

The tour gave Chaplin welcome relief from the scrutiny of the press into his political interests. He proved his mettle as a team player with the other studios by submitting to the production of propaganda supporting the war effort. Yet Chaplin saw no need to hide his political interests from the public.

Perhaps the single most intriguing dynamic of the relationship between Wagner and Chaplin was Wagner's zeal to introduce his friend to as many influential leftists as possible. Chaplin had already demonstrated his continuing intense interest in politics with his regular attendance at the Severance Club and his friendship, through Wagner, with Upton Sinclair. And another friendship would soon blossom.

On the evening of February 26, 1919, Wagner brought Chaplin to the Los Angeles Opera House to hear Max Eastman give a speech on the Russian revolution and the potential of an American intervention. Eastman opposed any involvement by the United States and urged his audience to support the Bolshevik cause.

After the speech, Wagner approached Eastman, gave him a handshake, and said, "Charlie Chaplin is in the wings and would like to meet you." [38]

Backstage, Chaplin was effusive in his praise. "You have what I consider the essence of all art – even mine, if I may call myself an artist – restraint." The two hit it off immediately and Chaplin invited Eastman to his film studio to watch how he made movies. Eastman had hoped to persuade Chaplin to invest in a start-up magazine that he founded with little capital. The US Postmaster General had forced Eastman's socialist magazine, *The Masses,* to fold in November 1917. Eastman and some of his staff were then tried in US District Court on sedition charges the following year. However, after two trials ended in hung juries, Eastman was free to establish his next magazine, *The Liberator*, but he had little cash.

Wagner, however, told Eastman privately that the prospects of getting Chaplin to provide funding for the new venture were dim. Chaplin, he said, was notoriously tight with his money and didn't have the commitment to be part of any long-term projects other than filmmaking. [39]

Wagner's presence at Eastman's speech did not go unnoticed by the Bureau of Investigation. The hostile climate toward leftists had begun after America's entry into the war when antiwar sentiment was deemed unpatriotic, and then worsened throughout 1919 when labor unions staged a series of strikes. Federal and local authorities commenced cracking down on any speech deemed subversive.

In May 1918 Congress passed the Sedition Act, an extension of the Espionage Act, that gave law authorities broad powers to arrest any person expressing anti-government opinions that would interfere with the sale of war bonds or impede the war effort. Furthermore, states passed versions of the "Criminal Syndicalism" bill that gave state and local law enforcement the ability to indict any individual who "knowingly associating oneself with a group which advocates, teaches, or aids and abets criminal syndicalism."

The primary targets of these laws were the IWW and members of the Socialist Party. Both organizations were fiercely antiwar. A series of strikes led by the IWW started with a walkout of 60,000 workers in the Seattle area in January 1919. Facing the potential of violence between workers and 3,000 police officers and federal troops, the IWW called off the strike on February 10. But walkouts followed in Boston, Pittsburgh and Gary, Indiana. Although there was no evidence of radicalism in the work stoppages, panic ensued that "Reds" were responsible.

In April 1919 federal authorities uncovered a bomb plot that targeted John D. Rockefeller, J.P. Morgan, United States Attorney General Alexander Mitchell Palmer and thirty-three other political and capitalist leaders. When eight bombs exploded nearly simultaneously in eight cities, including one at Palmer's Washington, D.C. residence, Palmer initiated what became known as the Palmer Raids to arrest anarchists across the country. The raids, however, also included socialists, communists and any individual suspected of anti-government sentiments.

Palmer also responded by forming the General Intelligence Division of the Bureau of Investigation on August 1. The division's sole purpose was to ferret out radicals. Over the years the bureau compiled files on an estimated 200,000 individuals. Anybody could have a file, from simply looking like a radical to making anti-capitalist statements. As a consequence thousands of people were arrested and jailed. [40]

Wagner, as we have previously discovered, was a fence sitter and could come off as wishy-washy when pressed to publicly declare his socialism. Remarking once about his radicalism, he said, "I never felt as stronger about things than I do now – but I got to live under this ridiculous, but, thank heaven, rapidly cracking up system." Whatever strong feelings Wagner had about radicalism, his personal philosophy was never to bite the hand that fed him. [41]

To be fair his beliefs focused more on the purity of art and giving the artist control over commerce of his art. He did not join his friend Upton Sinclair in throwing his support for the United States' role in the war, but he also didn't stand on soapboxes to oppose it. Instead, Wagner did what he did best since the day he took Emma Goldman into his home to protect her from the anti-Reds. He supported his leftist friends' right to free speech in expressing their opposition to the war and introduced radicals to influential Hollywood filmmakers. But he was more strident in his antiwar arguments in his private roundtable meetings. As we learn later, this made him a target of informants.

Supporting leftists like Prynce Hopkins and introducing Max Eastman to Charlie Chaplin put him in the crosshairs of the Bureau of Investigation's new anti-radical unit. And in October 1919 federal agents found the smoking gun they needed when they received a copy of a letter Wagner wrote to Charles Ashleigh, the IWW's chief publicist, who was serving a ten-year sentence on a sedition conviction at the Leavenworth Federal Penitentiary. To the Bureau of Investigation, it appeared that Wagner violated the Criminal Syndicalism law by "associating" with radicals, in this case the IWW. [42]

A British citizen and newspaperman who would gain fame as a prison journalist, Ashleigh had been with the IWW since 1912 when he arrived in the United States. In September 1917 he was jailed with other Wobblies for alleged subversive activity in Chicago. His sentence was later commuted and the US government deported him in 1921. [43]

Wagner's October 21, 1919, letter, a reply to Ashleigh, was innocent enough. Although there is no record of Ashleigh's original letter, he apparently asked Wagner to help a colleague get a job in the film industry. Wagner put him off, noting that he received "a hundred" such requests each week. But he promised to work on getting Ashleigh released. "As your countrymen say – in the politest circles, 'Keep your pecker up,' and we'll get you out or bust." [44] [45]

The mere fact that Wagner was corresponding on friendly terms with Ashleigh – a notorious "agitator and troublemaker," as the Leavenworth prison warden once called him – put him in violation of the new criminal syndicalism law. On November 24, Los Angeles County District Attorney Thomas L. Woolwine announced that he had issued a subpoena for Wagner to appear before the county grand jury on charges of sedition. Woolwine also subpoenaed reformers Kate Crane Gartz and Dr. John Randolph Haynes. [46] [47]

Gartz, at the age of fifty-four when she was summoned to testify, was a Pasadena millionaire whose family made their fortune in publishing. Active in the community, she was a co-founder of the Pasadena Playhouse and the American Civil Liberties Union. As a young woman she worked with Jane Addams at Hull House in Chicago. The experience deeply affected her and she committed her life to social reform. With Wagner and Haynes she was a regular at the Severance Club and held her own salon at her home. She hosted Albert Einstein, Max Eastman and Floyd Dell, the flamboyant editor for Eastman's *The Masses* magazine and who had stood trial with Eastman on sedition charges. Gartz heavily financed socialist causes, became a vocal antiwar activist, and published tracts that contained her protest letters to newspaper editors and state and federal officials. [48] [49]

Sixty-six years old at the time of his grand jury summons, Haynes had arrived in Los Angeles in 1887. In 1897 he formed the Los Angeles chapter of the Union Reform League, a Christian socialist organization committed to a non-revolutionary approach to public ownership of utilities, direct legislation and the women's suffrage movement. Throughout his career he participated in numerous socialist projects, and like Wagner, often preferred working outside formal socialist organizations to provide time and money to progressive causes. [50]

Wagner, Gartz and Haynes appeared at the hearing on Tuesday morning, November 25, at the Los Angeles County Courthouse at Temple Street and Broadway. Each witness was questioned at length by Woolwine's deputy, Asa Keyes, about their links to the IWW and their views on radicalism. After the first day of testimony Haynes feigned illness and did not appear again. Wagner and Gartz continued their testimony, but it was Wagner who spent the entire week on the witness stand denying that he had any links to the IWW or anarchists. [51] [52]

The pressure to subpoena the three socialists came from Frank Burke, the assistant director and chief of the General Intelligence Division of the Bureau of Investigation. Burke was aggressively pursuing all links to Bolshevism in general and the IWW in particular. But the bureau's agent in charge at the Los Angeles office, S.A. Connell, believed the local press was making people "unduly alarmed" over the activities of the IWW by paying too much attention to the union.

In a November 22 report to his superiors, Connell wrote, "As for myself, I am not alarmed at the excitement, which is now going on in Los Angeles, over the activities of the IWW but I believe it has been 'scared up' considerably by the newspapers which relate every arrest and incident connected with the IWW movement, printing large scary headlines in their papers, and thus alarming the people to such an extent that they believe that the IWW's are liable to attack them." [53]

It was in this climate of hysteria that Wagner, Gartz and Haynes faced an onslaught of allegations. But it's clear that the Los Angeles County District Attorney's office was doing the Bureau of Investigation's bidding, although somewhat unenthusiastically. Woolwine didn't bother to recall Haynes to the witness stand. And Keyes didn't seem interested in Wagner's relationship with the IWW simply because he had arranged with the union to give Emma Goldman safe haven in 1912, or the fact that Wagner promised Ashleigh that he would work on his release from prison. When Burke pressed Asa Keyes to draw a conclusion on Wagner's testimony, Keyes said there was nothing there.

On December 11, Agent George T. Holman in the Los Angeles office reported that, "Agent showed letter from Chief Burke and Mr. Keyes stated that they had had subject before the grand jury and questioned him at length, but nothing was disclosed in the examination that would warrant a prosecution of him, and in fact Keyes stated that subject disclaimed any radical views at this time." [54]

To Wagner, and probably to Keyes, that meant that Wagner didn't hold any radical views at the time of his testimony, but once he stepped outside the courthouse he may have had other thoughts. Keyes concluded to Holman that the case against Wagner "was not strong enough to do more than they had already done." [55]

While Wagner likely believed that he had a close call with the Bureau of Investigation, and feared that an arrest would end his career in films, it didn't deter him from continuing his leftist activities.

The Bureau of Investigation took notice, but did nothing when Wagner and Gartz attended a reception held in August 1922 by Charlie Chaplin for William Z. Foster, the director of the Communist Party of America on the eve of the party's convention at Bridgman, Michigan. At the reception, Bruce Rogers, described by an informant as a "money-getter," was to see film writer William C. deMille to collect cash for the communists. According to the informant attending the reception, Robert Morss Lovett, president of the Federated Press League, said, "these men," Wagner among them, "helped us before and will do it again." [56] [57]

* * *

Like many investigations into alleged disloyalty, betrayal played a part. The probe of Wagner's antiwar and alleged pro-German activities was partially based on evidence provided by some of Wagner's friends. Nora Sterry, an elementary school principal, reported to agents that she attended a party at Wagner's home where she met "some very queer people" discussing the European war. Wagner, she said, argued that he was a "pacifist," and did not believe in war. Agents made much of Sterry's report, describing Wagner's gatherings as an anti-government "secret society." Sterry's sister, Ruth, a prominent suffragette, told agents that Wagner told her sister that if Germany invaded the US, then Americans should "submit" to occupation. Wagner's artist friend Elmer Wachtel provided agents with Wagner's letters in which he said the US has no moral standing to criticize Germany given America's history of lynching blacks in the South.[58]

From early 1918 until the end of 1919, the War Department's Military Intelligence Branch conducted its probe. Agents placed Wagner under twenty-four hour surveillance during the Liberty Bond tour. Capt. Harry A. Taylor at the War Department described him as "a dangerous man." During the tour, agents considered recruiting Douglas Fairbanks to inform on Wagner, although there is no documentation the actor agreed to the proposal. During the tour agents searched every hotel room Wagner occupied.[59]

In one incident, while Wagner stayed at the Grunewald Hotel in New Orleans, agents recruited twenty-four-year-old Bella Hans, the daughter of a German immigrant, to seduce Wagner in an effort to gain access to his personal diaries. The plan was never executed, but agents eventually stole his diary while he was en route to Los Angeles. The diary proved a disappointment as it never mentioned his views on Germany.[60]

Although the surveillance provided no evidence of German espionage, information from the Sterry sisters, Wachtel, the Charles Ashleigh prison correspondence and Wagner's support of Prynce Hopkins made Wagner a perfect target for prosecution — successful or not — in an effort to send a message to other antiwar activists.

CHAPTER EIGHT

"Public censorship is killing bad pictures"

Rob Wagner was pushing fifty years old in 1920 when he attempted to turn his attention to working full-time in films. Although associated with the industry for nine years he had little practical experience behind the camera or in a studio's writer's department.

He was about to break into a young person's game and success – even with his vast connections to every studio head in Hollywood – was no guarantee. The competition was daunting. Young bucks like Raoul Walsh was just thirty-three years old in 1920 and had been making films for nearly a decade. The rising star Rex Ingram, who would go on to direct the seminal *The Four Horsemen of the Apocalypse* in 1921, was twenty-eight. Screenwriter Frances Marion was thirty-two and had been writing for films since 1912. Even Wagner's cousins, Jack and Blake Wagner, twenty years Rob's junior, had been shooting movies and writing scripts since 1910.

He joined actor and like-minded progressive Charles Ray in 1920 to write scenarios for two upcoming films to be directed by Ray. A considerable chunk of his time, though, was devoted to his personal ambition to shape the infant film industry's artistic direction and to defend studios at the behest of executives from calls to self-censor. He juggled the demands between industry observer and filmmaker, but saw his observer status consistently supplant his attempts at directing.

One of his first jobs at the start of the new decade was not writing scripts but joining the Palmer Photoplay Corporation as an adviser. The company, informally called Palmerplays, was a correspondence school for aspiring screenwriters founded in 1918 by former newspaperman and actor Frederick Palmer. He had appeared in numerous Thomas H. Ince films in the 1910s, and with Ince's blessing established the program. Ince and Cecil B. DeMille, among other high-profile filmmakers, supported the idea of developing a school that would produce original screenplays from unknown writers. Ince's father had once operated a reputable drama school and Ince firmly believed in supporting art conservatories. [1] [2] [3]

The school, even in its day, was controversial. Many such correspondence schools existed solely to separate naïve students from their money. By the 1920s movie studios had become hierarchical, elitist and difficult for amateurs to penetrate. Palmerplays would give aspiring writers no more of a chance at selling scenarios than if they had independently submitted them on spec. And Palmerplays subscriptions were as high as $90 (about $1,052 today) in the 1920s, up from $75 in 1918. The course took about one year and students received booklets, a dozen lecture tracts, newsletters with film industry updates and the monthly magazine *Photodramatist*, which had a circulation of 13,000. The school offered no guarantees that students' scenarios would be sold, but promised that as much as $1,000 could be earned for the right story. Palmer took a ten percent commission on any sold scenario.

Samuel Marx, who worked for Universal Studios in the 1920s and later became a producer for Metro-Goldwyn-Mayer, described Palmerplays as "rated an estimable school in the dubious business of teaching amateurs how to write for the screen."

Wagner appeared a curious choice to serve on the advisory council and contribute learning materials. He had only one directing credit, the documentary *Our Wonderful Schools*, to his name in 1920 and only three writing assignments, including the forgettable *Yoke of Gold* in 1916. But since his series of behind-the-scenes articles for the *Saturday Evening Post*, and subsequent publication of the book version, *Film Folk*, in 1918, he had been regarded as a movie authority. Frederick Palmer considered Wagner's marquee value as an important marketing tool. Joining Wagner on the advisory council along with DeMille and Ince were James R. Quick, a journalist with *Photoplay* magazine, Frank E. Woods with Famous Players-Lasky and Kate Corbaley, who had worked for Ince and later at MGM.[4][5]

Palmerplays figured in a wider debate within the film industry whether to produce films based on existing material or use original screenplays. The conservative nature of studio bosses usually leaned toward previously published material as a better bet toward bigger box office receipts. A proven story produced on stage or in literature reduced the risk of a flop. Wagner, of course, hated the idea of movie producers considering the bottom line at the expense of artistic merit. He complained that producers often relied on unappealing existing work for screenplays when audiences craved original stories. Ever the champion of the individual and unadulterated art, Wagner preferred that unproven writers providing original content should be given a chance.

But did Palmerplays actually produce scenarios that reached the screen? Palmer claimed that he sold $60,000 worth of scenarios, but there is little evidence that students had their stories made into movies. It's likely that most of that cash was prize money in student competitions. In 1924 Palmerplays released just three movies through its own production company. However, *Variety* panned one film, *His Forgotten Wife,* as "one of a series of yarns produced by the Palmer Photoplay School as an inducement to show those who take their scenario courses that there is a production chance for the work they turn out after paying to learn how it is done." [6] [7]

Wagner made no promises to students who contacted him to get their scenarios produced. He even hinted at the odds against success by telling one old friend from his Detroit days that, "It is by far the best school of its kind in America, and even if you do not become a professional through its studies I am sure you will get a lot of help and amusement out of your contact." [8]

* * *

If Palmerplays' educational philosophy was consistent with Wagner's pursuit of artistic integrity, then the burgeoning Little Cinema movement allowed him to apply the purity of that art in practical terms. By the early 1920s some filmmakers, among them directors Rex Ingram and Ernst Lubitsch, had become disenchanted with the commercialization of movies that sacrificed art to appeal to the lowest common denominator with formulaic plots and marketing actors as movie stars. Studio bosses had a tendency to lump films into two camps: artistic films that had no chance of turning a profit and commercial films that kept the big business of cinema rolling along.

Wagner was pessimistic that Hollywood had the wherewithal to develop a strategy in which studios could produce art films that were also commercially viable. He had seen the early rise of socialist-themed labor films, which he considered an art form of the political genre, before World War I, only to witness their disappearance in the postwar era. For every Charlie Chaplin and Buster Keaton there were dozens of directors and producers turning out western serials and slapstick comedies. Hollywood in the 1920s flooded movie houses with hundreds of pictures each year, most of which disappeared within a couple of months but turned tidy profits. More than eight-hundred movies, for example, were scheduled for production in 1927. Virtually all of those films targeted box office success and featured the same actors in the same roles they played previously and reciting lines from underdeveloped scripts.

Little Cinema, which derived from the Little Theater movement that started in 1912, promised to deliver art films with commercial appeal. The Little Theater movement was founded on the principle that non-commercial plays could be produced for intimate audiences with discriminating tastes. Stage companies produced these plays in small theaters with an informal plan to establish a string of playhouses across the United States. In 1922 the National Board of Review of Motion Pictures suggested a similar movement for the film industry in its magazine, *Exceptional Photoplays*. Wilson Barrett, secretary of NBR, was a champion of films with artistic merit and often discussed at the organization's annual meetings the conflict between art and the commercialization of films. Barrett was on a mission to improve the general public's taste in motion pictures. [9]

Initially called the Little Theater Film movement, the goal of Little Cinema was to showcase in small movie houses documentaries, foreign films and domestically produced avant-garde movies in response to growing demands from audiences for more original story-telling. The movement rejected big-budget pictures such as the Cecil B. DeMille spectacles in favor of small, more individual stories like the early work of Eugene O'Neill. [10] [11] [12]

There was an elitist element to the movement as it attempted to cultivate "modernity and chicness" with the discerning moviegoer. Such patrons may have had more progressive tastes but also more wealth than the average audience member. Admission prices were higher at smaller venues, which usually did not exceed six-hundred seats and often served coffee and cigarettes in the lounge while patrons browsed painting and sculpture exhibits during intermission. New York City was the center of the movement with society leaders like Gloria Gould, granddaughter of financier Jay Gould, showing Erich von Stroheim's *The Merry Widow* at the six-hundred-seat Embassy Theater for a $2 admission (about $26 today). [13] [14] [15]

Wagner didn't mind the high-brow aspect of the Little Cinema movement as long as it served the artistic purity of films. But he wanted to take the movement a step further. In early 1923 he co-founded Little Theatre Films, Inc. with Rex Ingram, Ernst Lubitsch, director Hugo Ballin and Paul Bern and Ralph Block, who were both writers and producers. The company was to work with distributors to bring European films to the United States. It was also to coordinate with about two-hundred little theater clubs throughout the country to screen films like Lubitsch's *The Cabinet of Dr. Caligari* and the German version of *Hamlet* featuring Asta Nielson. Little Theatre Films would handle the American release for foreign movies that had no distribution contract or find them a distributor. Civic organizations eager to screen art movies for selected audiences in communities outside urban centers included the Federation for Women's Clubs for Southern California, the Juvenile Protective League and the Friday Morning Club. The NBR was a sponsor. [16] [17]

The founders comprised the company's advisory board and immediately installed Curtis Melnitz, the Berlin representative for United Artists and a friend of famed German director Max Reinhardt, as its president. The board recruited screenwriter and Broadway lyricist George Marion Jr. to identify films in Europe for distribution while *New York Globe* drama critic Kenneth Macgowan worked with little theaters and university drama clubs to bring films to their towns. [18]

By July 1923, Wagner convinced Douglas Fairbanks, Mary Pickford, William deMille, Rupert Hughes and Charlie Chaplin to join the advisory board. D.W. Griffith and playwright and screenwriter Robert E. Sherwood also joined the company in an advisory capacity. Melnitz, Lubitsch and the German-born Bern were the key members for their

European connections. Bern was particularly important to the success of the venture because of his relationship with the Swedish film director Victor Sjöström (who also used the American spelling of Seastrom). Sjöström was scheduled to direct Bern's script for *Name the Man*, which was released in January 1924. The director was also committed to the distribution of his film, *Mortal Clay*, through Little Theatre Films to the American market in 1924. The movie had already been released in Europe in January 1922. [19] [20]

Little Theatre Films was only six months old when it fell apart. Melnitz abruptly resigned in January 1924 and his German contacts evaporated with his departure. At the same time Sjöström began a long and fruitful American career directing films at MGM, which did not require the fledgling company's services. Studio bosses, who agreed to have an employee or actor sit on the advisory board, were otherwise unwilling to provide financial support because they viewed foreign films as competition for box office receipts. [21]

Little Theatre Films was a noble effort by Hollywood insiders, but the financial considerations of the big studios undermined any chance for success. Many film critics also snubbed their noses at experimental cinema. John Hutchins in *Theatre Arts Monthly* complained that European movies were "static and inferior" and that too many Russian films were being screened. [22]

The demise of Little Theatre Films was hardly the death knell for silent avant-garde cinema on the West Coast, but it was only a matter of time before the Little Cinema movement lost steam. In 1928, Ragge Doran founded the 960-seat Filmarte Theater on North Vine Street south of Sunset Boulevard in Hollywood specifically to showcase art films. As the theater's director, Doran struggled to keep the movie house financially afloat and was forced to close it briefly. Filmarte reopened in September 1929 and began showing almost exclusively European and Russian films. [23]

Doran had hoped that exposing the Hollywood filmmakers to European imports would provide filming techniques for Americans. She screened such films as Sergei Eisenstein's *Battleship Potemkin* and *Ten Days That Shook the World*, which were more gritty and realistic than anything produced in Hollywood. Filmmakers who attended screenings were particularly impressed with the night photography of mob scenes. Still, Hollywood's cinematographers and directors had little interest in Soviet techniques, complaining they saw no value in jump cuts, short scenes moving back and forth between characters and montages. While some studios privately screened German and Russian films for movie crews to expose them to other techniques, most executives were indifferent if not hostile to European cinema. Lingering anti-German sentiment and an antipathy towards communism also played a part as revolutionary rhetoric and scenes of peasants overthrowing governments troubled Hollywood audiences. [24]

By 1929 it was clear that talkies had supplanted "silents" as the new motion picture in Hollywood. The dearth of avant-garde and experimental talking pictures prevented Filmarte Theater and other art movie houses from replacing silents with quality films. The stock market crash in October resulted in many art houses closing which effectively ended the Little Cinema movement. By 1930 only a handful of film critics championed Soviet films. *Experimental Film* magazine singled out Wagner, Arthur Millier of the *Los Angeles Times* and Frank Daugherty of *Film Spectator* as the only Los Angeles writers who countered the hostility aimed at Russian films by the Hollywood film establishment. [25] [26]

* * *

Wagner's moviemaking plans frustratingly remained on the back burner in early 1922 when he was asked by industry leaders to perform a different function. At the beginning of the decade the country fell into a deep economic recession. Film studios, once small operations willing to experiment with filmmaking and providing wide open job opportunities, had coalesced into Big Business as studios assumed complete control of production, distribution and exhibition. The war years and immediate postwar period proved profitable. Studios were willing to spend as much as $350,000 (about $4.9 million today) to produce a single film. But bloated budgets and the construction of ornate movie palaces left studios financially vulnerable. [27]

Although the US government declared the recession over in July 1921, the industry was still reeling from its effects when in September Roscoe "Fatty" Arbuckle hosted a party at the St. Francis Hotel in San Francisco. There, young actress Virginia Rappe became ill and later died. Rappe's friend accused Arbuckle of raping the starlet and contributing to her death. Arbuckle was charged with manslaughter.

The Arbuckle case gave rise to the birth of celebrity journalism as newspapers across the country engaged in a feeding frenzy over the details of the case. Led by managing editor Fred Eldridge and city editor Raymond Van Ettisch of the sensationalistic *Los Angeles Examiner*, the media covered every salacious detail and reported without evidence the actor's alleged penchant for "sex orgies" and that he raped the young woman with a soda bottle. Within days, the *Los Angeles Evening Herald* and the *Los Angeles Evening Express* followed by reporting one unsubstantiated rumor after another. Virtually every major US newspaper followed with lurid reporting. Joining the press were religious groups, including the Women's Christian Temperance Union and the Catholic Church, which had been anxious, as early as 1915, to impose government censorship of movies. The groups alleged the industry was a hotbed of immorality and demanded the industry clean itself up. [28]

Arbuckle would suffer through three trials. Two ended in hung juries and the third resulted in an acquittal with a formal written apology from the jury. While the comedian was in the third week of his second trial in San Francisco in 1922, another scandal rocked Hollywood when popular film director William Desmond Taylor was murdered on February 1 in his upscale Westlake Park bungalow in Los Angeles. Taylor's death was less a scandal than a murder mystery, but the *Examiner*, the *Herald* and the *Express* had learned from the Arbuckle case that stories of hapless actors embroiled in compromising sexual situations and secret trysts sold papers. *Examiner* editors, always believers in investigative journalism but reckless with facts, snared anybody with even a remote connection to Taylor. Soon media attention turned to actresses Mabel Normand, a longtime costar with Arbuckle and Charlie Chaplin, and Mary Miles Minter embroiling them in the growing scandal. Normand had a romantic relationship with Taylor and sought his help to beat her cocaine addiction. Minter was only nineteen years old when Taylor died and had professed her love for him in letters discovered by police in his residence. Taylor never returned her affections, but it didn't stop the press from speculating on whether her unrequited love for the director resulted in murder. Normand and Minter's film careers, like Arbuckle's, were destroyed.[29]

The Taylor homicide, which was never solved, added fuel to the chorus of self-appointed guardians' demand that if Hollywood couldn't police itself then the government should censor film content. Alarmed at declining box office receipts and the thought of losing control of studio independence, the Motion Pictures Producers and Distributors Association stepped in to counter the onslaught of bad publicity. The two primary leaders to develop a strategy were Frank Garbutt, a Paramount executive who was largely responsible for merging Famous Players-Lasky and Paramount in 1917 and a member of the association, and W.J. Reynolds, the organization's secretary. Panicked, Reynolds initially suggested that studios conduct surveillance on actors and film crew members suspected of immoral behavior. Cooler heads prevailed when Garbutt enlisted producer Sol Lesser and theater owners to put together a team of writers and speakers to wage a publicity campaign to put the industry in a positive light. Garbutt and Lesser recruited Wagner, then a member of the Writers' Club, who was named chairman of the group's publicity campaign. Joining Wagner were Will Rogers, Rupert Hughes, Frank A. Woods, screenwriter and president of the

Writers' Club, and journalist Elinor Glyn among others to write about Hollywood. The Motion Pictures Producers and Distributors Association also received the support of Dr. Herbert Booth Smith, pastor of Emanuel Presbyterian Church of Los Angeles, who was one of the few religious leaders to call for a fair trial for Arbuckle. [30] [31] [32] [33]

The strategy, in a series of speeches and articles, was to point out that Hollywood in 1922 employed up to 50,000 people and that the number of individuals engaged in immoral or criminal behavior was no higher or lower than any other group of professionals. The loosely organized team was charged with analyzing in the media the strengths and weaknesses of the industry and attempt to explain why it reputation had been tainted.

Elinor Glyn observed that by painting Hollywood with a broad brush and judging Arbuckle guilty without a trial was an assault on democracy. She deplored "the hysterical, illogical attack upon the moving picture community." [34]

Wagner noted that the insular nature of Hollywood contributed to its own unfavorable reputation. He told the *Hollywood Citizen*: "I think that much of the misconception that arises about Hollywood is due to the continued use of the word 'colony.' People in the east look upon us here as a remote, detailed 'colony,' probably with a fence around it, making our own morals and dominated by motion picture people who simply wallow in debauchery." Wagner argued that Hollywood was an "integral part" of Los Angeles largely populated by Midwest transplants that didn't observe "artificial boundaries" perpetuated by the media. [35] [36]

Unlike his previous support for antiwar activists, Wagner neither supported nor vilified Arbuckle, his onetime colleague and film collaborator. Arbuckle would have welcomed any kind words from the hundreds of men and women who had worked with him over the years, but none was forthcoming. Instead, Wagner and the writers on their propaganda blitz focused their arguments that whatever occurred at the St. Francis Hotel was not typical behavior of movie industry people.

This was the tone adopted by Wagner when he established *Script*: a community of hardworking people who had little time to engage in shenanigans and who contributed to the local economy. The film industry was a vital component to the financial health of Southern California. Indeed, the primary reason why actors sought to organize a union – a cause Wagner championed in *Script* – several years later was to curtail the grueling schedule of sixteen-hour days often seven days a week. There was little time in the schedule of a serious artist, whether an actor or technician, to engage in inappropriate behavior.

Later, Wagner must have pondered the irony of misbehaving Hollywood folk when his two cousins, Jack and Max Wagner, were involved in separate mini-scandals involving deaths. Jack Wagner was involved in a brawl with a bootlegger and three actors at the Hollywood Crescent Athletic Club in March 1927 when actor Eddie Diggins was fatally stabbed. The entire party had been drinking. The bootlegger, Charles Meehan, was suspected of stabbing Diggins, but no charges were ever filed. A month later Max Wagner was present when his roommate, actor Paul Kelly, beat to death another actor, Ray Raymond, during an alcohol-fueled party in their apartment. Max was the prosecution's star witness against Kelly. [37] [38] [39] [40]

While the publicity campaign to counter bad press was highly effective, Wagner was equally concerned that the potential fallout of the Arbuckle and Taylor scandals would lead to government censorship. Wagner always had an antipathy towards what he called "moralizers," members of the public whose sense of outrage over perceived indecency was disproportionate to what was actually portrayed on the screen. He had been collecting data on censorship since about 1915. He noted the many censorship cases involved special interest groups that objected to specific film content that had little to do with offending the sensibilities of the general public. He observed, for example, that Canadian censors cut eight reels of an American film because it had "too much American flag." [41]

He further noted: "More and more the films are becoming a form of publication in which economic and political interests advocate their causes. The sponsors of such publications should certainly be permitted the same freedom of speech as the newspapers or magazines, yet only last week a labor film was stopped in a district whose censor received his appointment from certain capitalistic interests."

He also deplored Pennsylvania's laws that banned scenes that implied pregnancy and the commission of crimes or violence. To Wagner, the censors rendered films attempting to address these issues as "absurd" because the deletions gutted the story and eliminated conflict and good versus evil. By enacting draconian censorship laws, filmmakers would sustain financial losses on movies that otherwise would earn a profit. [42]

Appearing on October 25, 1921, before the Los Angeles City Council, which was considering a censorship ordinance, Wagner said that "wildcat" films depicting immoral behavior would hurt the majority of film producers "making clean pictures." He said, "Public censorship is killing bad pictures." [43]

As is often the case with Wagner, there were caveats when self-interests were involved. Wagner, who adopted Santa Barbara as his hometown and where his mother Mary, Aunt Bess and brother Jim continued to reside, cut the city's residents some slack because his family was acquainted with members of the local censorship board. He told a Santa Barbara newspaper reporter that the city's "brand of censorship is ideal" because the censors comprised "cultured and intelligent women who keep abreast of the best in literature and current thought" and conferred with the California Theatre Company on appropriate films. [44] [45]

In March 1922, much to Wagner's disappointment, the Motion Pictures Producers and Distributors Association hired Will H. Hays, the former US Postmaster and chairman of the Republican National Committee, as the association's president to repair Hollywood's image and "clean up" movies to ward off government censorship. To the dismay of studio bosses Hays instituted the industry-wide Production Code to keep pictures clean. At the August 1922 reception for Communist Party leader William Z. Foster, Charlie Chaplin and Wagner voiced their opposition to Hays' appointment. "We are against any kind of censorship, and particularly against the Presbyterian censorship," Chaplin said. [46] [47]

Wagner continued his anti-censorship coverage in *Script*, reminding readers that special interest groups continued to plague the industry with political agendas. In 1930, Major Frank Pease, president of the Hollywood Technical Directors Institute, a group of technical advisers on military-themed films, sent a telegram to President Herbert Hoover demanding that director Lewis Milestone's antiwar film *All Quiet on the Western Front* be banned from theaters. According to Pease, the "filthy" film undermined the beliefs in the army and its chief source of inspiration originated from the Soviet Union. Wagner cited the Pease telegram as an example of mixing ethical and political opinion with art criticism. [48]

* * *

Whenever he could Wagner returned to the business of writing scripts that paid him a living wage. His first assignments were to work with Charles Ray on his two films. Ray was a star for many years at the Ince studio, but the actor wanted new challenges and established Charles Ray Productions in 1920. Ray had a reputation for being an egotist and difficult to work with, but his relationship with Wagner was close, and at least for a time, productive. [49]

Wagner produced two scripts for Ray, who would direct the films. *R.S.V.P*, released in December 1921, was a Wagner signature story about starving artist Richard Morgan who falls in love with a model (apparently Wagner discovered since his Paris art school days that some artists actually do fall in fall with their models) only to find that she is wealthy. He eventually wins the girl by demonstrating his considerable talent as an artist. *Smudge,* following in July 1922, told the story of a newspaperman using a little ingenuity to solve the problem of smudge pot smoke, used to keep citrus groves from freezing in the winter, from polluting a small community. Both films received middling reviews and did little to enhance Ray's reputation as a director. [50]

As he focused on writing scripts, Wagner's output in freelance magazine submissions dwindled to almost zero. His income in the early 1920s was derived from Palmerplays and taking freelance assignments from studios to doctor scripts, write gags and produce title cards. He scrounged around for any work available. While the assignments didn't provide the consistent income he found in magazine writing, it gave him what he desperately sought: hands-on experience in the mechanics of filmmaking. Despite the tepid critical responses to *R.S.V.P.* and *Smudge*, Ray had taught Wagner how a director organizes his film crew and shoots the script.

Although Wagner professed his ambitions to be a film director he was already well into Plan B in the early 1920s. If he were to establish a magazine covering the film industry it would require extensive knowledge of its operation. Unlike fan magazines, which focused on the minutia of movie stars, Wagner wanted to give the technical and political side of the industry equal weight. Los Angeles, Hollywood, North Hollywood, Culver City and Beverly Hills were communities to a growing population of film workers that would never be subjects in fan magazines, yet their contributions were equally important to the success of a picture.

Wagner envisioned a magazine that was all-inclusive. It would cover the public aspects of filmmaking with profiles of stars because that boosted circulation, but it would also give coverage behind the camera. The magazine would also profile the community they lived in. He would mix this coverage with political commentary on progressive causes, film, art and book reviews, mild gossip and an open-door policy that would give film people a soapbox to say what was on their minds. But to publish an authoritative magazine Wagner believed he had to start at the bottom and climb his way up to understand how the industry worked. He could have easily taken an administrative job with Charlie Chaplin or Jesse Lasky at Famous Players-Lasky, but he would have lacked the insight that could make *Script* stand out among the fan magazines. [51]

Instead, he took on freelance assignments. Following his stint with Charles Ray, Wagner moved to the low-budget studio Realart to write scenarios for Constance Binney. He penned a screenplay, *The Melancholiac*, on spec for Douglas Fairbanks that was never produced. He also accepted an entry-level job in Famous Players-Lasky's titles department, the lowest rung of the writers' ladder. Working with a roomful of men half his age, Wagner wrote titles and designed the cards for films during most of 1922. He also fleshed out scripts for the scenario department when asked. [52] [53] [54]

His only significant contribution to magazines was the serialization of "The Girl of the Films," in *Red Book* that began in July 1922. However, it was more of a Florence Wagner story about a young woman who struggles to make it big in motion pictures. Many of Florence's colleagues at the Kansas newspapers recognized her tart lines throughout the serial, including the protagonist saying, "I am more interested in a minimum wage for working girls than a maximum wage for movie queens." The Wagners had hoped a studio would pick up the story for a film, but instead turned it into a novel, *Tessie Moves Along*, published in 1927. [55] [56]

In late 1923, Blake Wagner invited his cousin Rob to the Mack Sennett Comedies lot to help write gags for the Ben Turpin two-reeler, *The Dare-Devil*. The director, Del Lord, had assigned Blake as the cinematographer. In turn, Blake told Rob there was a single-film assignment if he wanted it. Rob joined Mack Sennett and helped him develop the scenario about a hapless actor who performs one dangerous stunt after another completely by accident and frustrates the director who wants the stunts performed on command.[57]

Wagner and Sennett were friends since the Keystone days, but it had been nearly nine years since Wagner had worked for the comedy film producer on *Fatty and Mabel and the Law*. Sennett hired Wagner as a writer for his Keystone films, but fired him ostensibly for taking too many naps, a ridiculous assertion given that Sennett's writing team spent most afternoons goofing around. Sennett later wrote in his autobiography, *King of Comedy*, that Wagner's brand of humor was "several cuts too intellectual and satirical for our burlesque." In 1915, the novice Wagner had struggled with the genre. "Nothing makes sense," he complained to Sennett one day. "This place isn't a studio, it's a madhouse." By 1923, he understood "the exaggerated human conduct" of physical comedy and was better prepared to handle writing assignments.[58]

His collaboration with Sennett on *The Dare-Devil* proved successful as the film was one of Sennett's best comedies in the post-Keystone era. Wagner's success on *The Dare-Devil* led to an invitation in late 1923 to join Hal Roach Studios, which would become his most prolific period of directing and writing comedy films. His moderate success with Roach also led to a formal one-year contract with Sennett in September 1924 to write scenarios for comedians Ralph Graves and Edgar Kennedy.[59]

A less successful movie-making stint occurred with Famous Players-Lasky during the same period. Wagner signed a contract with Jesse Lasky on January 5, 1923, at $200 (about $2,724) per week to write and direct films. The contract was an extension of his job writing titles for Paramount under Famous Players-Lasky. His only directorial assignment, *Fair Week*, a rural melodrama set in Pleasanton, CA, was a box-office dud and did not lead to another directing job with Lasky. Five months after the film's release in March 1924, Wagner acknowledged to a colleague that he lost control of the picture. "I realize that I made a blunder in doing *Fair Week* with a bum cast and a rotten script and that is evidently the hardest thing I have to live down with Jesse. There is mighty little of me in *Fair Week*." [60] [61]

Wagner joined the directors' roster at Hal Roach not at the suggestion of Roach, but at the urging of Will Rogers. Towards the end of 1923, Florence Wagner's friend, actress Irene Rich, invited the Wagners and Will Rogers and his wife Betty for an intimate dinner. Rogers, who had been in Roach pictures for two years, complained of the physically demanding work and the limitations of mugging for the camera with pratfalls. "All I ever do on the Roach lot is run around barns and lose my pants," he told Wagner. [62] [63]

Rogers persuaded Roach to have Wagner direct him in a series of short comedies. The first was Rogers' idea to parody James Cruze's epic western, *The Covered Wagon*, produced earlier that year. Rogers and Wagner collaborated on the script. Wagner filmed *Two Wagons, Both Covered* at Lake Elsinore in Riverside County at the suggestion of Rogers in order to get away from meddling producers. Wagner delivered the two-reeler, about twenty minutes long, before deadline in November 1923 and under budget. But as Rogers feared, Roach executives couldn't keep their hands off it. They looked at a rough cut, announced the film was a flop and shut down post-production. Wagner quit the Roach lot in protest. A few weeks later, a film critic asked to see the rough cut and found it funny, suggesting to the Roach brass that they made a huge mistake. The film was hastily assembled and sneak-previewed in Santa Monica to an appreciative audience. It was Rogers' best silent film, prompting Roach to ask Wagner to return and collaborate with Rogers on more films. [64]

Three Wagner-Rogers comedies followed: *High Brow Stuff*, a send-up on little theater groups and released in April 1924, and two of the Alfalfa Doolittle trilogy films, *Going to Congress,* released a month later, and *Our Congressman*, which followed in July.

Going to Congress followed Doolittle, a country bumpkin backed by his district's powerbrokers to run for congress and do their bidding once elected. In *Our Congressman*, Doolittle emerges as an arrogant politician who had forgotten his roots. As envisioned by Rogers, the two films eschewed physical comedy for satire. Most of the jokes were told through title cards written by Rogers and designed by Wagner. *Going to Congress* received favorable reviews and was screened at the Republican National Convention in Cleveland and in New York at the Democratic National Convention. Rogers attended both conventions as a credentialed journalist. *Our Congressman* was weaker with watered down gags, although Wagner and Rogers managed to insert some of their favorite lines about Washington D.C.'s ignorance of Bolshevism. [65] [66] [67]

In one sequence, Doolittle is asked, "Do you think we will ever recognize Russia?" He responds, "We will never recognize them unless they shave." Doolittle is later questioned about his position on the Bolsheviks. He replies, "I never did favor these third party movements." [68]

Certainly Wagner had hoped that his collaboration with Rogers would result in films that achieved the artistic level that he had always sought in filmmaking. The two men possessed a sharp wit that would have worked well to skewer Washington's politicians. But the Roach lot was the wrong studio. Roach wanted "gentle inoffensive satire" with no partisanship. He wanted lively scenes even if it meant Rogers lost his pants. The studio head added Harley M. Walker, a longtime gag man for Roach, to *Our Congressman.* But Walker's slapstick approach conflicted with tone set by Wagner and Rogers. The story no longer belonged to Wagner and Rogers and was just another Roach comedy. Dissatisfied with the end result of *Our Congressman*, Roach assigned Hampton Del

Ruth, a veteran of the comedy lots, to the third one, *A Truthful Liar*, which had Doolittle as the ambassador to the Court of St. James. Del Ruth played Doolittle with a wide comedic brush and plenty of slapstick. The film was considered the best of the three, but it was also entirely different in tone and structure than Wagner's efforts.

Wagner ended his association with Roach in the summer of 1924, serving the remainder of his contract as an assistant director on the Our Gang comedies and teaming with Roach to write additional gags for Rogers' *Gee Whiz, Genevieve*.

Perhaps his greatest contribution to the Roach studio was not his films, but introducing Roach's chief director, Robert F. McGowan, to his former protégé, the Manual Arts High School alumnus Frank Capra. Wagner's former student had been working on the fringes of the film industry and had a handful of directing credits from a marginal production company. Capra had difficulty getting assignments on the comedy lots and Wagner's introduction set Capra on a path to write for Roach and, just two years later, to become director for the Harry Langdon comedies. At Sennett's studio for most of 1925, Capra wrote gags and teamed with Wagner to write the Edgar Kennedy vehicle, *Cupid's Boots*, which was released in July. [69]

The irony of Rob Wagner's film career was that his best days as a filmmaker were spent on the Sennett and Roach comedy lots. But it was those two studios that used formulaic scenarios essentially repeating the same stories and employing a small group of actors with star recognition. Film historians decades later would hail Sennett and Roach comedies as high art, but at the time they were throwaways with a short shelf life. When Wagner and Will Rogers attempted to break the mold and achieve a level of artistic integrity that Wagner so desperately wanted to accomplish, they were shut down to avoid losing the films' commercial viability. The result was that *Two Wagons* and the Alfalfa Doolittle trilogy were mere footnotes in Rogers' career.

Wagner moved to Harry Garson Productions, a small production company, and then to Universal Studios after his contract with Sennett expired in August 1925. Other than the Universal's mildly amusing forty-four-chapter *The Collegians* in 1926, Wagner's films were unremarkable. When it became clear in late 1926 and early 1927 that talkies were the films of the future, Wagner saw his filmmaking career draw to a close. He continued contributing title cards and scenarios to Universal through the summer of 1928, but he could no longer sustain an income that allowed him to live on North Crescent Drive in Beverly Hills, his home since 1923. By November 1927, he had returned to journalism, joining *Collier's* magazine as a Hollywood correspondent with many of his articles based on his experiences on the Sennett and Roach lots. He remained with *Collier's* through 1930 as a means to make a living while he and Florence began creating what would become *Rob Wagner's Script*.

Charlie Chaplin and his brother Sydney Chaplin, far right, with the Wagner family on *The Adventurer* set. With Charlie are Thornton at the center, front; Leicester to Thornton's left and Rob. Others unidentified. *(Author's Collection)*

Leicester and Thornton Wagner spent most of their youth as students at the radical Prynce Hopkins' Boyland school in Santa Barbara. *(Author's Collection)*

Charlie Chaplin entertains Rob's sons, Leicester, at right, and Thornton, on the set of *The Adventurer* in 1917. *(Author's Collection)*

Following his narrow escape from a grand jury indictment on sedition charges, Wagner joined Charles Ray to write two films. Here, Wagner goes over a script with Ray in 1921. *(Author's Collection)*

Prynce Hopkins was jailed and fined by a federal court for his antiwar activities during World War I. *(Courtesy David Petry)*

Charlie Chaplin, Edna Purviance and Rob Wagner join several children in Hawaii while on tour. *(Author's Collection).*

Rob Wagner and Charlie Chaplin, behind the automobile, during their Liberty War Bond tour in North Carolina in 1918. *(Carol Wagner Mills-Nichol Collection)*

Florence Welch Wagner with her stepson Leicester. It was not a happy relationship. *(Author's Collection)*

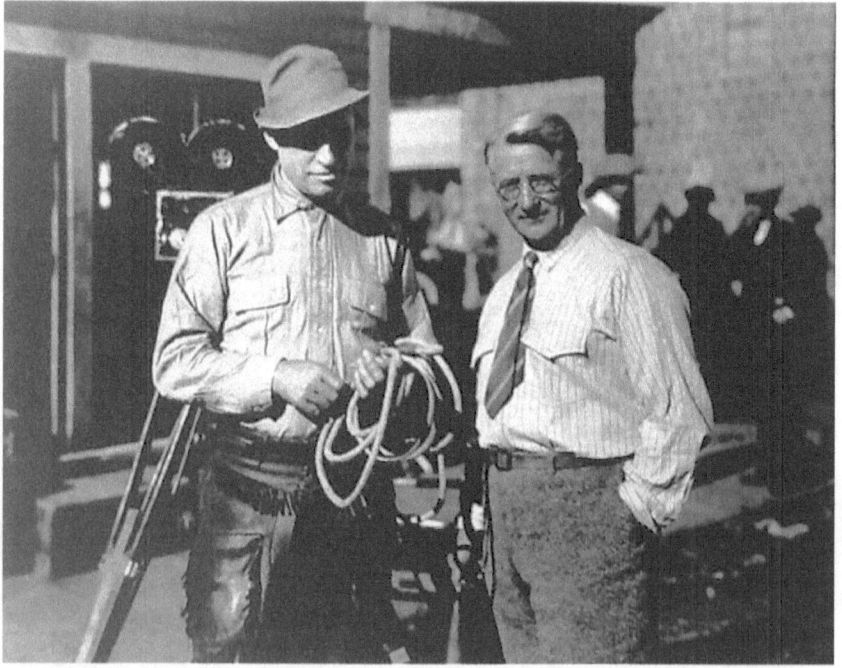

Wagner signed with Hal Roach to direct and co-write a series of films featuring Will Rogers as a country bumpkin congressman. From left: Roach, Wagner, unidentified, and Rogers on the Roach studio lot in 1923. *(Carol Wagner Mills-Nichol Collection)*

Will Rogers and Rob Wagner collaborated on four films together in late 1923 and 1924. *(Author's Collection)*

Wagner on location at Lake Elsinore, California, in late 1923 for the filming of *Two Wagons, Both Covered*. *(Carol Wagner Mills-Nichol Collection)*

In 1927 Rob Wagner was free-lancing and working on the Paramount film "Two Flaming Youths." Wagner, back to camera, discusses a scene with cast and crew from left: Assistant cameraman Al Williams, assistant director Otto Brower, and actors Jack Lundon and John Seresheff. *(Carol Wagner Mills-Nichol Collection)*

The film crew for *Fair Week* in Pleasanton, California, in 1924. Standing from left: Actor Walter Hiers, Irving Newmeyer, grip; Lloyd Tipple, grip; Tom Geraghty, writer and Bert Baldridge, cinematographer. Seated from left: Actress Constance Wilson, Mrs. Walter Hiers, Ethel Doherty, script assistant; and director Rob Wagner. *(Carol Wagner Mills-Nichol Collection)*

Frank Capra, a former student of Rob Wagner at Manual Arts High School, joins his old teacher on Wagner's short-lived radio broadcast at KFWB in 1936. Wagner felt uncomfortable on the air reading from a script and only conducted a few broadcasts. *(Carol Wagner Mills-Nichol Collection)*

Florence Wagner with Charlie Chaplin and his assistant, Tom Harrington, around 1918. *(Author's Collection)*

Kate Crane Gartz was called before the Los Angeles County Grand Jury with Wagner in 1919 on sedition allegations. She avoided an indictment, and later she was a likely investor in *Script* magazine. *(Courtesy Indiana State University)*

Leicester "Les" Wagner was working as a reporter for the United Press wire service when he helped his father launch *Script* in 1929. *(Author's Collection)*

Ye Ed and Ye Real Ed, Florence and Rob Wagner in 1938. *(Author's Collection)*

Rob Wagner in the mid-1930s. *(Author's Collection)*

Leicester Wagner with Gladys Lloyd Robinson, who scored a scoop by interviewing Leon Trotsky in 1938. *(Author's Collection)*

Script covers for many years used woodcut illustrations to save money. It wasn't until after 1938 that the magazine used photographs almost weekly for covers. *(Author's Collection)*

Leo Politi's illustrations of his regular characters were peppered throughout the magazine during the 1940s. *(Courtesy Paul Leo Politi)*

Leo Politi, left, and Rob Wagner on Olvera Street in about 1940. *(Courtesy Paul Leo Politi)*

Script sometimes skewered the "mannered" East Coast literary magazines of the early 1930s. The nattily dressed actor Adolphe Menjou and Rob Wagner in cords and a hickory shirt posed for the magazine's cover as the "best- and worst-dressed man in Beverly Hills" to emphasize *Script's* natural writing in contrast to the "stuffiness" of its competitors. *(Carol Wagner Mills-Nichol Collection)*

Ana May Wong followed Rob Wagner's counterintuitive advice and embraced her Chinese identity to score more acting roles. *(Carol Wagner Mills-Nichol Collection)*

Thornton Wagner took a different career path than his brother and father, becoming a pilot. At Willow Run, Ann Arbor, Michigan, he tested aircraft for the US military in 1942-43 before joining the Air Transport Command. *(Carol Wagner Mills-Nichol Collection)*

Leicester joined the Office of War Information in India in 1944. He returned to *Script* in 1946. *(Author's Collection)*

CHAPTER NINE

"Some little idiotic magazine"

With Rob Wagner's propensity for exaggeration to tell a humorous good story it's often difficult to determine where the truth stops and the tall tales begin. To hear Wagner tell it, he was ready to throw caution to the wind and establish a small weekly newspaper in the desert community of Indio east of Palm Springs.

He received a hefty salary from *Collier's* and *Liberty* to cover the film industry, but there was no creative fulfillment in writing for publications that allowed little wiggle room in their editorial policies. An Indio weekly newspaper was a daydream that gave him the freedom to write what he wanted. The fact was that Florence Wagner would have none of Rob's aspirations of editorial independence in the middle of the desert. She had spent sixteen years cultivating her social standing in the Beverly Hills and Hollywood communities and she was not about to give up her friends and position for a pipe dream.

Florence convinced Rob that his urge to establish a publication based on his socialist and artistic principles could be achieved in Beverly Hills. There was no reason to make it a national magazine or even compete with *Variety*. Instead it would be a publication for their friends – in the broadest definition of "friends" – and produced with the help of friends.

The Wagners likened *Script* to Hollywood actors who felt strongly about their art. Although actors earned hundreds of thousands of dollars in motion pictures, Rob said they often preferred to perform on stage before an intimate audience to satisfy their artistic ambitions. [1]

Rob used none of his income to fund *Script*. It's unlikely that Wagner's close friend Charlie Chaplin offered much financial help given his thrifty attitude towards money. More likely the source of the initial financing came from Kate Crane Gartz, Rob's comrade who faced the Los Angeles County Grand Jury with him in 1919, and from Upton Sinclair. Gartz was usually eager to donate money to progressive causes and *Script* seemed like a noble experiment to her. Sinclair felt the same way, recognizing that leftists needed all the friends they could get in an increasingly hostile environment in the growing conservative and insular film industry. Another source of early income came from an unlikely investor. Rob's son, Leicester, had inherited $25,000 (about $348,000 today) from his maternal grandmother, Jessie Willis Brodhead, who died in August 1929. At least a portion of that money ended up in *Script*.

Typical of journalists who aspire to own and operate their own publication, the Wagners almost doomed their project from the start with bad business instincts. Rob had a poor reputation among his family and friends for anything that required a skill beyond art and writing. He could not operate an automobile without it becoming a major production. In January 1923, he flipped his car while driving, breaking his collarbone. Two years later he overturned another vehicle with Florence beside him. She suffered a broken back. When it was time for the Wagners to take a road trip to Canada to visit Rob's relatives, Florence drove the entire 4,000 miles. He left all business decisions to Florence. Even the direction of his journalism and filmmaking career was left to her. Rob and Florence also had a reputation for being somewhat eccentric, or at least what passed as eccentricity in the late

1920s and early 1930s. They were often seen riding their bicycles around town, avoiding the use of a car whenever possible. Rob usually eschewed a suit and tie when on his own time or at the office, wearing a chicory shirt and corduroy trousers with one leg rolled up while riding his bicycle. [2]

Yet even Florence's business acumen abandoned her when they launched the magazine. Although she had income-generating land holdings in Kansas she failed to recognize that *Script* was about to become a money pit. At the end of 1928, the Wagners purchased a two-thirds interest in the Lynds Company, a small Beverly Hills print shop on Brighton Way owned by Benjamin M. Lynds, a World War I army veteran. Lynds, an alcoholic, did not disclose that his print shop was failing. The Wagners assumed all of its debts and accounts receivable for the new business, Wagner-Lynds Company, but discovered there was virtually no income. In addition, the equipment was not suitable for publishing a magazine. The Wagners could only build display advertisements and perform makeup duties. Linotyping was performed in Hollywood, and a Central Avenue shop twelve miles away did the printing. [3]

The Wagners sold the print shop to an experienced engraver, Jack Chancey, who turned it around to make it profitable. Meanwhile, the Wagners moved out of the Brighton Way building three months after *Script's* February 16, 1929, debut issue to the Brennan Building on Dayton Way at Rodeo Drive. Two real estate companies, a mortgage company, an architect and a general contractor were *Script's* neighbors. [4]

The editorial staff was miniscule. Florence recruited her old reporter colleague Florence Hayden from their days at the *Topeka Daily Capital* to report and write. Princeton University alumnus Jack Ainsworth Morgan was the associate editor, makeup artist, and wrote his "J.A.M. Berries" column. Leicester, while working for United Press wire service as a reporter, performed whatever editorial and production duties required. Typesetting was more or less performed by amateurs since no one had any real experience and the production budget could not afford a professional. On the evening the debut issue was going to print, Leicester was carrying two trays of type to the car when he tripped over the curb and spilled everything. The crew picked up the type, returned to the office and started over again before finishing at 2 a.m. In the meantime, Rob held on to his *Screenland* and *Collier's* contracts during the first two years of *Script's* existence to maintain an income and hedge against *Script's* potential failure. In December 1932, he signed a one-year contract with *Liberty* as film editor. [5]

The masthead of the new magazine was a mouthful: *Rob Wagner's Beverly Hills Script*. The magazine in its first year attempted to be everything for everyone. In addition to political comment, humor, film and theater coverage, the magazine also covered the city of Beverly Hills. Early articles included coverage of the city's plans to build a Civic Center on Santa Monica Boulevard between Rexford and Crescent drives as well as actress Gloria Swanson's anti-rabies campaign. [6]

The Wagners quickly realized that *Script* could not be a literary film magazine and a weekly newspaper at the same time. They abandoned city coverage with the exception of major issues and also dropped "Beverly Hills" from the masthead.

The fledgling magazine also attempted to market itself beyond industry players, signing a contract with KTM radio to float teasers on the publication's weekly content. Yet Wagner found that despite his years as a film industry booster, *Script* still had to earn the respect of insiders. Slights were common during those early years. Even the task of attending screenings to write reviews had a hierarchy and *Script* was clearly at the bottom of the heap. Studio publicity agents stood in the lobbies of Fox West Coast Theaters, the Beverly and Filmarte theaters handing out seating assignments and credit sheets. Wagner usually found himself at the rear of the theater next to the fire exit. It took several years to move front and center to view screenings. [7] [8]

Skepticism among industry insiders was not without foundation. By the end of the first year of publishing, *Script's* circulation was only 2,000 and barely attracting enough advertising to sustain it. At the end of 1930, circulation rose to 3,500, and then to 5,500 in February 1932. If Wagner wanted to attain his dream of running a "little weekly" he had accomplished his goal. Remarkably, *Script* remained in the black after the third issue, although it only earned enough to pay the printer one issue at a time with incoming subscriptions.

The Wagners didn't tout their publication as progressive or socialist, and only occasionally identified itself as a liberal magazine. But if they were to deliver on their progressive ideals as the standard bearers and defenders of art then they would have to take risks. Their first challenge was Major Frank Pease, the annoying anti-communist and anti-Semitic gadfly who wrote President Hoover in the spring of 1930 protesting that the film *All Quiet on the Western Front* was an affront to the US Army and inspired by communism.

Two months after attacking the war film, Pease sent several missives to Rob Wagner's old boss, Jesse Lasky, vice-president Paramount Studios, who had invited the Russian Jewish film director and avowed Bolshevik, Sergei Eisenstein, to write and direct movies. Eisenstein's *Battleship Potemkin* and *Ten Days That Shook the World* made him the darling of the American intellectual left and cinephiles for his expansive visuals and epic storytelling. The Russian government granted him permission to tour Europe in 1928, but gave him no funds for travel expenses. He earned money by lecturing. Eisenstein was virtually penniless when Lasky offered him a $100,000 contract to come to Hollywood to write and direct films for Paramount.

In a letter to Lasky, Pease demanded that Eisenstein be deported as a communist propagandist. "What are you trying to do, turn the American cinema into a Communist cesspool?" he wrote. Pease closed his letter by noting that, "Your unspeakable crime in importing Eisenstein should be as much resented and resisted by decent Jewish-Americans as it will be by all the other loyal Americans." He also wrote a vicious twenty-four-page pamphlet, *Eisenstein, Messenger from Hell*, to bolster his argument.

It was a xenophobic, anti-Semitic tirade in which he labeled Eisenstein as a sadistic Jew steeped in Bolshevik atrocities. Bringing Eisenstein to Hollywood would undermine the American way of life, Pease alleged. [9] [10]

As previously discussed, Wagner viewed the attack on *All Quiet on the Western Front* as political censorship. Only *Script* and the liberal *The Nation* weekly magazine covered Pease's attacks on the movie with any in-depth coverage. And only *Script* looked into Pease's background, albeit superficially. [11] [12]

An avid supporter of Russian cinema and a regular patron of European films screened at the Filmarte, Wagner was particularly upset over Pease's calls for Eisenstein's deportation. Impressed with *Ten Days That Shook the World*, he had eagerly waited for Eisenstein's arrival in the United States after hearing glowing reports about the state of films in Russia from Douglas Fairbanks and Mary Pickford, who had visited Eisenstein in the Soviet Union in 1926. Wagner was particularly intrigued with Eisenstein's method of creating the dramatic conflict of the masses by subordinating individuals and plot and bringing the background of that conflict into the forefront. Eisenstein's use of the montage, a filming technique ignored by American filmmakers at the time, also piqued Wagner's sense of film art. Russian filmmakers' lack of concern with box-office success and the competition between directors over artistic goals appealed to his socialism. Even in 1930, Wagner clung to the ideals that the 1917 Bolshevik revolution brought down a moribund royal empire and set its illiterate masses free. This romanticized view ignored the murderous oppressive rule of Joseph Stalin, which was beginning to manifest itself in 1930, but this was typical of Wagner's worldview. The cinematic artist, in this case Eisenstein, was untouched by the taint of Stalin as far as Wagner was concerned. [13]

But Pease's attacks on Eisenstein were more troubling than with broadsides against *All Quiet on the Western Front*. *All Quiet* was already released and a box-office hit. No amount of nasty invectives from Pease would undo the financial success of the film or place Universal Studios, which made the film, and its director, Lewis Milestone, in a vulnerable position with the public. However, Pease had made his reputation of standing up for American servicemen and he had his own military background to bolster his credibility.

Wagner, like most film folk, never heard of Pease until he attacked the Milestone film. And Wagner prided himself on knowing just about everybody in town. In *Script's* June 28, 1930, exposé on Pease's practices there is an underlying incredulity in Wagner's report that a man who purported to be a member of industry, as the president of the Hollywood Technical Directors Institute, was completely unknown to the close-knit film community. Wagner had good reason to be suspicious of Pease's film credentials, and he could find precious little information about him. [14]

As it turned out Pease was never a major in the Army, but a private first class. He enlisted in the Army in 1902 and was attached to the Hospital Corps. He was discharged three years later after his right leg was amputated. He also suffered from bronchitis and hemorrhoids. On August 11, 1927, he landed in Hollywood where he lived for a time at the Hotel Mark Twain with his wife, Mabel. By 1930, the couple and a daughter were living on Sunset Boulevard. [15]

Pease had grand plans, but he could never execute them. In 1907, he announced to the *San Jose Mercury News* that he would tour the world in his army uniform to study foreign armies to help implement reforms in the US Army. His project never materialized, nor was the army aware of it. After arriving in Hollywood he had a propensity to make wild, nonsensical speeches at Actors' Equity meetings and got into trouble selling souvenirs of movie stars, including Rudolph Valentino's private brand of cigarettes. In November 1929, he established the United Character Actors' Association, an agency for bit players, only to shutter it six months later when he discovered day actors only earned $15 a day. Next he opened the Hollywood Technical Directors Institute, which he operated out of his residence at 6557 Sunset Boulevard. By all appearances it had no members or employees. [16] [17] [18]

In a bizarre incident in December 1931, in a complaint to the French police in Paris, he represented himself as a former American diplomat who was drugged in a café and robbed of $1,000. Three years later British immigration officials deported Pease and his wife from England for inappropriately distributing anti-communist literature. He published through the American Defender Press in 1934 *What I Learned in Nazi Germany,* a fifty-nine-page booklet which completely misread the Third Reich by linking communism to Nazism. In 1935, he wrote *Pole to Panama* which defended American imperialism and urged the United States to rule from the North Pole to Panama as a means to solve its internal and foreign problems. The Jewish Telegraphic Agency, a wire service for Jewish media outlets, tracked and reported on Pease's anti-Semitic writings throughout the 1930s. [19] [20] [21] [22]

Given Pease's erratic behavior and poor track record in Hollywood, it's difficult to believe that any studio boss would take him seriously, let alone consider cancelling Eisenstein's contract and send him packing to Russia. Bud Schulberg, general manager of the West Coast productions at Paramount, told the Jewish Telegraphic Agency that he had no intention of recognizing Pease, the Hollywood Technical Directors Institute, or Pease's allegations. [23]

Film historians differ as to whether Pease had any influence in Hollywood. He certainly had no influence in banning *All Quiet* from movie theaters, but his role in getting Paramount to cancel Eisenstein's contract is a little murkier. Donald T. Critchlow, in his book, *When Hollywood was Right: How Movie Stars, Studio Moguls and Big Business*

Remade American Politics, argued that Pease had little sway with Paramount.

But studio bosses – Schulberg, MGM's Louis B. Mayer, Universal's Carl Laemmle, the Warner brothers, among others – were sensitive to anti-Semitic attacks and even more sensitive to charges that they may have communist sympathies. It didn't help Eisenstein that Paramount executives rejected every suggestion he made for a motion picture. He recommended adaptations of Theodore Dreiser's *An American Tragedy* and *Sutter's Gold*, and H.G. Wells' *War of the Worlds*. Paramount viewed these films as not commercially viable. Meanwhile, Pease's rants attracted the attention of New York Congressman Hamilton Fish's House Special Committee to Investigate Communist Activities and Propaganda. The committee focused its attention on Russian propaganda films infiltrating American theaters. [24]

Eisenstein's contract gave him wide latitude to choose whatever film he wanted to make. At least, on some level, Paramount wanted to see what he could do with his cinematic vision and American resources. But the studio couldn't see past conventional storytelling and viewed his scripts as too difficult to film. Faced with the Fish committee inquiries and Eisenstein's inability to come up with a shootable script, at least in Paramount executives' minds, the studio terminated his contract in November 1931. Wagner was disgusted with his former employer, complaining to Lasky that Paramount did not give Eisenstein enough time to prove himself. [25]

Returning to the Soviet Union was almost too much to bear for Eisenstein. Russians viewed him with suspicion because he embraced American capitalism to make pictures, but he had also failed to succeed. Charlie Chaplin and Wagner persuaded Upton Sinclair to finance a film for Eisenstein to be shot in Mexico. Sinclair's wife, Mary Craig Sinclair, raised $25,000 and persuaded Kate Crane Gartz to put up additional capital to fund the project. Both women would share producer credit. To keep tabs on their investment, Mary Craig Sinclair sent her alcoholic brother, Hunter Kimbrough, to accompany Eisenstein to keep him out of trouble. However, what was scheduled as a three-month shoot dragged on for fourteen months as Eisenstein shot 234,000 feet of film. It was a fiasco punctuated with drunken brawls and Kimbrough's growing alarm over Eisenstein's reckless behavior towards underage boys. Furious, the Sinclairs demanded that Eisenstein return to the United States and hand over the film. But Eisenstein's American visa had expired and he was left with no choice but to return to Russia. There, he was denied film assignments until 1938. [26] [27] [28]

The Sinclairs had an unimaginable amount of film to wade through to determine whether they even have a movie. They recruited Sol Lesser to supervise editing the film. Lesser brought in W. Donn Hayes and Carl Himm to cut the film. The result was *Thunder Over Mexico*, which was released on September 22, 1933. The film, which was silent, featured stunning natural photography and minimal use of title cards. It told the story of a young hacienda worker who discovers that his lover is imprisoned on a ranch and had been raped by a guest of his master. One scene that drew plaudits from critics for its realism was when three young men were buried in the ground up to the shoulders and then subjected to stampeding horses. [29]

Film purists heaped scorn on Upton Sinclair for having commercial filmmakers, the very people who booted Eisenstein from Hollywood, edit the film. Seymour Stern of *Experimental Cinema* magazine ignored the fact that it was Sinclair's money that financed the film and he had every right to edit it as he pleased. Stern attempted to wage a public protest. He lamented the "conventional version of Eisenstein's original majestic conception," which was "without a doubt the greatest tragedy in the history of film ..." [30]

Most critics, however, agreed the editing was skillful and the final film was exceptional. Wagner wrote that *Thunder Over Mexico* was "the greatest silent picture since *City Lights*" and "the offspring of a shotgun wedding of Hollywood and Moscow. And, as often happens, the child is more beautiful than either parent." [31] [32]

But in the end did Frank Pease's attack influence Paramount's decision to get rid of Eisenstein? Marie Seton, Eisenstein's biographer, argued that Pease was not an isolated "crank" and was not speaking solely for himself but for individuals and groups that held anti-Semitic views. Certainly Pease's anti-Semitism reflected the views of many people in prewar America, but he had no organized following. What Pease accomplished was to generate enough heat by using the loudest voice in the most profane terms to put pressure on the already skittish Paramount studio executives who wanted to avoid controversy and the taint of being labeled "red." In helping in some small part to jettison Eisenstein from Hollywood, Pease's actions helped damage the filmmaker's career in the Soviet Union and in effect prevented any possible return to Hollywood. Although *The Nation* and the trade publications treated Pease as a crank, *Script,* recognizing the damage "public moralizers" could achieve, treated his threats seriously.

***

Script fulfilled Wagner's dreams of artistic integrity, in placing art above commerce and purposely keeping the magazine's reach narrowed to California while keeping advertisers' influence on editorial content at a minimum. Wagner's sharp wit and keen observations on Hollywood politics was the foundation of the magazine's appeal. The writer, in his view, was the creator of celluloid art and possessed this exalted status above the director, producer and cinematographer. *Script* reflected this view as a writer's magazine and opened its pages to skilled artists, no matter their medium, to write on any topic they chose. Rob Wagner nurtured this editorial policy, but it was Florence Wagner who ran the magazine's day-to-day operations and likely exerted influence to go beyond the macro coverage of Hollywood to include editorials and reportage on the benefits of the Soviet system of government.

Rob Wagner, who had always said that Florence was the true editor of *Script*, more or less went along with Florence's broader view of the world although his belief in Bolshevism was more idealistic than her interest in the practical application of communism or socialism in government. Wagner's core belief in Bolshevism was rooted in the purity of art and he felt that Sergei Eisenstein had served as its poster child. Eisenstein's film *Old and New* encapsulated Wagner's feelings about the Russian revolution as the film dealt with "the transformation from feudal methods of farming to the great state farms alive with tractors, and including the sensational industrializing of a huge country that only yesterday was known as Dark Russia." He stubbornly held to the ideal that Russia's destiny lay firmly in the hands of farmers, although that hadn't been true except during a brief period in Vladimir Lenin's regime.

Moreover, the Soviet Union's education system was much admired by American leftists for what it accomplished in a short time. Wagner, since his meeting with the Russian diplomat, Baron Alexandre De Freedericksz, in Paris in 1903, had been convinced that the Soviet educational system was far superior to that of the United States.

Script would hammer this theme through the mid-1930s. When Anne Edwards, an old colleague of Rob's at Manual Arts High School and fellow liberal, traveled to Russia to study its educational system, she returned to write a glowing report for *Script* in 1936. She reported that the Soviets successfully taught five billion people in three years to read and write and that in 1935 alone 150 elementary schools opened in Moscow. She toured factory classrooms and noted the highly regimented schedules of university students. She was particularly impressed with the proliferation of bookstores. Absent from her report was that her trips to Odessa, Sebastopol, Yalta and Moscow were closely supervised by a minder. Her article also contained no references to the mandatory classroom indoctrination in communism and militarism under the Stalin regime. [33]

Edwards' report fit perfectly with Wagner's long-held belief that the Soviet Union accomplished what no Western nation could by virtually erasing illiteracy. Perhaps conscious of Edwards' glowing account of the Soviet educational system and an attempt at balance, Wagner sought permission from journalist and the former American spy, Marguerite Harrison, to publish a version of her experiences in a Russian prison.

Wagner had met Harrison on the Paramount Studios lot in 1925 when he was in the studio's writing department and she was working on a documentary on Iranian nomadic tribes called *Grass: A Nation's Battle for Life*.

Harrison gained celebrity status when she was a correspondent for The Associated Press. She eventually became a spy for the American government in 1920 and was sent to Russia to gather intelligence on the Soviet economy and the condition of American political prisoners. She was imprisoned for ten months at the notorious Lubyanka Prison. Following her release, she wrote the book *Marooned in Moscow: The Story of an American Woman Imprisoned in Russia*. For the April 29, 1927, issue of the *Canadian Jewish Review*, she wrote an article, "Evraika," that told the story of the arrest and imprisonment of a Jewish woman who became disillusioned with communist Russia's false promises of a classless society and the virulent institutionalized anti-Semitism in the Soviet government. [34]

Wagner repurposed Harrison's story for *Script* readers just two weeks after Edwards' article that argued, perhaps clumsily because the *Canadian Jewish Review* version of the story was better written with a stronger message of Soviet hypocrisy, that the Soviet ideal of a classless, educated society didn't apply to all of its people.

Most American publications typically demonized Russia as a threat to democracy, but *Script* never did. There may be some justification that *Script* was a dupe for communist propaganda because some of its arguments were simply wrong-headed. But the truth was closer to the fact that Wagner preferred to play devil's advocate by presenting a viewpoint contrary to conventional wisdom. He wasn't seeking to be right, but to poke holes the prevailing position that every communist was determined to subvert American ideals.

In 1938, Gladys Lloyd Robinson, the wife of actor Edward G. Robinson, was a columnist for *Script*. On a trip to Mexico to visit Diego Rivera, she asked the artist to arrange an interview with his friend Leon Trotsky, the Marxist revolutionary and a founder of the Red Army who was living in exile in Mexico under heavy armed guard following his expulsion from the Soviet Union in 1929. Although a vehement opponent of Stalin's regime, he gave few media interviews.

Robinson's interview with Trotsky was a major scoop for *Script*, although the article itself contained a series of softball questions that did little to shed light on how communism or socialism could provide jobs and feed people during an economic catastrophe. Nor did Robinson address the most obvious question in 1938, that of the well-publicized purge of hundreds of Soviet writers, artists and intellectuals, many of whom were imprisoned and executed for their loyalty to Trotsky. *Script* also did itself no favors by writing a jocular headline over the question and answer interview that trivialized its content. Yet Trotsky did provide some insight into the allure of fascism to a population experiencing societal and economic upheaval, but which would ultimately fail in the long run. However, he vastly overstated in his argument that the "crisis of capitalism" during the Depression would "transform into a grave crisis of democracy." [35]

But like many great scoops, it almost didn't matter what the elusive subject had said. Trotsky was accessible to *Script* at a time when he was rebuffing pleas for interviews from other publications.

Years later and after the death of her husband in 1942, Florence Wagner approached the subject of the Soviet Union in a much more aggressive manner. Screenwriter and Communist Party member Dalton Trumbo, the author of *Johnny Got His Gun* and an occasional contributor to *Script*, submitted a lengthy essay on the "Russian Menace" for the May 25, 1946, issue in which he wrote from the perspective of a Russian, and attempted to debunk the assertion from anti-communists that the Soviet Union threatened the security of the United States. Trumbo's facts were accurate, but his message was naïve. He argued that the Russian military was deployed in positions that were nowhere near US interests.

Trumbo, like many leftists in postwar America, believed that the Soviet Union had no interest in a conflict with the West, and it was only America that was hawkish. "If I were a Russian ... I would be alarmed, and I would petition my government to take measures at once against what would seem an almost certain blow aimed at my existence. This is how it must appear in Russia today," he wrote. [36]

Trumbo's article reflected the politics of leftist film writers and particularly Florence Wagner, who took a more direct approach than her husband to advocate that Russia posed no threat to the United States. The attitude of screenwriter Ring Lardner, Jr., who joined the Communist Party in 1937 but had become disillusioned with Stalin's brutal regime, reflected Florence's feelings about the new Cold War: "... It seemed to me then that the Soviet leaders were more serious than ours about wanting peaceful relations," he wrote in his autobiography, *I'd Hate Myself in the Morning*. [37]

As sole publisher of *Script* after 1942 until she sold the magazine in 1947, Florence published articles sympathetic to the communist cause with little concern over maintaining balance or even the executions of thousands of writers and artists. She even found Bolshevik inspiration in unlikely subjects. In 1945 Florence published a profile of actress Angela Lansbury, a newcomer to Hollywood. Lansbury was the granddaughter of British Labour Party leader, socialist and Bolshevik sympathizer George Lansbury, editor of the *Daily Herald*, whose newspaper was partially funded with Soviet money. Her father was Communist Party member Edgar Lansbury. The article spent less column inches on the actress, and more on the family's political accomplishments.[38]

Rob always softened the message of the magazine's flirtations with communism with humor and balance as he did with Marguerite Harrison's experiences in Lubyanka Prison following the laudatory article on the Soviet school system. It made for palatable reading for *Script's* largely conservative Beverly Hills readership. Florence, however, dispensed with such nuances and allowed leftists wide latitude to write whatever they pleased. For example, Trumbo used *Script* to publicize the work of the liberal labor group National Citizens Political Action Committee (NCPAC) whose membership consisted of many Communist Party members. This organization worked to re-elect President Roosevelt in 1944 and supported the 1946 re-election of Congressman Jerry Voorhis, who lost to Richard Nixon and his red-baiting campaign.[39]

Rob had insisted on soft-pedaling socialism and Bolshevism by framing his politics as artistic expression in a deprecating manner. He won many friends and admirers who may have otherwise dismissed *Script* as a socialist rag. Florence did not have that skill. Her stepson, Leicester, with his journalistic training in objectivity, also acted as a counter-balance to Florence's communist sympathies. But since he wasn't involved in the day-to-day operations, it left *Script* devoid of Rob's personality and intellect.

* * *

Script was on firmer ground when it covered local issues and left global politics to the national publications. Its progressive take on Hollywood politics foreshadowed many issues that shaped the film industry long after the magazine had folded. If *Script* earned the reputation as the West Coast *New Yorker*, then Leicester and Florence Wagner after Rob's death brought it to a new level as the West Coast version of *PM*, the left-leaning New York City daily newspaper published between 1940 and 1948 which had initially accepted no advertising to free itself of business interests.

But *Script* in the 1940s did not mimic *PM*. *Script,* from its inception, was at its best championing young artists and was far ahead of its rivals in recognizing talent in minority actors like Ana May Wong and artists David Alfaro Siqueiros and Leo Politi. Florence also employed the Modernist and abstract artist Stanton Macdonald-Wright as art critic, whose weekly columns appeared from 1942 to 1946. (Macdonald-Wright repaid Florence by describing *Script* twenty-two years later as "some little idiotic magazine" and Florence "a sort of Hollywood this-and-that.") [40]

Script advocated collective bargaining for actors and technicians and exposed animal cruelty practices nearly a decade before the film industry took measures to end dangerous animal stunts. And it was prescient in recognizing that independent film production in which the director, writer and actor accepted lower salaries for a percentage of the box office receipts would be Hollywood's future.

Following Rob's death, Leicester and Florence built on that type of advocacy journalism which tackled the problem of Japanese American internment during World War II, the Los Angeles Zoot Suit riots, housing discrimination against American Indians and the resurgence of the Ku Klux Klan in California.

This type of reportage *Script* performed in the mid-1940s was born from Rob Wagner's insistence in 1929 that it challenge studios' treatment of actors, directors and writers. An early organizer of the Screen Writers Guild when it was a club in 1920 (it unionized in 1933), Wagner was determined that writers were represented as a group in determining salaries and screen credit. [41]

In May 1927 Wagner was among 275 film industry insiders invited by MGM's Louis B. Mayer, actor Conrad Nagel and directors Cecil B. DeMille and Fred Niblo to the Biltmore Hotel's Gold Room to hear and ultimately join in forming the Academy of Motion Pictures Arts and Sciences. Throughout most of the 1920s, the studios stymied the efforts of its artists to unionize, and Mayer had hoped the Motion Picture Academy would put to rest the question of unionization. Certainly from the beginning the Academy shied away from labor issues and instead focused on "awards of merit." To Wagner, the proposed Academy was a naked attempt to silence labor with a powder-puff organization that handed out awards. [42]

Wagner wrote in *Script*: "At the time there were all sorts of troubles brewing within the industry – the cinematographers were organizing to the hilt, the actors were chafing under intolerable conditions, and the writers who heretofore had been merely a lot of white rabbits too frightened to organize, taking anything that was handed to them, had begun to wake up to their own powers." He was incensed that film producers formed an organization that could "handle" the disparate groups with a "pretty invention." He was one of only fifteen attendees at the meeting who refused to join the Academy. [43]

His attitude changed with the advent of sound, which arrived at about the same time the Academy was forming. Wagner argued four years after that meeting at the Biltmore that "science saved the Academy" because the Academy was forced to find a solution to producing sound without ambient noise that bedeviled directors, film budgets and shooting schedules. By solving technical issues with – and eventually including film technicians in its awards categories – the Academy proved itself to be more than a vanity group. The film industry booster that he was, Wagner felt duty-bound to sing the Academy's praises, but he was never fully onboard because the Academy never committed itself as a labor advocate for artists. In May 1931 Fred Niblo invited him to join the Academy after a number of previous entreaties had failed. Wagner declined, citing *Script's* editorial policy against memberships and the fact that he hadn't worked on a film since 1928. [44] [45] [46] [47]

When producer and agent Mike Levee, who was heavily involved in the Theater Guild, founded the Screen Guild in April 1932, Wagner found a kindred spirit, although Levee's motives for his new enterprise was more of an economic practicality than an artistic one. The Screen Guild anticipated independent film production as many producers, directors and actors found themselves jobless as the Great Depression cut deep into studio budgets. Producers who were casualties of studio shakeups could raise money from investors to produce a film and defer the salaries of the directors, actors and writers for fifty percent of the film's net receipts. To Wagner this allowed producers and directors artistic freedom and experimentation. Merian C. Cooper used funds from wealthy benefactors to produce *Becky Sharp* which featured Technicolor's new three-strip color process. Producer Frank Borzage also took advantage of the Screen Guild, filming *Man's Castle* and *No Greater Glory* and releasing the films through Columbia Pictures. [48] [49]

The Screen Guild's formation reminded Wagner of his efforts to establish a Little Theater Film group, where he had hoped to produce films solely on an artistic level. The Guild performed a similar service on a larger scale and provided an environment that encouraged greater freedom of expression. "In Hollywood, the Screen Guild, composed of, owned and operated by the profession itself, will have no difficulty in casting the best talent of the cinema and stage, and as the participants will all be working for themselves, they will have an enthusiasm impossible in the great industrial studio owned by Wall Street," he wrote in *Script*. The Guild's lofty ambitions did not survive the 1930s, but it did serve as a template for future independent production that flourished in the decades that followed. [50]

Script often placed itself in fighting losing battles. The Motion Picture Academy flourished (and indeed became the vanity organization Wagner had feared), the studio system remained invincible in the prewar era and its editorials against animal cruelty were largely ignored in the 1930s, although the number of animal deaths grew in alarming numbers. As movie studios in the 1920s solidified their strength and profits and film budgets soared, new genres developed that employed large numbers of animals. Century Films in 1922 produced a series of animal pictures featuring the Century Dogs. Rob's cousin, Blake Wagner, was the cinematographer on several Century pictures and reported that the canine cast often fought amongst themselves causing injuries. In 1926 about 100 horses were killed during the filming of *Ben Hur*.

"We have seen running horses tripped by wires, thrown over cliffs and killed; we have seen lions stirred to violent action by charging a wire-meshed floor with electricity; we have seen comedy dogs driven almost mad with rubber bands about their muzzles …," Wagner wrote in the April 4, 1931, issue of *Script*. [51]

Advances in special effects reduced such cruelty, but sound brought the practices back as filmmakers began expanding topics to include nature and jungle movies. One such film, *Trader Horn*, was filmed in Mexico, Africa and on the MGM lot. In his editorial, Wagner noted that because the African film footage did not provide enough "punch," additional scenes were filmed in Mexico. The Mexican footage depicted lions fighting among themselves who were reportedly starved to force them to attack and eat monkeys, deer and hyenas. *Script* exposed MGM's move to avoid American animal protection laws by filming slaughter scenes in Mexico. Richard Schayer, who wrote the screenplay for *Trader Horn*, said in a letter to *Script* that that he and director W.S. Van Dyke developed a story against "wanton destruction" of wildlife, but implied that MGM employed "more brutal handling" of the animals without their consent. It was not until nearly a decade later that film studios took the issue of animal cruelty seriously. Will Hays' office intervened in 1939 when horses were killed on the sets of *Northwest Mounted Police* and *Jesse James*. In 1940 the American Humane Association was finally allowed on film sets to monitor the treatment of animals. [52]

* * *

Rob and Florence Wagner's greatest test of their faith as socialists, and perhaps their greatest failure, was the mess they involved themselves in when Upton Sinclair ran for governor of California in 1934. A committed Christian socialist, Sinclair was no stranger to running for political office. He ran for Congress in 1920 and the United States Senate in 1922 on the Socialist Party ticket and lost. He tried again as a socialist in a bid for California governor in 1926. But for the 1934 California gubernatorial election, he registered as a Democrat in September 1933, while establishing his End Poverty in California (EPIC) campaign. Much to everyone's surprise he secured the Democratic nomination in the August 1934 primary over the favored George Creel. [53]

Rob Wagner was an early and enthusiastic – although mostly private – supporter of EPIC. He designed the organization's bumble bee logo and discussed EPIC strategy with Sinclair during long walks on Sunday mornings near Sinclair's Pasadena home. He described Sinclair in *Script* as "utterly incorruptible" and "the greatest 'brain-truster' in America" He even attended an early Sinclair campaign rally. As governor, Sinclair pledged to have the state take over factories and farms idled during the Depression and develop cooperative factories and farms as part of a "production for use" plan. He argued for a $50 per month pension plan for the elderly and said he would implement a state income tax and establish a state-managed cooperative economy. [54]

Wagner, of course, was a believer. However, he committed the journalistic sin of failing to understand his readership and alienating the ultra-conservative studio heads like Louis B. Mayer who felt threatened that Sinclair would implement a form of nationalization of the film studios. MGM produced phony newsreels depicting thousands of Dust Bowl refugees arriving in California to take advantage of entitlements. The *Los Angeles Times* galvanized big business, politicians and the media to wage a smear campaign. It was an ugly, unprecedented political attack that would foreshadow future political campaigns. Sixteen years later Richard Nixon used similar tactics against Helen Gahagan Douglas in the California Senate race.

Wagner had jeopardized his relationship with the studios that provided him with a living. He further compounded his misjudgment by failing to anticipate reader reaction. *Script* subscribers, for the most part, were sufficiently conservative in a company town to fear that their jobs were in jeopardy if Sinclair were elected. Even closet liberals were not about to defy their studio employers by supporting Sinclair. Some studio workers who sympathized with Sinclair gladly wore incumbent Frank Merriam campaign badges to work.

When the *Literary Digest* reported in its August 23, 1934, issue that *Script* was the only publication "backing" Sinclair's candidacy, subscription cancellations poured in. Florence was livid. Subscriptions generally did not make or break the financial health of a magazine, but *Script* was no ordinary publication. Column inches for the display of advertising were always minimal, originally by design to avoid subjecting the publication to the whims of advertisers. Later on, as the Depression deepened, advertising money simply dried up. Subscriptions for *Script* were the magazine's lifeblood and Florence recognized the magazine was at risk of going under. [55]

The *Literary Digest* report stemmed from *Script's* positive coverage of Sinclair and in part from a letter written by organizer Frank Scully on Authors' League letterhead that implied the League was endorsing Sinclair. The Authors' League was formed in August 1933 to work with the US government's campaign to increase employment, raise salaries, and reduce working hours. Wagner was a founding member along with his old friend Rupert Hughes and authors Zane Grey, Nunnally Johnson, Anita Loos and Edgar Rice Burroughs among others. Dorothy Parker, Will Rogers, Robert Benchley and Gene Fowler later joined. [56]

Scully's letter, written without the knowledge of fellow Authors' League participants, asked members to serve on a committee to endorse Sinclair. The letter implied it was sent by Parker, Wagner, Scully, Morrie Ryskind, Jim Tully and Lewis Browne. Awkwardly worded, the letter asked recipients to check their name listed on the left if they endorsed Sinclair or cross it out if they rejected the endorsement. [57]

The Wagners began to receive calls both at home and at the magazine's office from League members demanding an explanation as to why their names were listed as Sinclair supporters. Rob Wagner was just as surprised as everyone else. Wagner pressed Scully for an answer. "Considering the fact that I – *Script* – have not publicly taken sides, I'm in a pretty bad spot," Wagner wrote Scully. He elaborated by telling Scully that he thought that while Sinclair's intentions were pure, he would make "a bum executive" and is "scared to death" of winning the election. [58]

Scully angrily replied that, "I asked you if you wanted to come in (to support Sinclair), or stay on the sidelines. You said you wanted to come in. So I put you in. Knowing how close you've become to this Epic thing, I couldn't imagine you out of it. But if you say out, okay." [59]

The *Literary Digest* article and Scully's letter damaged Wagner's credibility in the film community. The booster of all things Hollywood was endorsing a socialist who allegedly wanted to distribute film profits to the poor, which threatened jobs and pushed studio bosses to declare that they would move their operations to Florida. Letters from readers were blistering.

"If your friend Sinclair is all you claim he is, he certainly has fooled the public in more ways than one," wrote A.L. Lumbard, a reader with a typical reaction to *Script's* favorable coverage of Sinclair's campaign. "Just think what a man of his ability could do if he would preach the fundamentals which up to now have made America the finest country in the world in which to live." [60]

The incident wasn't entirely Wagner's fault, although he didn't help himself by sending mixed signals to Sinclair. Wagner could be gushing about his support for Sinclair one moment, then tell his friends that *Script* was neutral. As early as December 1933, Wagner made it clear to Sinclair that no endorsement for political office would be forthcoming. "As an editor I've decided that I'm in a stronger position if I don't join parties and organizations ... I've never said in *Script* I'm a Socialist, with the result I can slip over Socialism. I'll be able to boost our candidacy better that way." [61]

Sinclair was understandably confused. Perhaps Wagner had forgotten, but Sinclair certainly remembered, that he received a very public endorsement from Wagner when he ran for California governor on the Socialist Party ticket in 1926. To Sinclair, eight years changed little on how the two friends viewed socialism and its potential benefits to the public. In a letter to Wagner, Sinclair was alternately angry and hurt that Wagner claimed to take no sides in the campaign. Sinclair noted at the beginning of 1934 that, "I invited you to become one of a group of Californians who were publicly taking the stand for my candidacy for governor, and I have before me your signature in red pencil to that document. You will see that it is an unqualified campaign endorsement." [62]

It was an awkward episode for the two men, but Florence demanded that if *Script* was to stem the flow of fleeing readers, her husband had to take an unequivocal stand that the magazine was neutral in the election. For most of September and October of 1934, Wagner spent a large chunk of his time writing letters to his readers trying to convince them that *Script* was not endorsing Sinclair. "We personally did not wish him to run, and we dreaded his victory," Wagner explained. "Not for what he might do to California, but for what California might do to him. We did not wish to see a sensitive artist crushed in the political mill." [63]

On the eve of the election, Wagner complimented Sinclair in an editorial on a well-run campaign and lamented the nasty attacks from his opponents. Yet it was the magazine that was foremost in his mind, noting that after the election, "*Script* can go on its jaunty way, kidding this and that and behaving like its own foolish self."

Sinclair garnered an impressive 879,000 votes, but was far outdistanced by Merriam who won 1,138,000 votes to win the election. Wagner and Sinclair's relationship survived and they continued their friendship as if Wagner's waffling over the endorsement issue was just a blip.

CHAPTER TEN

"Beverly Hills Scratch Sheet"

Throughout the 1930s, Rob Wagner hustled his celebrity friends to write for his magazine. Charlie Chaplin finally consented by submitting an outline, which Wagner fleshed out: the whimsical story of a scientist who discovered a cure for all diseases and gave poets priority treatment because "they are the high priests of the soul." The story appeared in the fifth anniversary edition of *Script*. Walt Disney contributed Mickey Mouse and Donald Duck illustrations exclusively for the magazine cover.

Much of the journalism practiced by film celebrities in *Script*, including efforts by actors Tom Mix and Eddie Cantor, were attempts at marketing to gain readership and today fail to stand the test of time. However, other contributions helped burnish *Script's* reputation as a literary publication and provide a forum for untested, as well as veteran, writers. The vagabond pugilist writer Jim Tully, with his withering interview techniques, was a regular contributor between 1932 and 1936, including his 1934 profile of the up-and-coming director Frank Capra. Dancer and choreographer Agnes de Mille covered modern dance and Upton Sinclair wrote favorably on technocracy, although its economic model differed from his own EPIC plan. Cinematographer James Wong Howe discussed film lighting techniques and Western novelist Louis L'Amour wrote of his postwar experiences from Europe in a series of letters to Florence. In addition to his writing about his unabashed sympathies for the Soviet Union, Dalton Trumbo profiled African American screenwriter, actor and director Carlton Moss, who wrote the screenplay for *The Negro Soldier,* the groundbreaking 1944 recruitment film directed at the black community. The still relatively unknown William Saroyan received wide exposure long before he wrote the novel *The Human Comedy* in 1943. Tarzan creator Edgar Rice Burroughs wrote a series of murder mystery puzzles between 1932 and 1935 in which he asked readers to solve the murders. The series was later published in the book, *Murder, a Collection of Short Murder Mystery Puzzles.* [1] [2] [3]

While Rob was responsible for attracting his film friends and experienced writers to pen stories for his magazine, it was Florence who recognized the talent in young writers like Saroyan and Ray Bradbury and published their early work.

Bradbury, who had one of his first stories *It's Not the Heat, but the Hu –* published in *Script,* never met or spoke with Rob. His contact was solely with Florence who nurtured his work as he struggled to get broader recognition for his writing. Bradbury, who had his first story, *Hollerbochen's Dilemma,* published in the fanzine *Imagination!* in 1938 and published his own magazine *Futuria Fantasia,* had become acquainted with the fantasy and science-fiction writer Robert Heinlein through a literary club. Heinlein suggested to Bradbury that he pitch his stories to *Script.* In the summer of 1940 he submitted *It's Not the Heat, but the Hu –* and it was Florence who first read the story and published it on November 2. In the spring and early summer of 1941, Florence published two more of his stories. Although Bradbury was never paid for his work, his early contributions for *Script* marked a transitional period for the young writer from amateur to professional. Florence, Bradbury said years later, gave him the confidence to write on broader themes and the exposure that attracted the attention of publishers, such as Arkham House, which published his first collection of short stories in *Dark Carnival* in 1947. [4] [5] [6]

***

In 1940, *Script* was about to enter a new phase in how it presented itself to its readers. Politics, film coverage and humor remained the foundation of the magazine, but its tone shifted with the addition of the Fresno-born Italian artist Leo Politi. Born in 1908, the young artist, in the late 1930s, was earning a meager living selling sketches of tourists on Olvera Street east of downtown Los Angeles and across the street from Union Station. Politi, who later became well known as an author of illustrated ethnic children's books, was heavily influenced by the Mayan culture and painted almost exclusively Mexican themes. [7]

Many Southern California artists had a deep appreciation in the 1920s and 1930s for paintings and murals by Mexican and non-Latino painters whose art focused on Latin American culture. By the early 1930s Los Angeles had become a vital cultural and artistic center. José Clemente Orozco, David Alfaro Siqueiros and Alfredo Ramos Martinez developed some of the most important art projects in the city. The French artist Jean Charlot, who was at the center of the Mexican art movement during this period, and who was later chaperoned by Wagner and *Los Angeles Times* art critic Arthur Millier during his 1939 visit to Los Angeles, was also a contributor to the local art scene. It was also a time of great political upheaval. Between 1930 and 1935 Los Angeles County law authorities apprehended and deported as many as 80,000 Mexicans, many of whom were United States citizens, in an effort to deny them public assistance during the Depression. Left-leaning artists politicized much of the Latino art during this period. [8]

Siqueiros, a Marxist and radical union organizer, was expelled from Mexico in 1932 and arrived in Los Angeles for a six-month stay to complete three murals: *Street Meeting* at the Chouinard School of Art, *América Tropical* at the Sons of Italy building on Olvera Street and *Portrait of Present Day Mexico* at a Pacific Palisades home.

América Tropical, completed in October 1932, proved to be Siqueiros' most controversial project with its allegorical depiction of a crucified Indian peon on a double cross topped by an American eagle representing his oppression by the United States. The Sons of Italy found the mural "ugly." Christine Sterling, the Los Angeles matron responsible for reviving Olvera Street in the early 1930s as a tourist attraction with a sleepy Mexican street vibe, demanded that it be whitewashed.

Shortly after Siqueiros' arrival in Los Angeles, Wagner met him at Chouinard and persuaded the artist to write an article for *Script* on his advanced painting techniques for his murals. Siqueiros responded with a piece on using technology to paint murals with cameras for projection of the models on the walls. He also discussed the use of pneumatic drills to roughen the surface before painting, the use of air brushes and how working with a group of assistants with specific talents efficiently completed the project. The article provided the only documentation of Siqueiros' methods in the English-language Los Angeles media during the summer of 1932. [9]

Throughout the 1930s and indeed until the end of *Script's* life the magazine covered the contributions of Mexican artists to the culture of Los Angeles. *Script* art critic Stanton Macdonald-Wright championed Alfredo Ramos Martinez's work as offering "the best of the Mexicans to exhibit" their art in Southern California. Muralist and sculptor Buckley MacGurrin, *Script's* chief art critic in the 1930s, was an early advocate of Politi. [10] [11]

The Michigan-born MacGurrin studied art in Paris and moved to Hollywood after World War I to become a designer for movie studios. By 1934, he was working at Paramount Pictures. He later succeeded

Macdonald-Wright in the supervision of the Federal Art Project in Los Angeles and Santa Barbara counties. MacGurrin often publicized Politi's exhibits in *Script*. He observed in 1940 that, "Leo became proficient in the use of many media – oil, watercolor, wood-carving, wood engraving, lithography, book illustration; he had a very fine artistic education. His training was modern as opposed to academic; it tended to develop originality rather than subservient to the art forms of bygone eras. His own artistic philosophy drew him toward the genuine and the earthy; toward people whose contact with the soil was still fresh, intimate, satisfying." [12]

Likely following a recommendation from MacGurrin, Wagner offered Politi – at no salary – an opportunity to become the principal illustrator and later art director of his magazine. The magazine not only allowed Politi to ink hundreds of illustrations over an eight-year period, but it also provided him the freedom to express his pacifist nature and to comment on social issues. *Script* was also the first home for Little Pancho, Politi's creation of an adventurous little Mexican boy. To Politi, Wagner was a mentor and kindred spirit.

Politi and the Wagners' *Script* proved to be a perfect match. The magazine's free-thinking attitude appealed to the artist. For Wagner, Politi's art gave his magazine a much needed sense of place. Politi's largely Mexican themes gave the magazine a unifying voice and validated its motto as the "sunshine magazine of the great southwest." Wagner thought so highly of Politi's love of Mexico and Latin American themes that he brought in Gisella Lacher Loeffler, an artist from Taos, New Mexico, who was known for her decorative Latino child folklore figures and illustrations, to complement Politi's contributions. Gisella, as she was known in the art community, and Politi often alternated cover illustration duties.

Wagner peppered the inside of the magazine with Politi's tiny ink sketches of Little Pancho, Lupita, Rosa and other Mexican characters. And Politi wrote autobiographical tales of the Plaza, Olvera Street or his

Bunker Hill neighborhood in his own handwriting accompanied by full-page illustrations.

For *Script*, Politi could tackle larger, grittier themes that were absent from his later work as a children's book author. In the May 25, 1940, issue, Politi provided six illustrations to accompany a fictional tale of a Mexican soldier who kidnapped, raped and murdered an American nurse at a small village. Politi's full-page illustration of the village demonstrates his passion for movement with perhaps a dozen vignettes, from young mothers drawing water from the village fountain to a mother breastfeeding her child to another mother and child praying at an altar of Our Lady of Guadalupe. His depiction of the tragic nurse opposite the village illustration conveys a sense of angelic virginity not unlike Our Lady of Guadalupe. But it's his treatment of the murderer that speaks of the character's remorse and his abandonment of humanity, yet gives the reader a sense of tolerance and understanding.

He reveled in recording street scenes, capturing tiny slices of Los Angeles. He could also examine with pathos the flip side of Mexicans' lives in Los Angeles. In one illustration he passed a neighborhood bar and sketched the despair of its patrons. The magazine allowed him to illustrate and write of the places and people in his neighborhood without making judgments or editorializing, observing the drunks, prostitutes and dirty, barefooted children on Temple Street. And without rancor he noted that as he walked home from Olvera Street, police officers forced him against a wall and searched him without provocation.

"Still, I like this section (of the city)," he wrote in the September 28, 1946, issue of *Script*. "I don't know why, but I just do." It was his neighborhood and he loved not just the beauty that he discovered, but also its warts. His nudes were equally non-judgmental. An ink drawing of young Mexican women lying naked in hammocks could convey innocence and a hint of eroticism. Or he could be playful with a blushing nude model entering a studio full of male art students. His wartime political art for *Script* usually skewered the hypocrisy of Tojo, Stalin and Hitler. After Germany invaded Poland in 1939, most of his characters over several months wore gas masks, a comment on their imprisonment by the conditions of war and the dictators who ruled their lives. By the standards of the day, Politi's political art was moderate in contrast to daily newspaper cartoonists because he preferred less confrontational messages. He stayed on course with this message that only cultural and ethnic understanding could solve the world's ills.

Politi's pacifism fit perfectly with *Script's* editorial policies of the late 1930s and early 1940s, which could be interpreted as isolationist, but more accurately was antiwar. But more importantly, Politi's numerous illustrations providing slices of the daily lives of a disenfranchised community broadened the magazine's scope by not only including central and East Los Angeles as part of *Script's* community, but also embraced Mexican culture as Southern California's identity.

* * *

On July 19, 1942, Rob and Florence arrived in Santa Barbara to allow Rob a much-needed rest at the El Encanto Hotel, a luxury hotel atop a bluff overlooking the Pacific Ocean. He was tired and suffering from a cold that he couldn't shake. The next morning at 7:30, as he was preparing with Florence in their cottage for breakfast in the hotel's dining room, he suffered a fatal heart attack. Leicester, who was the night wire editor of the United Press in San Francisco, flew down to Los Angeles to be with the family. Thornton, flying for the Air Transport Command, flew in from New Orleans. [13] [14]

That evening Charlie Chaplin arrived at the Wagner home on North Crescent Drive in Beverly Hills to offer support to Florence after she returned from Santa Barbara. Florence, Leicester, his wife, Lucy, and Thornton, sat around the dining room table making funeral arrangements to be held at Forest Lawn Memorial Park in Glendale. Chaplin stayed in the living room with

Leicester and Lucy's two children, Howard and Georgia, and entertained them with shadow puppets and playful stories as the Tramp. It was a kind gesture that Lucy never forgot. She later observed that Chaplin spent more time with her children in a single evening than Rob and Florence had in an entire year. [15]

The jobs of editor, publisher and business manager of *Script* now fell squarely on the shoulders of Florence, but she needed help and turned to Leicester to share responsibilities. Leicester's relationship with his stepmother remained unchanged over the decades. She made demands on his time when he was needed to help edit copy and write for *Script*, but had kept Rob away from Leicester's children and spent little time socializing with her stepson's family. Leicester, on the other hand, even into his 30s and 40s, was eager to please Florence.

Leicester, or "Les" as his friends called him, had established a highly regarded career as a Los Angeles journalist. After working for the *Santa Barbara News Press*, he initially covered crime for the United Press in Los Angeles, which had offices in the *Los Angeles Daily News* building on Pico Boulevard and Los Angeles Street. By 1932, he was given the coveted Hollywood beat and wrote a series of "As Told To" articles about movie stars, including profiles on Jean Harlow and Mae West. In 1934, he joined 20th Century-Fox's publicity department. A short man, standing just 5 feet, 3 inches tall, slight in build weighing 110 pounds with a broad, open friendly face, Leicester was a natural publicity man. But in a company town he never escaped the shadow of his popular father. His membership inside the Hollywood Movie Machine prompted comparisons to his father, making it difficult to shed the identity of "Rob Wagner's son." [16] [17]

One morning in 1938, Les Wagner simply refused to get out of bed, and there he stayed for days. Suspecting that he was suffering from a nervous breakdown, although the family never received a formal diagnosis from a physician, Rob, Florence and Lucy decided to send Les with his family to Marin County for some much needed breathing space.

Rob asked his niece, Harriet Wagner, now married to Gregory Jones, a Sonoma County rancher, to keep an eye on him and report his condition from time to time. In letters to Rob, Harriet reported that Leicester had recovered quickly and was flourishing in the United Press' San Francisco office. [18]

With Rob death, the checks and balances in place that provided some sense of objectivity to the magazine's otherwise near slavish devotion to the leftist point of view disappeared. Florence did not possess the humor or inclination to soften the magazine's ideological liberal editorials to make them palatable to readers. Les Wagner, however, was *Script's* saving grace. Taking over with the new title of news editor in July 1942, he took a more news-oriented approach to the magazine's coverage of California events and politics. Pages One and Two, once the domain of his father's editorials splashed with humor and satire and a wink and a nod, now featured a mix of advocacy journalism and opinion. The one element the son kept of his father's editorials was a contrarian attitude towards the conservative establishment and the media reporting news in Los Angeles, especially the William Randolph Hearst-owned *Examiner* and *Herald-Express*. Wagner was particularly interested in covering topics largely ignored by the newspapers such as racial discrimination. But he also wanted to expose what he saw as the blatant racism in the fascist-leaning *Examiner* and *Herald-Express*.

Like anyone who contributed to *Script*, Les Wagner received little or no compensation for his work. After his return to Los Angeles from San Francisco, he took as regular employment a job at the *Los Angeles Daily News*, the city's only liberal voice competing against the conservative powerhouses *Times, Examiner* and the gaudy *Herald-Express*. His spare time was devoted to *Script*. Most of the reporters and editors at the *Daily News* were liberal, but they often described themselves as students of the US Constitution and the Bill of Rights. The Constitution and Bill of Rights, at least to the *Daily News* staff, which included an African American and two Asians, in the 1940s applied to all American citizens regardless of race or religion. This by no means meant that the

Daily News possessed an enlightened editorial policy or that it always practiced fair and balanced journalism. At times it could be just as insensitive as the race-baiting Hearst papers, but the strength of conviction among its editorial staff made the *Daily News* more intellectually honest than its competitors in its coverage of the minority communities. [19]

* * *

The *Daily News* didn't provide Wagner with a forum to attack the Hearst papers, but *Script* did. Perhaps no more offensive to Wagner was the *Examiner's* treatment of his family's old friend, Charlie Chaplin, who lost a paternity lawsuit brought in 1943 by Joan Barry, an actress and his protégé. Although a blood test arranged by Chaplin's attorney, the celebrity lawyer Jerry Giesler, showed that Chaplin did not father Barry's daughter, a Superior Court judge ruled that he was the biological father and ordered that he financially support her until the age of twenty-one.

A federal grand jury followed the court order by indicting Chaplin on February 10, 1944, on two counts of violating the Mann Act (he would be acquitted of the charges). Chaplin, who had a loyal fan base despite his modest film output after the advent of sound, was stunned at the vehement attacks and scorn heaped upon him from the LA press. *Ad hominem* attacks colored the coverage as any pretense of objectivity and fairness fell away. Even the *Daily News'* liberal and much admired journalist Florabel Muir engaged in some ugly attacks on Chaplin's personal appearance and clothing choices. [20]

Chaplin supporters fell into two camps, either believing he was being persecuted by the federal government, particularly by FBI director J. Edgar Hoover, for his proclivity for dating young girls often twenty to thirty years his junior, or for his leftist politics. Chaplin believed fascist forces were behind the indictment because he ridiculed Adolf Hitler in *The Great Dictator*.

Les Wagner agreed, writing the week before the grand jury indictment, that Chaplin was a "shining target for the fascist clique in America." It was not a wild-eye allegation grasping for an explanation. The FBI thought his satire on fascism in which he equated dictatorships with the exploitation of big business was "nothing more than subtle Communist propaganda." In his final speech in *The Great Dictator*, the text of which was published in *Script*, the Jewish barber mistaken for Hitler urged the unity of Jews, gentiles, blacks and whites. In a 1942 essay for *Script*, which the FBI described as a "Beverly Hills scratch sheet," Chaplin urged Europeans to stand against dictatorships. Conservatives, particularly isolationists, attacked him for his progressive politics. Les Wagner replied in an essay for *Script*: "In making *The Great Dictator* ... Chaplin made himself a threat to Fascists, even those in America who have leanings toward Fascism, under no matter what name." The Mann Act trial was a "convenient situation" to discredit Chaplin, he added. [21] [22]

When Wagner compared Chaplin to Jesus Christ in his article, the FBI took notice. Wagner observed: "There are men and women in far corners of the world who never have heard of Jesus Christ; yet they know and love Charlie Chaplin. So when Chaplin makes a picture like *The Great Dictator*, his thoughts reach a far greater audience than do the newspapers, the magazines or the radio – and in picture words that all can understand." [23]

Hedda Hopper, the gossip columnist for the *Times*, replied acidly, "I'm wondering how the coupling of the buffoon's name of that of a Diety [sic] will improve his standing with the public, whose good opinion he is assiduously courting for the first time." [24]

At a time when liberals joined big business and encouraged capitalism as part of the war effort, dissent among leftists was viewed by the FBI as disloyal. Chaplin's leftist tone in *The Great Dictator* made him suspect. By extension, *Script's* defense of Chaplin was also perceived as disloyal. Yet Wagner brought into the debate of Chaplin's guilt or innocence that the

Mann Act violations leveled against the actor were politically motivated. FBI files released many years later confirmed what Wagner and Chaplin's supporters long believed: Federal authorities were more interested in Chaplin's politics than his interest in young girls. And it was his politics, more than his personal life, that eventually led the government in 1952 to deny Chaplin a visa to remain in the United States. [25]

* * *

Script's increasing progressive political editorials under Les Wagner coincided with the arrival of African Americans by the thousands into Los Angeles to find wartime factory jobs, Mexican Americans were being drafted into the military and sent to war, and Japanese Americans were interned in relocation camps.

Perhaps cowed by the anti-Japanese rhetoric in the media following the attack on Pearl Harbor on December 7, 1941, *Script* under Rob Wagner was unsure how to approach the Japanese internment. President Franklin Roosevelt's executive order on February 19, 1942, to deport or relocate an estimated 120,000 Japanese Americans to internment camps throughout the American West should have been a cause worth fighting. For Rob, who was once the target of anti-German sentiment during World War I and who felt persecuted by the government with accusations of sedition in part because of his surname, it's mystifying that *Script* did not take a more aggressive position under his editorship regarding the government's role in subverting due process and the constitutional protections guaranteed to American citizens.

The magazine's initial coverage was promising when it published a sensitive piece by Yori Wada, a Nisei serving as a private in the US Army, for the April 11, 1942, issue. He wrote: "Thrown in the maelstrom of the war, they (Nisei) gave vent to vocal declarations of loyalty to the Stars and Stripes. But to their dismay and confusion, they found a growing wave of suspicion directed against them and their parents. Truly, they were men without a country, shunning allegiance to Japan, their love for America unbelieved. Inside they felt empty; they knew not which way to turn." [26]

It was a bold piece at a time when the *Examiner* dominated Japanese American coverage with unrestrained racism. Inexplicably two weeks later, *Script* pulled the rug from underneath the Japanese American community with a much less supportive article from Rob's acquaintance, Alfred Cohn, a former newspaperman and writer who penned the screenplay for *The Jazz Singer*. Providing an "eye witness" account of the round-up of Japanese Americans at Santa Anita racetrack in Arcadia, which served as a staging area to deliver the internees to camps, Cohn used offensive stereotypical language to describe the prisoners and implied they were content with imprisonment. "You get the impression that this new life is a welcome change from squatting over rows of carrots and onions twelve to fourteen hours a day," Cohn wrote in the lead paragraph, reporting there is a "general air of gaiety" at the makeshift prison. [27]

Under Les Wagner, though, *Script* took a much sharper tone, directing its ire over the *Examiner's* racism and what he saw as the government's gross human rights violation. At the end of 1942, the Martin Dies Committee, part of the House on Un-American Activities Committee, announced that it would investigate allegations of mismanagement in the War Relocation Authority following incidents of unrest at Manzanar, CA, and Poston, AZ. The hearings held in 1943 provided a forum to bash the WRA by favoring testimony from critics and suppressing support for the agency as well as to air anti-Japanese sentiment.

In two editorials for *Script*, Wagner complained that the Dies Committee was heavily influenced by the Hearst papers and had determined long before testimony was given that the WRA was incompetent. When the committee called witness after witness to support allegations that the WRA was "coddling" internees, Wagner wrote, "Anyone who could speak a damning word about the Japs was welcomed with open arms;

those who sought to give the Japs an even break were refused a hearing. Such is the working of democracy in A.D. 1943." Later, he observed sarcastically, "After the war we shall have to do one of two things with the Japanese in this country. We can either amend the Constitution to permit statutory expression of racial intolerance and ship every person of Japanese blood to Japan, or we can give them the protection of the Bill of Rights." [28] [29]

In January 1944, the Office of War Information recruited Wagner to write and broadcast radio reports in the China-Burma-India Theater (CBI) from its Calcutta, India, headquarters. He wrote weekly dispatches for *Script* during this period and managed to continue in part to have contributing writers provide Los Angeles area commentary to the editorial pages. From India, he continued to defend Japanese Americans' loyalty to the United States by profiling Nisei soldiers' work as interpreters, interrogators of Japanese POWs and their role in Merrill's Marauders, the US Army 5307th Provisional Composite Unit fighting in CBI. In the July 1947 issue, six months after the Wagners had sold the magazine, San Diego Municipal Court Judge Dean Sherry, an Army major who survived the Bataan Death March and was a prisoner of war, wrote a first-person account of his experiences and the kindness of a Japanese army lieutenant, Kazuhito Uemura, who protected him and provided food during his captivity. [30] [31]

* * *

Before Les Wagner's departure for New York in 1944 to join the OWI, he and Florence performed a more direct version of advocacy journalism. Les' coverage of the Dies Committee and his support of Japanese Americans didn't extend beyond the editorial page. However, *Script's* approach to the Sleepy Lagoon murder case, which resulted in nearly two-dozen young men being charged with murder with little or no evidence, and the Zoot Suit riots involving US servicemen and Mexican

American youths commonly referred to as "pachucos," vastly differed from the Dies Committee editorials.

Violence between servicemen and Mexican Americans erupted on June 3, 1943, following some previous minor skirmishes between the two groups. The servicemen, mostly sailors, were incensed by media coverage, which in most cases turned out to be false, of young Mexican Americans assaulting white women in downtown. The teenagers and young men wore Zoot Suits, which featured jackets with wide shoulders, narrow-cuffed and pleated trousers and flat-brimmed hats. They wore key chains down to the knee and often wore their hair in a pompadour. African American and Filipino youths often wore the same outfits, but it was the Mexican Americans that earned the enmity of servicemen.

To defend the honor of Anglo women, or because they were Mexican and wore flamboyant suits – the motive was never made clear – sailors took to the streets in taxi cabs to hunt down and assault luckless youths out on the town. The *Examiner* and *Herald-Express* gleefully portrayed these attacks as necessary vigilante behavior to protect the city. Few servicemen during the early coverage were named or quoted and virtually no Mexican Americans were given the opportunity to voice their opinions about the attacks through the ten days of violence. The *Times* and *Daily News* were marginally more circumspect in their coverage, but also sometimes fell on the side of the military version of events. [32]

As the attacks continued, young Mexican American women, girlfriends of pachucos or who had been victims of the attacks, began calling the *Daily News* city desk demanding that their voice be heard. On one night Wagner answered the phone and listened to a young woman describe the rape of her thirteen-year-old friend by a serviceman. The fighting ended on June 13, but towards the end of the street violence Mexican American organizations began putting pressure on the *Daily News* and *Times* to provide context to the violence and at least to consider the institutional racism that led to the attacks. Such coverage followed in the *Daily News*, and Wagner used his phone conversation with the young woman to write a quasi-opinion news article in the magazine about the plight of minorities in the city. [33]

"Our minority groups in Los Angeles have been shabbily treated," he wrote for the June 26, 1943, issue, pointing out that the city jail was crowded with servicemen charged with violent crimes against members of the Mexican American community. The evidence against the servicemen was "alarming" and contained page after page of arrest sheets from the Los Angeles Police Department. Writer and author Carey McWilliams, an activist in the Mexican American community and head of the Sleepy Lagoon Defense Committee, recalled nearly forty years later that the editorial was "unusual" for a literary magazine. "They (*Script*) didn't usually get into issues of this sort," he said. [34] [35]

Wagner's article could be dismissed as one of dozens published in the liberal media and lost in the din of a vehement anti-Mexican climate, but Florence backed up *Script's* position with cash. For nearly a year, Los Angeles had been inundated with coverage of the Sleepy Lagoon murder case. On August 2, 1942, Jose Diaz suffered a fatal injury near a pond near the Delgadillo Ranch at Atlantic and Slauson boulevards. About 600 Mexican American youths were rounded up and twenty-two were charged with murder, although there was scant evidence that a murder even took place. Twelve defendants were convicted of murder and five of felony assault in January 1944 following a racially charged trial. McWilliams and activist Alice Greenfield helped form the Sleepy Lagoon Defense Committee to solicit support and funding for the defendants' defense. In October 1943, Florence, author Emil Ludwig and actors Joseph Cotten and Rita Hayworth donated $600 ($8,220 today) to the defense committee. The appeal process continued through the rest of 1943 and most of 1944. In October 1944, the California District Court of Appeal in the Second Appellate District reversed the convictions setting the stage to release the defendants who had been incarcerated at San Quentin state prison. [36]

The prevailing editorial policy during this period was that the Constitution and Bill of Rights mattered. No single individual in a position of authority like Superior Court Judge Charles W. Fricke, who presided over the Sleepy Lagoon trial and suppressed evidence that favored the defendants, or Judge Ruben S. Schmidt, who ruled that a Native American family could be evicted from their home, should be permitted to defy the rule of law, according to the magazine.

Schmidt had presided over a lawsuit filed by six homeowners in West Hollywood who wanted the court to enforce a covenant in the original deed of the home that denied non-Caucasians ownership. The covenant, according to the lawsuit, applied to the Harry Crocker family. Crocker was French-Canadian, but his wife, Isabel, was three-quarters American Indian. Schmidt ruled that Isabel Crocker and the couple's three daughters, Muriel, Alicia and Jeanne, were not Caucasian. He denied the Crockers' contention that the covenant violated public policy, was not in conformity with the guarantees of the Fourteenth Amendment of the US Constitution and violated the state Constitution.

In one of Les Wagner's last *Script* articles, which was more a news story than opinion piece, he observed the hypocrisy of the ruling: "The other day Indians of sixteen tribes gathered to discuss the paradox of white citizens owing them millions of dollars (in) land while denying them the right to live on it." [37]

In a similar vein, Florence Wagner turned the editorial page over to M.J. King in 1946 who outlined the resurgence of the Ku Klux Klan in California, particularly in the mountain community of Big Bear and in Los Angeles, exposing the terrorist group's attacks on African Americans, Chinese and Jewish residents. There had been considerable media coverage of the Klan in 1946, but none from any magazine connected with the film industry or the arts. California Attorney General Robert Kenny outlawed the group for failing to follow its articles of incorporation and because it was not a benevolent organization but instead spread racial hatred through violence and intimidation. King broke no new ground and as an opinion piece it was rather mild, but he outlined a litany of Klan violence and provided solutions to minimize the threat of civil rights violations. [38]

*　*　*

Had Rob Wagner lived would he have followed a similar path as his son in exposing the civil rights violations against Los Angeles' minority population? Rob Wagner's track record of publishing accounts of discrimination against minorities is almost non-existent. Like so many old radicals active before World War I any consideration of the economic difficulties minorities faced was an afterthought to poor and white middle-class workers. His own journalism since his days at the *Detroit Free-Press* are almost completely absent of any discussion of race relations aside from his association with Charles Bertrand Lewis, who wrote under the byline "M. Quad" and had earned his reputation for writing his racist series "Brother Gardner and the Lime Kiln Club," a brutal parody of African American society. Yet Rob Wagner never subscribed to the prevailing opinion among whites, who came of age during the Victorian Era, that African Americans were intellectually inferior.

In 1918, Wagner was perhaps the only writer covering the film industry who wrote about minority movie extras and the dangers they faced in performing stunts. Wagner wrote: "The Mexicans are the queerest bunch that work extra. They are employed by a patrón, and consequently take orders from him alone. A director can shout his fool head off, even in bad and violent Spanish, but they won't do a thing until their patrón tells 'em to. They work best in the battle stuff, for they are naturally better actors and more dramatic than Americans. The lowest-browed dub in the bunch has some artistic sense and will take a fearful drubbing for art's sake."

Then Wagner would undermine his reporting by using flippant language to describe one extra as "half Indian, half Mex., and half Chink." [39]

However, Rob Wagner's reporting can be separated from what his more personal thoughts were on race and how it was perceived in the film community. Around 1915 Wagner befriended the ten-year-old daughter of a Chinese laundry shop owner in Chinatown. Wagner noticed Anna May Wong, who would later become a film star, with her sisters trundling bundles of clothes from customers to their shop. A friendship blossomed as Wagner encountered Wong on her daily trips between Chinatown and downtown Los Angeles. The neighborhoods surrounding Chinatown were often jammed with film crews shooting movies and Wong stopped to watch scenes being filmed. She was so enamored with the magic of movie-making after watching Pearl White and Mary Pickford work on location that she eventually confided in Wagner her dreams to become an actress.

Wong began her film career in 1919 at the age of fourteen and considered Wagner, who encouraged her acting, as her mentor. He lobbied film producers to cast her in their films, but he was often met with that "old squawk about racial prejudice" of moviegoers. To Wagner any racial prejudice was in the minds of the producers. Wong longed to play roles given to Caucasian women, but found herself playing versions of the same exotic Asian often as a character with some name variation of "Lotus Blossom" or "Lotus Flower." [40] [41]

Feeling suffocated in her limited roles she left for Europe in about 1928 where she discovered that she was accepted not for being an exotic Chinese woman but for her intellect, charm and wit. She appeared in a number of films, including the British movie *Piccadilly* in 1929, but returned to the United States by 1930. She frequently traveled between the United States and Europe. Like expatriates Paul Robeson, Josephine Baker and Louise Brooks living in Europe, she might have found a home there if not for the rise of Nazism.

She continued to play stereotyped Asian roles, which frustrated her further. But during this period she became more vocal about her parents' homeland China. She wrote an opinion piece for *Script* in 1932 condemning Japan's invasion of Manchuria and the Mukden Incident in which the Japanese staged the bombing of a railroad and blamed it on Chinese insurgents as a pretext to invade. She raised funds for the United China Relief and became an advocate for Chinese American causes. She lamented the dearth of quality film roles for Chinese actors, who were often reduced to playing villains or temptresses. When Metro-Goldwyn-Mayer studios passed her over for the lead role of O-lan in Pearl S. Buck's *The Good Earth* in 1935, she was crushed. She spent 1936 touring China in an effort to get in touch with her roots. [42]

Frustrated with Hollywood's dismissive attitude towards Asians, casting white actors as Asian characters and her own struggles as an American actor, she turned to Wagner for advice.

Wagner suggested that if she were to be successful as an actress then she should embrace her Chinese identity. In contemporary Hollywood the suggestion would smack of being a sell-out. But in the 1930s it made sense if Wong wanted to work and to prevent Caucasian actors from taking Asian roles.

"I urged her to 'can' her Hollywood feathers and be Chinese," Wagner later recalled. "I suggested that she even burn incense in her hotel room, to add to her exotic charm." By the mid-1930s, many China-born women had embraced the West, followed the fashions accordingly, were Western educated and spoke flawless English. Yet Wong followed Wagner's suggestion. She exaggerated her exotic nature with the burning incense, red-lacquered fingernails, bowls of flowers floating in water and kept a reserved demeanor during press interviews. It was stage-managed self-promotion, but she successfully conveyed her American intellectual qualities and Asian sexuality. The move by Wong worked as she landed numerous roles, many which minimized Chinese stereotypes, in the mid to late 1930s, although a fair number were in B-movies. For the most part she pushed past the dragon lady parts. [43] [44]

After Rob's death, *Script* remained loyal to Wong even as her popularity declined. In April 1943 producer David O. Selznick, who headed the Hollywood chapter of the United China Relief, organized a reception and pageant to honor Madame Chiang Kai-shek, wife of the leader of the Republic of China. Top tier Hollywood actresses – among them Loretta Young, Ingrid Bergman, Barbara Stanwyck and Ginger Rogers – appeared on stage with the guest of honor. Wong, who worked tirelessly for the UCR, was not invited at the request of Madame Chiang Kai-shek, perhaps because many Chinese objected to her portrayals of Asians on the screen. Outraged, Les Wagner wrote that, "There wasn't a single representative from the Chinese colony, except for the Consulate staff." He added that there was "no more faithful worker for the cause of United China than Anna May Wong." [45]

Would Rob Wagner have championed Wong as he did if he hadn't known her since her childhood? It's not likely. There is little evidence in *Script* to suggest that he editorialized on the racial injustices against other Asians, or African American or Mexican actors.

Los Angeles, however, was a vastly different city in the years leading up to World War II, both in demographics and attitudes about race. It took the influx of African Americans into the city to find wartime employment and the rising tensions between Mexican Americans and whites to bring about the discussion of minority rights. As previously discussed, appointing Leo Politi as art director of *Script* and slowly changing direction to explore the margins of Los Angeles society was the first indication that *Script* was moving to a more inclusive readership. But there were financial considerations as well. By 1940, *Script* was receiving advertising from MGM and Fox studios, but desperately needed national advertising revenue that could come from the other studios. To get the studios interested, *Script* would have to broaden its readership to include subscribers and advertisers not normally associated with Beverly Hills, Hollywood, or the film industry.

This problem weighed heavily on Les and Florence Wagner after Rob's death. *Script's* advertising policy prohibited the magazine from accepting advertising from actors or directors and especially eschewed "congratulatory" advertising of individuals. As a consequence, the *Hollywood Reporter* and *Variety* had only to compete against each other to solicit and receive such ads. *Script* alleged the two trade publications "blackmailed" actors and directors into placing ads or risked having their names placed on a no-publish list. The policy put *Script* in financial jeopardy, leaving Florence to explore other options, including wider coverage to attract more far-flung advertisers. [46] [47]

Meanwhile, Les recognized that Los Angeles had changed since he had returned from San Francisco. The African American population exploded from just 50,200 in Los Angeles, San Francisco and Oakland in 1930 to 254,120 just in those three cities in 1950. It was no longer an issue of expanding the readership to attract more advertising, but the new demographics demanded different coverage. Les was no stranger to living on the margins of society. As a child roaming the Santa Barbara streets unsupervised he engaged in petty crimes. He spent a year in state custody when he was sixteen. He gravitated to the crime beat as a reporter and wasn't above getting into the occasional street brawl. These were not necessarily the experiences of most members of the minority community, but he had an affinity for the disenfranchised. Les was much like his cousins, Jack and Blake Wagner, who grew up in Mexico and spent much of their youth on their own. Les was just as comfortable talking to a busboy as he was interviewing a prime minister. He also was not above taking advantage of his position as a reporter and editor at the *Daily News* to use the newspaper's sources and contacts within the community to flesh out his own editorial pieces on minority affairs. He saw no conflict of interest because in many cases complaints from minority readers to the city desk never materialized into a news story. In 1946, following his return from India, he became a member of the National Association for the Advancement of Colored People. He believed in the NAACP's civil rights cause, but it also didn't hurt to have access to the city's most prominent African American leaders.[48] [49]

***

On a brisk February afternoon in 1947, Florence Wagner drove from her Beverly Hills home to the *Daily News* building at Los Angeles Street and Pico Boulevard. As she rounded the block and the building on the northwest corner came into view, she saw dozens of fire trucks, hoses, ambulances and patrol cars jamming the area. A terrific explosion that morning had leveled the nearby O'Conner Electroplating plant on East Pico Boulevard and destroyed an entire city block.

Robert L. Smith, the *Daily News'* forty-two-year-old brusque general manager, was sitting at his desk when the blast blew out two windows near his office and lifted him from his seat. When Florence arrived at Smith's office, city crews were deep in mop-up operations and the *Daily News* room was in chaos as reporters and editors scurried about to get out an afternoon edition.

Florence arrived at the newspaper plant to meet Smith to sell *Script*. The magazine's circulation dropped to an embarrassing 817 readers. It was unable to secure national advertising and Florence couldn't, nor did she try to, duplicate Rob's personality that was the essence of the magazine. Les Wagner was aware as early as 1946 that the *Times* was likely to launch a tabloid newspaper as the liberal answer to the *Herald-Express* and to tap into the growing market in the San Fernando Valley. The *Los Angeles Mirror* would debut in October 1948 with a circulation that averaged about 100,000 readers. Wagner joined as a columnist. He would have no time for *Script*. Florence, meanwhile, was preparing for her second wedding. In February 1948 she and James Lawrence Breese, a naval pilot during World War I and the state commander of the Civil Air Patrol in New Mexico during World War II, were married in a private ceremony in Pasadena.

Smith had political ambitions and often worked for candidates at the local and state level. The cynical *Daily News* staff perceived him as opportunistic, but for fifteen years he managed to keep the newspaper in the black. Joining Smith as a buyer in *Script* was Ralph K. Davies, the former director of the Federal Petroleum Administration for War and senior vice-president at Standard Oil. Davies had a good track record in investments and had the money to back the new venture. On the editorial side, Smith recruited the newspaper's liberal city editor James Felton to run the editorial side of *Script*. Felton was the city editor of the *Sacramento Bee* and a staunch unionist. While working as an editor for the *San Diego Sun*, management fired him for his union activities, but the newspaper was forced to rehire him after the National Labor Relations Board ruled in his favor following a hearing. [50] [51]

Smith planned to boost *Script's* circulation to 50,000, add writers with national reputations and have Salvador Dali contribute cover art. Smith did indeed increase circulation to his stated goal, but he had no national advertising to support it. The magazine began paying for editorial contributions and attempted to nurture young undiscovered writers. Smith never got Dali to illustrate the covers. He attempted to transform *Script* into a virtual clone of the *New Yorker*, ignoring the fact that what made the Beverly Hills magazine a modest success in the first place was its casual, and oftentimes low brow, approach to writing about politics and filmmaking.

Script limped along for two years. It attempted to mimic the advocacy journalism during the war years, but Smith was politically conservative and the magazine's efforts to give a voice to the voiceless fell flat. Without the necessary advertising to sustained its circulation, the magazine folded in 1949.

For eighteen of its twenty-year existence *Script* adhered to its socialist principles of turning down advertising and not paying its contributors to avoid compromising its editorial content. Even after 1940 when the economic realities demanded more traditional financial means to keep the magazine viable, *Script* retained its integrity but also sealed its fate. It was a hybrid of film entertainment coverage with liberal political commentary and it worked longer than anyone could have anticipated. There was no other magazine like it in the country. The socialist *The Masses* and its successor, *The Liberator*, helmed by Max Eastman, came close when the publications focused on the arts and literature and less on political theory. Eastman's two magazines were run as cooperatives in which contributors had a say in management operations. In fact, it's likely that Rob Wagner adopted some of Eastman's management techniques for his own operation. But *The Liberator* was gone by the time *Script* arrived on the literary landscape.

Script's failure was a direct result of Rob's death and Florence's inability or unwillingness to harness his energy to continue. But the conservative postwar political climate, the rise of McCarthyism and the Hollywood blacklist made *Script's* old-school radicalism an anachronism. Few people outside the Communist Party thought of the Soviet Union as progressive. And although Les Wagner's advocacy journalism was a natural outgrowth of his father's progressive politics and prescient in giving the minority community a voice, the magazine's efforts were perceived by conservatives as disloyal to American ideals.

In the end, *Script* was a product of its time. The socialism and Bolshevism admired by Rob Wagner in the 1910s and 1920s were virtually unrecognizable by the 1940s. The idea of artistic purity seemed almost quaint in the face of the brutal Stalin regime and the growing threat of Soviet spying. The timing of magazine's founding in 1929 on the eve of economic and political upheaval until its death twenty years later when the economy boiled with unrestrained capitalism were almost perfect in time and place for the little publication. But in a hawkish late-1940s America preoccupied with the Cold War and communist infiltration there was little profit for publications indulging in idealistic leftist causes.

AFTERWORD

The events of 1918-1919 had a profound impact on Rob Wagner, resulting in a ten-year journey to publish a magazine that cherished free thought. Wagner cooperated with the Bureau of Investigation's probe into his antiwar activities and he was likely aware that he was under surveillance during the April 1918 Liberty Bond tour with Charlie Chaplin, according to the nearly 100 pages of declassified Justice Department documents.

However, it's unlikely that he knew that Nora and Ruth Sterry and Elmer Wachtel had informed on him, or that federal agents had hoped to recruit his good friend Douglas Fairbanks as an informant. With the exception of Ruth Sterry's hearsay testimony that Wagner said the US should surrender if Germany invaded American soil, which even in its most conservative interpretation amounts to treason, Wagner's pacifism and neutrality during World War I didn't quite reach the level of sedition. He acknowledged to federal agents that he broke away from the Socialist Party when many prominent members threw their support to the war effort, and joined a "militant" faction to oppose the war. But his opinions did not match the fiery rhetoric of Emma Goldman or Max Eastman.

In fact, he bought Liberty Bonds, supported Red Cross work and even encouraged some young men to join the military if that is how they wanted to express their patriotism, according to Justice Department documents. Wagner's comments were limited to private conversations and private correspondence. Rob and Florence enjoyed being contrarians and provocateurs (Wachtel reported that Florence told him that she rather "shoot" Wagner's sons "with her own hand" to prevent them from being drafted into the military), and it would have stung if he had learned that his and his wife's comments were not taken with the lively spirit that it was intended in roundtable discussions.

Bureau agents and military intelligence aggressively pursued Wagner during the Liberty Bond tour (they seemed much less interested in Chaplin) by burglarizing his hotel rooms and rifling through his correspondence. Yet not once did Wagner, Chaplin or Charles Lapworth ever make pro-German statements. And when agents finally took possession of Wagner's diary, they discovered a man who didn't like large parties, took long solo walks in the early morning, and kept to himself when not obligated to accompany Chaplin to an event. He also didn't particularly care for his Southern hosts. [1]

Separate investigations by the Bureau of Investigation and the Los Angeles County District Attorney's office concluded there was no evidence that Wagner was disloyal, engaged in pro-German activities or offered aid and support to the radical IWW.

On July 24, 1918, federal agent Frank Turner wrote in a report that based on his interview with Wagner at his Avenue 39 studio there was no evidence that he was a German spy. "From conversation with the subject I could find no reason for his being reported as pro-German ... " Turner wrote.

Edwin Van Wirt, who assisted Turner in interrogating Wagner, wrote in separate report that Elmer Wachtel's allegations against Wagner were "either made with spiteful intentions or that the informant was unduly suspicious." [2]

The District Attorney's decision not to indict Wagner on sedition charges came seventeen months later.

The federal investigation and subsequent Los Angeles County Grand Jury hearing in November and December 1919 taught Wagner that free speech was an illusion, censorship was more dangerous than anti-government speeches and the government had a capricious streak when it came to protecting personal liberties.

Building upon these experiences, Wagner sought to establish a publication that gave writers free rein to express their thoughts. His experiences during the Red Scare shaped *Script's* editorial policies. He ridiculed the elites, mocked state and federal government policies and took the Hollywood studio machine to task for its failures to treat its workers equitably.

As America geared up for war in 1938, *Script* published an antiwar essay by Paul Gerard Smith who warned young men enlisting in the military that war belonged to the politicians and businessmen who profited from conflict.

"If you go to war, you are a chump as I was (during World War I)," Smith wrote, adding: "If they try to bully you into enlisting or force you by draft into a set-up which is 100 per cent fraudulent, tell them to go to hell even if they shoot you in your tracks. At least you will die honest."[3]

Script was not joining the isolationists, but cautioning young men that if they chose to fight, it had to be their war based on their own values and ideals, and not one that allowed big business to engage in profiteering and political leaders promote graft.

The magazine's tone was less sharp than Wagner's previous antiwar rhetoric because the distance of two decades didn't soften the accusations of "spy" and "traitor" hurled at him. If anything, the debacle involving *Script* and Upton Sinclair's EPIC campaign served as a nasty reminder just how quickly the political winds could shift.

ACKNOWLEDGMENTS

———•◆•———

I always considered my forty-plus years of off-and-on research of *Rob Wagner's Script* magazine to be a hobby. Writing a book about the history of the magazine and my great-grandfather, its founder, was not a serious consideration because I believed it to be a conflict of interest. After all, I was not writing a memoir so objectivity would always be an issue.

There was also the fact that in the 1970s film historians wrote little about the magazine because cinema scholarship was more or less still in its infancy. *Script's* impact on the film industry was virtually unknown. This changed beginning in the 1980s with four important books: *Chaplin: His Life and Art* by David Robinson (1985), *The Best of Rob Wagner's Script* edited by Anthony Slide (1985), *Campaign of the Century: Upton Sinclair's Race for Governor of California and the Birth of Media Politics* by Greg Mitchell (1991) and *Frank Capra: The Catastrophe of Success* by Joseph McBride (1992). Each provided early details of Rob Wagner's relationship with some of the most important film artists of the silent and early sound era. Film scholars now routinely study Wagner's papers held at UCLA's Charles E. Young Library.

The one element missing in scholarly discussions of *Script* was how and why the magazine came to be. It seemed reasonable that after a distance of nearly seventy years that I could objectively explore the origins of this early literary film publication. This book attempts to put

Script's impact on the film industry between 1929 and 1947 into context by building on the original research of film and political historians. It examines the origins of Rob Wagner's politics that date to his childhood when his maternal grandfather spoke of the oppression of the Irish by the British. It examines how Wagner advocated for the artistic integrity of motion pictures through independent film production and arguing that the screenwriter was the most important member of any film crew.

My gratitude goes to those four authors for introducing *Script* to a new generation of film scholars, and it's my hope that this book puts a definitive stamp on the magazine's legacy.

This book in many ways wrote itself thanks to two diaries Rob Wagner kept shortly after the turn of the twentieth century. His family album traced the history of the Wagners and his mother's side, the Greaves and Hornbook families, to provide insight into how it shaped Wagner's attitudes about government, landownership and art.

Following his marriage to Jessie Brodhead, Wagner also wrote a honeymoon diary in 1903 and 1904 while living in London and Paris during his art school studies. It offers glimpses into the day-to-day lives of Rob and Jessie as expatriates. Of particular note from this diary are Rob's attitudes about religion, art, the relationships between artist and model, the beginnings of his leftist ideology and his deep interest in Russia.

I wish to thank the staff at the Charles E. Young Research Library at the University of California at Los Angeles for helping me access my great-grandfather's papers. Since the mid-1980s I have visited the library often to read his letters and literary work and to make copies. There are at least two generations of student staff members who had assisted me over the years. My last visit was in 2015 and my first occasion to conduct research specifically for this book. My special thanks to Peggy Alexander's staff.

My thanks also goes to my cousin, Carol Wagner Mills-Nichol, granddaughter of Rob Wagner and daughter of Thornton Wagner. An author, Carol edited my manuscript and provided much needed guidance on writing, research and how to approach my subject. She also provided me with several photographs from her own collection for the book.

I also wish to thank another cousin, Kathleen Wagner Starrett, granddaughter of Robert Hawley Wagner, a cinematographer for First National Pictures during the silent era, for providing photographs of cousins Jack, Blake, Max and Bob Wagner.

My gratitude also goes to my publisher Jim Skidmore at Janaway Publishing for taking a chance on a book with a subject that is usually not in his catalog. It's a risk I hope he doesn't regret.

To my wife, Dr. Sabria Salama Jawhar, my special appreciation for her encouragement and patience during this lengthy project.

ENDNOTES

INTRODUCTION

[1] "Chaplin May Testify," *Variety*, Dec. 3, 1919.
[2] Tom Sitton, *John Randolph Haynes: California Progressive* (Redwood City, CA: Stanford University Press, 1992), 146.
[3] Max Alvarez, "Cinema as an Imperialist Weapon: Hollywood and World War I," *World Socialist Web Site*, Aug. 5, 2010. Accessed January 5, 2015, https://www.wsws.org/en/articles/2010/08/holl-a05.html.
[4] Paul Burnett, "The Red Scare," *University of Missouri-Kansas City, School of Law*. Accessed Apr. 22, 2015.
http://law2.umkc.edu/faculty/projects/ftrials/SaccoV/redscare.html.
[5] *The Western Comrade*, Vol. 1, No. 1, April 1913, pp.114-115.
[6] Rob Wagner letter to Upton Sinclair, Dec. 8, 1933, Rob Wagner Papers, 1925-1942, UCLA: Library Special Collections, Charles E. Young Research Library (Stored off-site at University of California Southern Regional Library Facility).
[7] Rob Wagner letter to Will Hays, Feb. 15, 1940 (Rob Wagner Papers 1925-1942).
[8] Upton Sinclair, *The Brass Check: A Study of American Journalism* (Champaign, IL: University of Illinois Press, 1919), 398-399.
[9] Florence Wagner, "Here's to Script," *Script*, March 1947, p. 14.
[10] "Censorship Goes On and On," *Rob Wagner's Script*, June 28, 1930, pp. 1-2.
[11] Greg Mitchell, *Campaign of the Century: Upton Sinclair's Race for Governor of California and the Birth of Media Politics* (New York: Random House, 1992), 132-133.
[12] Sergei M. Eisenstein, "The Russian Cinema," *Rob Wagner's Script*, Aug. 9, 1930, pp. 16-17.
[13] Anne Edwards, "Light in Dark Russia," *Rob Wagner's Script*, March 7, 1936, pp. 8-9.
[14] Marguerite Harrison, "Evraika the Jewess," *Rob Wagner's Script*, March 21, 1936, pp. 6-7.

[15] Gladys Lloyd Robinson, "An Exile in Mexico," *Rob Wagner's Script*, Sept. 10, 1938, p. 5.
[16] Alfred Cohn, "Santa Anita – Sukiyaki Style," *Rob Wagner's Script*, April 25, 1942.
[17] Les Wagner, "Japanese-American Heroes," *Script*, Jan. 5, 1944.
[18] Les Wagner, "Who Greeted the Mayflower?" *Script*, March 1947, p. 4.
[19] Rob Leicester Wagner, *Red Ink, White Lies: The Rise and Fall of Los Angeles Newspapers, 1920—1962*, (Upland, CA: Dragonflyer Press, 2000).

CHAPTER ONE

[1] "Encyclopedia of Detroit," *Detroit Historical Society*, (http://detroithistorical.org: accessed May 1, 2015).
[2] Peter Gavrilovich, and Bill McGraw, *The Detroit Almanac*, (Detroit. MI: Detroit Free-Press, 2006).
[3] Robert Leicester Wagner, *Wagner Family History Book and Photo Album* (unpublished), MS, 1908, Author's collection.
[4] Thomas Hughes, *History of Blue Earth County and Biography of its Leading Citizens*, (Chicago, IL: Middle West Publishing Co., 1901).
[5] William R. Plum, *History of the Military Telegraph in the Civil War*, (Chicago, IL: Jensen McClurg & Co., Publishers, 1882); Robert Leicester Wagner, *Wagner Family History Book and Photo Album* (unpublished), MS, 1908, Author's collection.
[6] 1870 U.S. federal census, Wayne Co., MI, pop. sch., Detroit Ward 1, Roll: *M593_712*; p. *26B*; Robert Wagner household, Dwelling # 341, Family # 404, digital image #56, *Ancestry.com (*http://www.ancestry.com: accessed 4/2015), citing Family History Library Film: *55221;* and 1880 U.S. federal census, Wayne Co., MI, pop. sch., Detroit, Roll: 612, p. 215A; Robert Wagner household, dwelling #234, family #247 (420 Second Ave.) digital image, *Ancestry.com* (http://www.ancestry.com: accessed 4/2015), citing Family History Film: *1254612; Wagner Family History Book and Photo Album.*
[7] Robert Leicester Wagner, *1903-1904 Honeymoon Diary of Robert Leicester Wagner and Jessie Willis Brodhead* (unpublished). N.d., MS. Author's collection; *Wagner Family History Book and Photo Album.*
[8] *Keramic Studio* magazine, Volume V, May 2, 1900; *Wagner Family History Book and Photo Album.*
[9] Robert Leicester Wagner, "A Famous Author Talks about Fraternities Thirty Years Ago," *The Greek Review*, June 1930; *Wagner Family History Book and Photo Album.*
[10] *Rob Wagner's Script*, April 26, 1930.
[11] "Youth and the Big Adventure," *Rob Wagner's Script*, March 28, 1931, p. 23.

CHAPTER TWO

[1] Robert Leicester Wagner, *Wagner Family History Book and Photo Album.*
[2] John H. Wagner, Bureau of Pensions government document, Feb. 18, 1907; also, "Civil War and Later Veterans Pension Index," Record of John H. Wagner, 6th Minn., Co., "I," digital image, *Fold3.com* (http://www.fold3.com: accessed May 26, 2015).
[3] "The Civil War, Battle Unit Details, 6th Regiment, Minnesota Volunteers," *National Park Service* (http://www.nps.gov/civilwar/search-battle-units-detail.htm?battleUnitCode=UMN0006RI: accessed Feb. 12, 2015).
[4] 1900 U.S. Census, Dupage Co., IL, pop. sch. York, Roll: *298,* Page: *14A,* E. D. *0039,* John H. Wagner household, Elmhurst Village, dwelling #249, family #277, digital image, *Ancestry.com* (http://www.ancestry.com: accessed 4/2015) citing FHL microfilm: *1240298.*
[5] Author interview with Greg Jones, great-nephew of James R.H. Wagner, Sonoma, Calif., September 1, 1992.
[6] *Notables of the Southwest, Being the Portraits and Biographies of Progressive Pen of the Southwest*, (Los Angeles, CA: *Los Angeles Examiner,* 1912), 123.
[7] Sigma Phi membership roster, University of Michigan, 1895. Author's collection.
[8] *Michiganensian* Yearbook, University of Michigan, Class of 1915.
[9] Wilfred B. Shawn, editor. *The University of Michigan, An Encyclopedic Survey* (Ann Arbor, MI: University of Michigan, Digital Library Production Service, 2000).
[10] *The Michigan Alumnus*, Vols. 1, 5 and 6; Earl D. Babst, "Back in the Nineties," *The Alumnus*, March 16, 1909.
[11] Robert Leicester Wagner, "A Famous Author Talks about Fraternities Thirty Years Ago," *The Greek Review*, June 1930.
[12] *The Wrinkle*, Vol. 1, 1893.
[13] *The Wrinkle*, Vol. 2 1894.
[14] "Robert Wagner Dead," *Detroit Free-Press*, Dec. 5, 1894, p. 2.
[15] Robert Leicester Wagner, "*Wagner Family History Book and Photo Album.*
[16] Memorandum of Agreement between Robert Wagner and John T. Woodhouse, May 2, 1887. Author's collection.
[17] Articles of Agreement, Robert Wagner Land Contract, July 28, 1891. Author's collection.
[18] "The Why and Wherefore of Script," *Rob Wagner's Script*, Feb. 16, 1935, p. 1.
[19] "City Directories, Michigan, Detroit," Charles F. Clarke & Co. (1867-1868, 1871-1872; R.L. Polk & Co., (1886, 1887, 1896), Entries for Robert Wagner, *Fold3.com* (http://www.fold3.com: accessed 5/2015).
[20] Peter Brooker and Andrew Thacker, editors. *The Oxford Critical and Cultural History of Modern Magazines: Volume II: North America 1894-1960* (Oxford, England: Oxford University Press, 2012).
[21] Frederick Winthrop Faxon, *Ephemeral Bibelots: A Bibliography of the Modern Chap-Books and Their Imitators* (Boston, MA: Boston Book Co., 1903).

[22] Mike Ahley, *The History of the Science Fiction Magazine, Vol. 1*, (Chicago, IL: NTC/Contemporary Publishing, 1976).
[23] *The Scranton Journal*, April 8, 1897.
[24] *The Washington, D.C. Times*, April 11, 1897.
[25] *The Sacramento Record-Union*, Sept. 20, 1896.
[26] *The Clack Book*, Easter 1897.
[27] James O. Kemm, *Rupert Hughes: A Hollywood Legend*, (Portland, OR: Pomegranate Press, 1997).
[28] *Periodyssey Press, Oldmagazines.com* (http://www.oldmagazines.com) accessed December 1, 2000.
[29] *The Criterion*, Oct. 1, 1898.
[30] *The Criterion*, Nov. 5, 1898.
[31] "The Vanity of a Great Man," *Rob Wagner's Script*, Feb. 15, 1930, p. 22.
[32] *University of Michigan* Alumni, 1923.
[33] Joyce Milton, *Tramp: The Life of Charlie Chaplin*, (Boston, MA: Da Capo Press, 1998).
[34] *Detroit Free-Press*, May 31, 1898.
[35] *Richmond Dispatch*, May 29, 1898.
[36] "Whatcha Scairt Of?" *Rob Wagner's Script*, May 7, 1936, p. 1
[37] Emanuel Julius, "Rob Wagner, The Artistic Red," *The Western Comrade*, July 1913, pp. 114-115
[38] Arnold T. Schwab, *James Gibbons Huneker, Critic of the Seven Arts* (Redwood City, CA: Stanford University Press, 1963).

CHAPTER THREE

[1] *Periodyssey Press, Oldmagazines.com* (http://www.oldmagazines.com: accessed Dec. 1, 2000.
[2] Robert Leicester Wagner, *1903-1904 Honeymoon Diary.*
[3] Ibid.
[4] Ibid.
[5] Clarence Monroe Burton, William Stocking and Gordon K. Miller, associate editors, The City of Detroit, Michigan, 1701-1922, Vol. 2 (Ann Arbor, MI: University of Michigan Library, 2006), 600.
[6] Ibid.
[7] "Prominent Detroit Woman Stricken by Hand of Death," *Detroit Free-Press*, March 29, 1910.
[8] Methodist Episcopal Church, *Minutes of the Annual Conferences of the Methodist Episcopal Church.* (New York: T. Mason and G. Lane for the Methodist Episcopal Church, 1840-1940).
[9] United States Congress, Andrew R. Dodge, Betty K. Koed, *Biographical Directory of the United States Congress, 1774-2005* (Washington, D.C.: Government Printing Office, 2005).
[10] Clarence Monroe Burton, William Stocking and Gordon K. Miller, associate editors, The City of Detroit, Michigan, 1701-1922 (Vol. 2), p. 600.

[11] Robert Leicester Wagner, *1903-1904 Honeymoon Diary.*
[12] Ibid.
[13] Ibid.
[14] "Wagner-Brodhead," *Detroit Free-Press*, Dec. 6, 1902.
[15] Robert Leicester Wagner, *1903-1904 Honeymoon Diary.*
[16] Ibid.
[17] Ibid.
[18] Estelle Lawson Lindsey, "Artist Condemns False Ideas Set Up by Robt. W. Chambers and His Ilk," *Los Angeles Record* (Editorial Page), month and day unknown, 1911.
[19] Robert Leicester Wagner, *1903-1904 Honeymoon Diary.*
[20] Ibid.
[21] Ibid.
[22] Ibid.
[23] Ibid.
[24] Ibid.
[25] Ibid.
[26] Ibid.
[27] Ibid.
[28] *Notables of the Southwest, Being the Portraits and Biographies of Progressive Men of the Southwest*, p. 123.
[29] "Mrs. Rob Wagner Passes Way Suddenly," *Santa Barbara Morning Press*, Aug. 20, 1906.
[30] "Famous Portrait Painter Here," *Los Angeles Herald*, Aug. 17, 1906.
[31] "Mrs. Rob Wagner Passes Way Suddenly," Aug. 20, 1906.
[32] "Jessie Willis Wagner" certified death record, Santa Barbara County, CA, copy obtained June 25, 1987.

CHAPTER FOUR

[1] "Art Notes," *Los Angeles Herald*, Nov. 15, 1909.
[2] Lee Shippey, "Personal Glimpses of Famous Southlanders," *Los Angeles Times*, Nov. 2, 1930.
[3] E.E. Hitchcock, "The Intercollegiate Socialist Society," *The Western Comrade*, September 1913, Vol. 1, No. 6, p. 202.
[4] "In Old Santa Barbara," *Santa Barbara Morning Press*, Dec. 20, 1958.
[5] Hanna Astrup Larsen, "The Artist Colony of Santa Barbara," *San Francisco Call*, June 28, 1908.
[6] "League Notes," *Keramic Studio*, May 1900, pp. 109, 148.
[7] "Club Notes," *Keramic Studio*, May 1903.
[8] "League Notes," *Keramic Studio*, May 1894, pp. 52, 145.
[9] Beth Gates Warren, *Artful Lives: Edward Weston, Margrethe Mather, and the Bohemians of Los Angeles* (Malibu, CA: J. Paul Getty Museum, 2011), 106, 156.
[10] Tom Sitton, *John Randolph Haynes, California Progressive*, (Redwood City, CA: Stanford University Press, 1992), 146.

[11] E.E. Hitchcock, "The Intercollegiate Socialist Society," *The Western Comrade*, September 1913, Vol. 1, No. 6, p. 202.

[12] Leonard Pitt and Dale Pitt, *Los Angeles A to Z: An Encyclopedia of the City and County*, (Oakland, CA: University of California Press, 1997), 474.

[13] Rob Wagner, "My Own Dope," a scrapbook collection of newspaper clippings of Rob Wagner (*Los Angeles Citizen*, undated), Author's collection.

[14] "Art Notes," *Los Angeles Herald*, Jan. 16, 1909.

[15] "Art Notes," *Los Angeles Herald*, May 1, 1910.

[16] Elizabeth Waggoner, "Art Notes," *Los Angeles Herald*, July 17, 1910.

[17] Leonard Pitt and Dale Pitt, *Los Angeles A to Z: An Encyclopedia of the City and County*, 219, 474.

[18] "A Mirage in Mojave," *Rob Wagner's Script*, June 13, 1931, p. 23.

[19] Unknown newspaper clipping of Los Angeles city election socialist slate, 1913 (Rob Wagner Papers, 1925-1942).

[20] Ibid.

[21] "A Mirage in Mojave," *Rob Wagner's Script*, June 13,-1931, p. 23.

[22] Ibid.

[23] Emma Goldman, *Living My Life*, (New York: Knopf Publishing, 1931).

[24] John A. Farrell, *Clarence Darrow: Attorney for the Damned*, (New York: Doubleday Random House, 2011).

[25] Penny A. Weiss and Loretta Kensinger, *Feminist Interpretations of Emma Goldman* (University Park, PA: Penn State Press, 2010).

[26] Rob Wagner, *The Graphic*, May 11, 1911, p. 4,

[27] Matthew Bokovoy, *The San Diego World's Fairs and Southwestern Memory, 1880-1940* (Albuquerque, NM: University of New Mexico Press, 2005).

[28] Jeff Smith, "The Big Noise: The Free Speech Fight of 1912," *San Diego Reader*, July 4, 2012.

[29] Ibid.

[30] "San Diego Has a Tar Party for Dr. Reitman," *San Francisco Call*, May 17, 1912, p. 1.

[31] Upton Sinclair, *The Brass Check: A Study of American Journalism*, (Champaign, IL: University of Illinois Press, 1919), 203.

[32] Lee Shippey, "Personal Glimpses of Famous Southlanders," *Los Angeles Times*, Nov. 2, 1930.

[33] Ibid.

[34] "The Artist's Sons," *The Moving Picture World*, Oct. 6, 1911.

[35] *The Artist's Sons* playbill, Oct. 6, 1911, author's collection.

[36] "The Artist's Sons," *The Moving Picture World*.

[37] Gene Fowler, *Father Goose: The Story of Mack Sennett*, (New York: Covici-Friede, 1934), 107-108.

[38] Rob Wagner, "An Heroic Heavy," *Rob Wagner's Script*, April 25, 1931, p. 23.

[39] State Board High School Credential, Rob Wagner, Sept. 27, 1913, Author's collection.

[40] *California Society of Secondary Education, Vol. 11*, (Burlingame, CA: California Journal of Secondary Education, 1936), 274.

[41] Anne Edwards, "Light in Dark Russia: A Survey of the Schools in the USSR," *Rob Wagner's Script*, March 7, 1936, pp. 8-9.
[42] Emanuel Julius, "Rob Wagner, the Artistic Red." *The Western Comrade*, July 1913, Vol. No. 4.
[43] Joseph McBride, *Frank Capra: The Catastrophe of Success*, (New York: Simon & Schuster, 1992), 61.
[44] Ibid.
[45] Ibid, 61-62, 140, 143.
[46] Ibid.
[47] Ibid.
[48] Ibid.
[49] Ibid.
[50] "Hueneme Notes," *Oxnard Daily Courier*, May 15, 1915.
[51] Robert Leicester Wagner, *Wagner Family History Book and Photo Album*.
[52] William Wallace Wagner, conductor, Southern Pacific Company Blacklist, May 12, 1892.
[53] Robert Leicester Wagner, *Wagner Family History Book and Photo Album*.
[54] "Not Ambitious to be Dime Novel Bandits," *Los Angeles Herald*, June 11, 1906.
[55] Author's interview with Richard L. Wagner, son of Robert Hawley Wagner, Danbury, CT, November 1, 1991.
[56] *The Gray Goose*, March 1907; *The Bellman*, Nov. 9, 1912; *The Smart Set*, May 1915.
[57] Author's interview with Richard L. Wagner, November 1, 1991.
[58] Jackson J. Benson, *The True Adventures of John Steinbeck, Writer* (New York: Viking Press, 1984), 17, 28, 78, 402-403, 450-452.
[59] Author's interview with Richard L. Wagner, Danbury, Connecticut, November 1, 1991.
[60] Rob Wagner letter to "Nick," July 18, 1926 (Rob Wagner Papers, 1925-1942).

CHAPTER FIVE

[1] "A Mirage in Mojave," *Rob Wagner's Script*, June 13, 1931, p. 23.
[2] Rob Wagner letter to Jack London, Oct. 13, 1913 (Rob Wagner Papers 1925-1942).
[3] *The Western Comrade*, Vol. 1, No. 1, April 1913.
[4] Jeffrey D. Stansbury, *Organized Workers and the Making of Los Angeles, 1890-1915*, a dissertation submitted in partial satisfaction of the requirements for the degree Doctor of Philosophy in History (University of California, Los Angeles, 2008).
[5] Cecilia Rasmussen, "A Socialist Who Almost Was Mayor," *Los Angeles Times*, Oct. 31, 1999.
[6] Robert V. Hine, *California's Utopian Colonies* (New York, NY: W. W. Norton & Company, 1973), 114-121.
[7] Ibid.

[8] Rob Wagner letter to Jack London, Oct. 7, 1913 (Rob Wagner Papers 1925-1942).

[9] *The Western Comrade*, June 1913, Vol. 1, No. 3, pp. 90-91.

[10] Emanuel Haldeman-Julius, *My First 25 Years, Instead of a Footnote – An Autobiography* (Girard, KS: Big Blue Book B-814, 1949).

[11] Ibid.

[12] Rolf Potts, "The Henry Ford of Literature," *Believer* magazine, September 2006 (accessed July 11, 2015).

[13] Emanuel Haldeman-Julius, *My First 25 Years, Instead of a Footnote – An Autobiography* (Girard, KS: Big Blue Book B-814, 1949).

[14] Frank E. Wolfe, "The Movie Revolution," *The Western Comrade*, July 1913, Vol. 1, No. 4., p. 125.

[15] David E. James, *The Most Typical Avant-Garde: History and Geography of Minor Cinemas in Los Angeles,* (Oakland, CA: University of California Press, 2005), 99.

[16] Frank E. Wolfe, "The Movie Revolution, *The Western Comrade*, July 1913, Vol. 1, No. 4, p. 125,

[17] Steven J. Ross, *Working-Class Hollywood: Silent Film and the Shaping of Class in America*, (Princeton, NJ: Princeton University Press, 1999), 27, 36.

[18] David E. James and Rick Berg, editors. *The Hidden Foundation: Cinema and the Question of Class,* (Minneapolis, MN, University of Minnesota Press, 1996), 34.

[19] Steven J. Ross, *Working-Class Hollywood: Silent Film and the Shaping of Class in America*, p. 110.

[20] Rob Wagner, "A Unique Melange of Red and Black," *The Western Comrade*, October 1913, Vol. 1, No. 7, pp. 235,236.

[21] Errol Wayne Stevens, *Radical L.A.: From Coxey's Army to the Watts Riots, 1894-1965,* (Norman, OK: University of Oklahoma Press, 2009), 106-109.

[22] Ibid.

[23] "A Mirage in Mojave," *Rob Wagner's Script*, June 13, 1931, p. 23.

[24] "*Western Comrade* Has New Owners," *Western Federation of Miners*, Vol. XIV, No. 54, December 25, 1913.

[25] Ibid.

[26] N. W. Ayer & Son, *American Newspaper Annual and Directory: A Catalogue of American Newspapers*, 1916, Vol. 1, p. 76.

[27] *The Western Comrade*, May 1917, Vol. 5, No. 1, p. 5.

[28] Upton Sinclair, *The Brass Check: A Study of American Journalism*, (Champaign, IL: University of Illinois Press, 1919), 203.

CHAPTER SIX

[1] Rob Wagner letter to Winifred Wendell of Detroit (with handwritten notations from Florence Wagner), March 31, 1925 (Rob Wagner Papers, 1925-1942).

[2] Rob Wagner letter to Prynce Hopkins (with handwritten notations from Florence Wagner), June 28, 1926 (Rob Wagner Papers, 1925-1942).

[3] 1900 U. S. federal census, Shawnee Co., KS, pop. sch. Topeka, Ward 4, Roll: 500, p. 11A, James Welch household, Dwelling #237, Family #274, digital image #22/23, *Ancestry.com* (http://www.ancestry.com: accessed 11/2015), citing Family History Library Film #1240500.

[4] *Ancestry.com*. "Kansas State Census Collection, 1855-1925" [database on-line]. Provo, UT, USA: Ancestry.com Operations, Inc., 2009.

[5] "Society," *Topeka State Journal*, May 27, 1911, p. 17.

[6] "Society," *Topeka State Journal*, January 7, 1914, p. 8.

[7] "Society," *Topeka State Journal*, January 19, 1914, p. 8.

[8] "Their Goodbye Speeches," *Topeka Daily Capital*, May 9, 1905, p. 5.

[9] "Senior Class Play, *Topeka Daily Capital*, March 10, 1905, p. 9.

[10] "Leave for Europe," *Topeka State Journal*, June 5, 1911, p. 3.

[11] "A Kansan Aboard," *Topeka Daily Capital*, August 13, 1911, p. 3.

[12] "A Kansan Aboard," *Topeka Daily Capital*, July 30, 1911, p. 19.

[13] "Florence Welch Talked to K.U. Journalism Class," *Topeka Daily Capital*, Feb. 27, 1909.

[14] Peter Churchill, "Our Cover Girl (Angela Lansbury)," *Script*, July 7, 1945, pp. 2,3.

[15] Dalton Trumbo "The Russian Menace,", *Script*, May 25, 1946, pp. 2,3.

[16] "In Society: Welch-Wagner," *Topeka Daily Capital*, January 6, 1914, p. 6.

[17] "In Society," *Topeka State Journal,* January 6, 1914, p. 8.

[18] "Society," *Topeka State Journal*, January 19, 1914, p. 8.

[19] "In Society," *Topeka Daily Capital*, January 14, 1914.

[20] "Society," *Topeka State Journal*, January 19, 1914, p. 8

[21] Ibid.

[22] Ibid.

[23] Michael Redmon, "Prynce Hopkins: Distinctive Home at Garden and Pedregosa," *Santa Barbara Independent*, August 19, 2014.

[24] Boyland, Santa Barbara, CA, Report Card of Leicester Wagner, Feb. 15, 1915 (Rob Wagner Papers, 1925-1942).

[25] Boyland, Santa Barbara, CA, Report Card of Leicester Wagner, March 28, 1915 (Rob Wagner Papers, 1925-1942).

[26] Boyland, Santa Barbara, CA, Report Card of Thornton Wagner, Feb. 16, 1915 (Rob Wagner Papers, 1925-1942).

[27] Leicester Wagner letter to Rob and Florence Wagner, May 18, 1915 (Rob Wagner Papers, 1925-1942).

[28] Leicester Wagner letter to Rob and Florence Wagner, May 14, 1915 (Rob Wagner Papers, 1925-1942).

[29] Rob Wagner letter to J.E. Elliot, March 26, 1928 (Rob Wagner Papers, 1925-1942).

[30] James R.H. Wagner letter to Leicester Wagner, Oct. 6, 1919 (Rob Wagner Papers, 1925-1942).

[31] Leicester Wagner letter to Rob and Florence Wagner, July 12 1922 (Rob Wagner Papers, 1925-1942).

[32] Robert Leicester Wagner, "A Famous Author Talks about Fraternities Thirty Years Ago," *The Greek Review*, June 1930.

[33] Author interview with Carol Wagner Mills-Nichol via email, January 20, 2015.
[34] Author interview with Lucy Howard Wagner, Bradbury, CA, November 22, 1986.
[35] Author interview with Harriet Wagner Jones, Sonoma, CA, Oct. 15, 1992.
[36] Rob Wagner letter to Winifred Wendell of Detroit (with handwritten notations from Florence Wagner), March, 1925 (Rob Wagner Papers, 1925-1942).
[37] Rob Wagner letter to Prynce Hopkins (with handwritten notations from Florence Wagner), June 28, 1926 (Rob Wagner Papers, 1925-1942).
[38] Ibid.
[39] Author interview with Carol Wagner Mills-Nichol via email, January 20, 2015.
[40] Ibid.
[41] James R.H. Wagner letter to Rob Wagner, June 3, 1933 (Rob Wagner Papers, 1925-1942).
[42] James R.H. Wagner letter to Rob Wagner, Jan 14, 1934 (Rob Wagner Papers, 1925-1942).
[43] Rob Wagner self-portrait in oil, dated April 14, 1914 (author's collection).
[44] Certificate of Bronze Medal for "Painting in Oil," 1915 Panama-Pacific International Exposition (author's collection).
[45] "About Mr. and Mrs. Wagner," *Topeka Daily Capital*, Nov. 3, 1914, p. 6.
[46] "Wagner house burned," *Los Angeles Herald*, December. 30, 1922.
[47] "A Film Favorite" (Parts 1 and 2), Rob Wagner, *Saturday Evening Post*, October 9 and 16, 1915.
[48] "The Quickie," Rob Wagner, *Saturday Evening Post*, Nov. 15, 1926.
[49] *Woman's Home Companion*, October 1920; House advertisement *Screenland*, October 1928 and; *Red Book Magazine*, July 1922; *Blue Book Magazine*, December 1924; *Liberty*, Sept. 20, 1924, April 3, 1926 and weekly from Dec. 31, 1932 to Oct. 21, 1933; *Collier's*, various issues from October 29, 1927, through May 14, 1932.
[50] "Social and Personal," *Topeka Daily Capital*, December 2, 1917, p. 17.

CHAPTER SEVEN

[1] Brent E. Walker, *Mack Sennett's Fun Factory: A History and Filmography of His Studio and His Keystone and Mack Sennett Comedies with Biographies of Players and Personnel*, (Jefferson, NC: McFarland & Co., 2013), 309.
[2] Joyce Milton, *Tramp: The Life of Charlie Chaplin*, (Boston, MA: Da Capo Press, 1998).
[3] Ibid
[4] Ibid
[5] Brent E. Walker, *Mack Sennett's Fun Factory: A History and Filmography of His Studio and His Keystone and Mack Sennett Comedies with Biographies of Players and Personnel*, 309.

[6] Joyce Milton, *Tramp: The Life of Charlie Chaplin*.
[7] Ibid.
[8] Upton Sinclair, *The Brass Check: A Study of American Journalism* (Champaign, IL: University of Illinois Press, 1919), 398-399.
[9] Mary Craig Sinclair, *Southern Belle* (Jackson, MS: University Press of Mississippi, 1957), 208-209.
[10] Brent E. Walker, *Mack Sennett's Fun Factory*, p. 309.
[11] Beth Gates Warren, *Artful Lives: Edward Weston, Margrethe Mather, and the Bohemians of Los Angeles* (Malibu, CA: J. Paul Getty Museum, 2011), 106-107, 156, 158.
[12] Ibid.
[13] Ibid.
[14] "The Strange Case of John Bovingdon," *Life* magazine, August 16, 1943, p. 34.
[15] "John Bovingdon, former local dancer, is fired," *Berkeley Daily Gazette*, July 31, 1943, p. 23.
[16] Lauren Coodley, *Upton Sinclair: California Socialists, Celebrity Intellectual* (Lincoln, NE: University of Nebraska Press, 2015).
[17] Steven J. Ross, *Hollywood Left and Right: How Movie Stars Shaped American Politics* (New York, NY: Oxford University Press, 2011).
[18] M. Keith Booker, *Film and the American Left: A Research Guide* (Westport, CT: Greenwood Press, 1999), 199.
[19] Kenneth Schuyler Lynn, *Charlie Chaplin and His Times* (New York, NY: Simon and Schuster, 1997), 224-225.
[20] Theodore Huff, *Charlie Chaplin* (New York, NY: Henry Schuman, Inc., 1951), 4.
[21] Joyce Milton, *Tramp: The Life of Charlie Chaplin*, (Boston, MA: Da Capo Press, 1998).
[22] *Honolulu Star-Bulletin*, Oct. 16, 1917, p. 5.
[23] *Honolulu Star-Bulletin*, Nov. 6, 1917, p. 6.
[24] Rob Wagner draft of letter to unknown publisher, January 22, 1918 (Rob Wagner Papers, 1925-1942).
[25] Ibid
[26] Chaplin letter to Rob Wagner, May 15, 1918 (Rob Wagner Papers, 1925-1942).
[27] Rob Wagner, "Mr. Charles Spencer Chaplin: The Man You Don't Know," *Ladies' Home Journal*, August, 1918.
[28] *Charlie Chaplin Goes to War*, Roy Rosenzweig Center for History and New Media (chnm.gmu.edu.com), accessed October 1, 2015.
[29] Max Alvarez, "Cinema as an Imperialist Weapon: Hollywood and World War I,"*World Socialist Web Site*, August 5, 2010. (https://www.wsws.org/en/articles/2010/08/holl-a05.html.: accessed Jan. 5, 2015)
[30] Ibid.
[31] Real Southern Hospitality, *Rob Wagner's Script*, June 21, 1930.
[32] Michael Redmon, "Prynce Hopkins: Distinctive Home at Garden and Pedrogosa," *Santa Barbara Independent*, August 19, 2014.

[33] Beth Gates Warren, *Artful Lives: Edward Weston, Margrethe Mather, and the Bohemians of Los Angeles*, 140.
[34] Paul Avrich, *The Modern School Movement: Anarchism and Education in the United States* (Princeton, NJ: Princeton University Press, 1980), 248.
[35] Beth Gates Warren, *Artful Lives: Edward Weston, Margrethe Mather, and the Bohemians of Los Angeles*, 140.
[36] Patriots of Fear, *Rob Wagner's Script*, April 19, 1930.
[37] Real Southern Hospitality, *Rob Wagner's Script*, June 21, 1930.
[38] Max Eastman, *Love and Revolution: My Journey Through an Epoch* (New York, NY: Random House, 1964), 146.
[39] Beth Gates Warren, *Artful Lives: Edward Weston, Margrethe Mather, and the Bohemians of Los Angeles*, 153-154.
[40] Paul Burnett, "The Red Scare" (http://law2.umkc.edu/faculty/projects/ftrials/SaccoV/redscare.html), accessed October 2, 2015.
[41] Joyce Milton, *Tramp: The Life of Charlie Chaplin*, (Boston, MA: Da Capo Press, 1998).
[42] Letter from Division Superintendent, Leavenworth, Kansas, Federal Penitentiary, to S.A. Connell, Esq., Los Angeles, Calif., Oct. 28, 1919, *Fold3.com* (https://www.fold3.com/image/5203649?terms=rob%20wagner:_____ accessed August 15, 2015.
[43] Ibid.
[44] James McGrath Morris, *Jailhouse Journalism: The Fourth Estate Behind Bars* (Livingston, NJ: Transaction Publishers, 2001), 92.
[45] Mark W. Van Wienen, editor, *Rendezvous with Death: American Poems of the Great War* (Champaign, IL: University of Illinois Press, 2002), 285.
[46] "Threaten M.P. Snyder with Death," *Oxnard Press-Courier*, November 24, 1919.
[47] Upton Sinclair's Page, "The Clouds are Breaking," *Appeal to Reason Weekly*, December 20, 1919.
[48] Jane Apostol, "From Salon to Soap-Box: Kate Crane Gartz, Parlor Provocateur," *Southern California Quarterly*, Vol. 89, No. 4 (Winter 2007-2008), pp. 373-390.
[49] Kevin Starr, *Inventing the Dream: California through the Progressive Era* (New York, NY: Oxford University Press, 1986), 212.
[50] Tom Sitton, *John Randolph Haynes, California Progressive* (Redwood City, CA: Stanford University Press, 1992), 146.
[51] Ibid.
[52] Justice Department agent George T. Holman report, "In Re: Robert Wagner, alleged IWW and socialistic activities," December 11, 1919, *Fold3.com* (https://www.fold3.com/image/5203652: accessed October 22, 2015).
[53] Regin Schmidt, *Red Scare: FBI and the Origins of Anticommunism in the United States, 1919-1943* (Copenhagen, Denmark: Museum Tusculanum Press, 2000), 37, 188.
[54] Justice Department agent George T. Holman report, "In Re: Robert Wagner, alleged IWW and socialistic activities," December 11, 1919.

[55] A. Hopkins report, "Charlie Chaplin, et al. Los Angeles, Cal.," Federal Bureau of Investigation, August 14, 1922 (Freedom of Information Act, author's collection), pp. 2, 6.

[56] Ibid.

[57] Richard Merrill Whitney, *Reds in America: The Present Status of the Revolutionary Movement in the United States Based on Documents Seized by the Authorities in the Raid Upon the Convention of the Communist Party at Bridgman, Michigan on August 22, 1922* (New York, NY: Beckwith Press, 1924), 157.

[58] Old FBI Case Files. Batch of miscellaneous reports totaling 74 pages from the Department of Justice, Bureau of Investigation, War Department and the Military Intelligence Branch on "Rob Wagner, suspected German spy" and "suspect in pro-German activities" dated April 1, 1918 through July 30, 1918. (https://www.fold3.com/search/#query=robert+wagner&offset=1&preview=1&t=74) Accessed April 25, 2016.

[59] Ibid

[60] Ibid

CHAPTER EIGHT

[1] Anne Morey, "Have you the Power? The Palmer Photoplay Corporation and the Film Viewer/Author in the 1920s," *Film History* (Indiana University Press, Vol. 9, No. 3, 1997), 300-319.

[2] Anne Morey, *Hollywood Outsiders: The Adaption of the Film Industry, 1913-1934* (Minneapolis, MN: University of Minnesota Press, 2003).

[3] Brian Taves, *Thomas Ince: Hollywood's Independent Pioneer* (Lexington, KY: University Press of Kentucky, 2011).

[4] Anne Morey, "Have you the Power? The Palmer Photoplay Corporation and the Film Viewer/Author in the 1920s," *Film History*.

[5] Anne Morey, *Hollywood Outsiders: The Adaption of the Film industry, 1913-1934*.

[6] Ibid.

[7] Ibid.

[8] Rob Wagner letter to Winifred Wendell, March 31, 1925 (Rob Wagner Papers, 1925-1942).

[9] Wheeler W. Dixon and Gwendolyn Audrey Foster, eds., *Experimental Cinema: The Film Reader* (London and New York: Routledge, 2002), 22-23.

[10] Ibid.

[11] Symon Gould, "The Little Theater Movement in Cinema," *The Educational Screen*, February 1927, pp. 68-70.

[12] Marguerite Tazelaar, "The Story of the First Little Film Theater," *Movie Makers*, July 1928, pp. 441-442.

[13] Tino Balio, *The Foreign Film Renaissance on American Screens, 1946-1973*, (Madison, WI: University of Wisconsin Press, 1996), 26.

[14] Tino Balio, *Grand Design: Hollywood as a Modern Business Enterprise, 1930-1939* (Madison, WI: University of Wisconsin, 1996), 390-391.

[15] "Gloria Gould to Run Embassy Theatre to Pre-View Showings," *Exhibitors' Trade Review*, August 8, 1925.

[16] "Little Theatre Films Completes Formation of Its Advisory Board," *Exhibitors Herald*, July 21, 1923, p. 21.

[17] Constance Palmer Littlefield, "New Hope for the American Photoplay," *Screenland*, October 1923, pp. 62-63.

[18] "Films Little Theatre," *Variety*, May 1930, p. 1

[19] Ibid.

[20] E.J. Fleming, *Paul Bern: The Life and Famous Death of the MGM Director and Husband of Harlow* (Jefferson, NC: McFarland Press, 2009), 78-79.

[21] "Curtis Melnitz Quits Little Theatre Films," *Exhibitors Herald*, January 12, 1924, p. 24.

[22] Wheeler W. Dixon and Gwendolyn Audrey Foster, *Experimental Cinema: The Film Reader*.

[23] "Hollywood Bulletin," *Experimental Cinema*, June 1930, pp. 12-14.

[24] Ibid.

[25] Ibid.

[26] David James, *The Most Typical Avant-Garde: History and Geography of Minor Cinemas in Los Angeles*, (Oakland, CA: University of California Press, 2005), 214-215.

[27] Tino Balio, *Grand Design: Hollywood as a Modern Business Enterprise, 1930-1939*, pp. 390-391.

[28] Rob Leicester Wagner, *Red Ink, White Lies: The Rise and Fall of Los Angeles Newspapers, 1920—1962* (Upland, CA: Dragonflyer Press, 2000).

[29] Ibid.

[30] Benjamin B. Hampton (Benjamin Bowles), *A History of the Movies* (New York: Covici, Friede, 1931), 289-290.

[31] " 'Movie Revue' production is failure," *Modesto Evening News*, August 9, 1923, p. 2.

[32] Nathan Miller, *New World Coming: The 1920s and the Making of Modern America* (Boston, MA: Da Capo Press, 2004), 242.

[33] Steve Neale, editor, *The Classical Hollywood Reader* (London & New York: Routledge Press, 2012).

[34] Elinor Glyn, "Justice and Fair Play for Film Folk," *Los Angeles Examiner*, February 20, 1922.

[35] *Hollywood Citizen*, February 22, 1922.

[36] Rob Wagner, "The Shame of Sleepy Hollywood," *Silverscreen*, March 30, 1922, pp. 28-29.

[37] Tony Luke Scott, *The Stars of Hollywood Forever* (Unknown, CA: Tony Scott Publishing, 2001), 14.

[38] "Kelly's Chum Testifies to Booze Parties," *Santa Ana Register*, May 17, 1927, p. 1.

[39] "Another Indictment in Death of Raymond Looms, *Modesto News-Herald*, April 29, 1927, p. 1.

[40] "Dot Mackaye and Kelly Trysts at Apartment to be Bared by Valet," *Oakland Tribune*, May 16, 1927, p. 1.

[41] Rob Wagner, ten-page undated, unpublished draft, "Censorship" (Rob Wagner Papers, 1925-1942).

[42] Ibid.

[43] "Censorship 'Goes West' at Los Angeles Public Hearing," *Exhibitors Herald*, November 5, 1921, p. 39.

[44] "Rob Wagner Thinks Censorship as Applied Here is Ideal Arrangement," *Santa Barbara Daily Independent*, September 15, 1921.

[45] "Fatty Arbuckle Does Not Typify Real Moving Picture World," Wagner, undated newspaper clipping, *Santa Barbara News Press* (Rob Wagner Papers 1925-1942).

[46] "Will Hays Ungratefully Takes a Rap at Film Producers," *Manitowac Herald-Times*, March 3, 1924, p. 3.

[47] Joyce Milton, *Tramp: The Life of Charlie Chaplin*, (Boston, MA: Da Capo Press, 1998).

[48] "Censorship Rages On and On," *Rob Wagner's Script*, June 28, 1930, pp. 2-3.

[49] Joseph McBride, *Frank Capra: The Catastrophe of Success*, (New York, NY: Simon & Schuster, 1992), 64.

[50] American Film Institute, *The American Film Institute Catalog of Motion Pictures Produced in the United States, 1921 to 1930*, Part I (Oakland, CA: University of California Press, 1997), 627.

[51] "The Big Producer," *Rob Wagner's Script*, May 17, 1930.

[52] "Rob Wagner Original," *The Photodramatist*, January 1921, p. 33.

[53] "Paramount Studio Feature is Offered Exhibitors Gratis," *Exhibitors Herald*, June 3, 1922, p. 36.

[54] "What Picture Will Walter Hiers Start Next Week?" *The Norwalk Hour*, January 27, 1923, p. 8.

[55] "Wagner Serial Epic of Screen Life," *The Photodramatist*, August 1922.

[56] "Society Notes," *Topeka Daily Capital*, March 21, 1922, p. 6.

[57] Warren M. Sherk, *The Films of Mack Sennett* (Lanham, MD: Scarecrow Press, 1998), 43.

[58] Mack Sennett and Cameron Shipp, *King of Comedy: The Lively Art* (New York, NY: Doubleday, Inc., 1954), 129-130.

[59] "Coast Film News," *Variety*, September 3, 1924, p. 23.

[60] Famous Players-Laky Corporation contract between Rob Wagner and Jesse Lasky dated January 5, 1923 (Rob Wagner Papers 1925-1942).

[61] Rob Wagner letter to "Hec," Aug. 27, 1924 (Rob Wagner Papers 1925-1942).

[62] Betty Rogers, *Will Rogers: His Wife's Story*, (Norman, OK: University of Oklahoma Press, 1979), 157-158.

[63] Ben Yagoda, *Will Rogers: A Biography* (Norman, OK: University of Oklahoma Press, 2000), 206.

[64] Ibid.

[65] "Chatter of the Make-Believers," *Oakland Tribune*, February 12, 1924, p. 29.

[66] "Will Rogers Directed by Rob Wagner," *Oakland Tribune*, December 30, 1923, p. 1 (Amusement Section).

[67] "Will Rogers to Burlesque American politicians," *Exhibitors Trade Review*, April 12, 1924, p. 29.
[68] Michael Slade Shull, *Radicalism in American Silent Films, 1909-1929: A Filmography and History* (Jefferson, NC: McFarland Press, 2009), 294.
[69] Joseph McBride, *Frank Capra: The Catastrophe of Success*, (New York, NY: Simon & Schuster, 1992), 61.

CHAPTER NINE

[1] "The Why and Wherefore of Script," *Rob Wagner's Script*, Feb. 16, 1935, p. 2.
[2] Milton Weiss, *Star Gazing in Hollywood: Reminiscence of a Beverly Hills Restaurateur* (self-published, 2001), 9.
[3] "The Why and Wherefore of Script," *Rob Wagner's Script*, Feb. 16, 1935, p. 2.
[4] Ibid.
[5] "21" *The Princeton Alumni Weekly* (Princeton University), June 7, 1929, p. 1072.
[6] Gloria Swanson letter to Rob Wagner, Dec. 12, 1930 (Rob Wagner Papers 1925-1942); *Broadcasting*, May 15, 1932, p. 21.
[7] James P. Cunningham, "Asides and Interludes," *Moving Picture Herald*, May 1, 1937, p. 45.
[8] "Attack Jews for Film Production, 'All Quiet on the Western Front,' " *The Wisconsin Jewish Chronicle* (Jewish Telegraphic Agency), June 27, 1930, p. 7.
[9] Thomas Doherty, *Hollywood's Censor: Joseph I. Breen and the Production Code Administration* (New York, NY: Columbia University Press, 2009).
[10] Andrew Kelly, *All Quiet on the Western Front: The Story of a Film* (London, UK: I. B. Tauris, 2002).
[11] "Self-Styled Hollywood Technical Directors Institute Also Wants Eisenstein Out of the Country," *Exhibitors Herald-World*, June 28, 1930, p. 12).
[12] "Censorship Goes On and On," *Rob Wagner's Script*, June 28, 1930, pp. 1-2.
[13] "The Russian Cinema," *Rob Wagner's Script*, Aug. 9, 1930, p. 16.
[14] "Censorship Goes On and On," *Rob Wagner's Script*, June 28, 1930, pp. 1-2.
[15] Richard Bart, "Major Frank Chester Pease," Sept. 26, 2011 *Genealogy.com*, (http://www.genealogy.com/forum/surnames/topics/pease/3178/ : accessed Nov. 9, 2015).
[16] "Censorship Goes On and On," *Rob Wagner's Script*, June 28, 1930, pp. 1-2.
[17] "Bit Agent Quits," *Variety*, April 30, 1930, p. 5.
[18] *Film Daily Year Book*, 1930, p. 588.
[19] "American Defies Great Britain's Ouster Demand," *Fresno Bee*, July 24, 1933, p. 9.
[20] "U.S. Ex-Diplomat is Robbed in Paris," *Oakland Tribune*, Dec. 19, 1931, p. 2.
[21] Phineas J. Biron, "Strictly Confidential," *The Wisconsin Jewish Chronicle*, Jan. 1, 1937, p. 1.
[22] "Pole to Panama," *Xenia Daily Gazette* (Ohio), March 21, 1935, p. 35.

[23] "Paramount Officials and Sergei Eisenstein to Ignore Deportation Threat, Anti-Semitic Attack," *The Wisconsin Jewish Chronicle* (Jewish Telegraphic Agency), June 27, 1930, p. 7.
[24] Donald T. Critchlow, *When Hollywood was Right: How Movie Stars, Studio Moguls and Big Business Remade American Politics* (London, UK: Cambridge University Press, 2013), 18-20.
[25] Joyce Milton, *Tramp: The Life of Charlie Chaplin*, (Boston, MA: Da Capo Press, 1998).
[26] Ibid.
[27] Lauren Coodley, *The Land of Orange Groves and Jails: Upton Sinclair's California* (Berkeley, CA: Heyday Press, 2004), 95-96.
[28] Harland Fend, "Thunder Over Mexico Much Discussed Film," *Cincinnati News*, April 20, 1934.
[29] Ibid.
[30] Marie Seton, *Sergei N. Eisenstein: A Biography* (London, UK: The Bodley Head, 1952), 168, p. 200.
[31] William M. Drew, *The Last Silent Picture Show: Silent Films on American Screens in the 1930s* (Lanham, MD: Scarecrow Press, 2010), 115.
[32] "The Russian Cinema," *Rob Wagner's Script*, Aug. 9, 1930, p. 17.
[33] Anne Edwards, "Light in Dark Russia: A Survey of the Schools in the U.S.S.R.," *Rob Wagner's Script*, March 7, 1936, p. 9.
[34] Marguerite Harrison, "Evraika, the Jewess: A Story of a Bolshevik Prison," *Rob Wagner's Script*, March 21, 1936, p. 7.
[35] Gladys Lloyd Robinson, "An Exile in Mexico," *Rob Wagner's Script*, Sept. 10, 1938, p. 5.
[36] Dalton Trumbo, "The Russian Menace," *Script*, May 25, 1946, p. 10.
[37] Ring Lardner Jr., *I'd Hate Myself in the Morning* (New York, NY: Nation Books, 2001), 113-114.
[38] Peter Churchill, "Our Cover Girl," *Script*, July 7, 1945.
[39] Dalton Trumbo, "The Real Meaning of the NCPAC, *Script*, Feb. 3, 1945, p. 24.
[40] Oral History Interview with Stanton Macdonald-Wright, 1964 April 13-Sept. 16, Archives of American Art, Smithsonian Institution.
[41] "The Screen Guild," *Rob Wagner's Script*, April 21, 1932, p. 2.
[42] Ibid.
[43] Ibid.
[44] Alfred Hustwick, "The Guild Forum," *The Photodramatist*, Oct. 1921, pp. 7-8.
[45] "Technical Bureau Served to Preserve M.P. Academy," *The Motion Picture Projectionist*, Aug. 1931, pp. 31-32.
[46] Fred Niblo letter to Rob Wagner, May 22, 1931 (Rob Wagner Papers, 1925-1942).
[47] Rob Wagner letter to Fred Niblo, May 27, 1931 (Rob Wagner Papers, 1925-1942).
[48] "The Screen Guild," *Rob Wagner's Script*, April 21, 1932, p. 2.

[49] Thomas Schatz, *Hollywood: Critical Concepts in Media and Cultural Studies, Vo. 1* (London and New York: Routledge, 2003), 187.

[50] "The Screen Guild," *Rob Wagner's Script*, April 21, 1932, p. 2.

[51] "Movieland Goes Roman," *Rob Wagner's Script*, April 4, 1931.

[52] "Richard Schayer letter to Rob Wagner, April 20, 1931 (Rob Wagner Papers, 1925-1942); Susan McCarthy, "Hollywood's Long History of Animal Cruelty," *Salon*, April 2, 2012, (http://www.salon.com/2012/04/02/hollywoods_long_history_of_animal_cruelty/): accessed Feb. 6, 2016.

[53] Leonard Pitt and Dale Pitt, *Los Angeles A to Z: An Encyclopedia of the City and County*, (Oakland, CA: University of California Press, 1997), 470.

[54] "A Trustful Brain Truster," *Rob Wagner's Script*, March 17, 1934, p. 1

[55] Kenneth Stewart, "Upton Sinclair and His Epic Plan for California, *Literary Digest*, Aug. 23, 1934, p. 10

[56] "Authors United Under Banner of Blue Eagle," United Press, Aug. 30, 1933.

[57] Undated Author's League letter from Dorothy Parker, Rob Wagner, Frank Scully, Morrie Ryskind, Jim Tully and Lewis Browne (Rob Wagner Papers, 1925-1942).

[58] Rob Wagner letter to Frank Scully, Oct. 6, 1934 (Rob Wagner Papers, 1925-1942).

[59] Frank Scully letter to Rob Wagner, Oct. 10, 1934 (Rob Wagner Papers, 1925-1942).

[60] A.L. Lumbard letter to Rob Wagner, Oct. 1, 1934 (Rob Wagner Papers, 1925-1942).

[61] Rob Wagner letter to Upton Sinclair, Dec. 8, 1933 (Rob Wagner Papers, 1925-1942).

[62] Upton Sinclair letter to Rob Wagner, Oct. 17, 1934 (Rob Wagner Papers, 1925-1942).

[63] Greg Mitchell, *The Campaign of the Century: Upton Sinclair's Race for Governor of California and the Birth of Media Politics* (New York: Random House, 1992), 133.

[64] "Darkness Before Dawn, *Rob Wagner's Script*, Sept. 29, 1934, p. 1

[65] *The undersigned Californians endorse the announced candidacy of Upton Sinclair for the governorship of our state* (1926) Signers: A. Bruce Anthony, Herman Lissauer, Mark Lee Luther, Rob Wagner, Lewis Browne, Myna Browne, Jim Tully. Upton Sinclair (1878-1968) Papers, University of Indiana, Lilly Library.

CHAPTER TEN

[1] Jim Tully, "Frank Capra," *Rob Wagner's Script*, March 3, 1934.

[2] "A Number of Writers," *Rob Wagner's Script*, Dec. 23, 1939.

[3] William Saroyan, "The Broken-Hearted Comedian and the Girl Who Took the Place of His Unfaithful Wife," *Rob Wagner's Script,* Oct. 8, 1938.

[4] Author interview with Ray Bradbury, Jan. 14, 1992, San Dimas, Calif.
[5] Ray Bradbury, "It's not the Heat, It's the Hu –," *Rob Wagner's Script*, Nov. 2, 1940.
[6] Jonathan R. Eller, *Becoming Ray Bradbury* (Champaign, IL: University of Illinois Press, 2011), 43.
[7] Author interview Paul Leo Politi, May 20, 2007, Pasadena, Calif.
[8] David Alfaro Siqueiros, "The New Fresco Mural Painting, *Rob Wagner's Script*, July 2, 1932.
[9] Ibid.
[10] "Art," Stanton Macdonald-Wright, *Rob Wagner's Script*, April 14, 1945.
[11] Buckley MacGurrin letter to Leo Politi, Dec. 29, 1940.
[12] Buckley MacGurrin, "Our Cover Boy," *Rob Wagner's Script*, May 25, 1940.
[13] Death Certificate of Rob Leicester Wagner, July 22, 1942, Santa Barbara, Calif., Author's Collection.
[14] Author interview with Lucy Harvey Wagner, Feb. 3, 1986.
[15] Ibid.
[16] Leicester Wagner application letter to Office of War Information, Feb. 27, 1942 (Rob Wagner Papers, 1925-1942).
[17] "Prominent Newsman, Les Wagner, Succumbs," *Pasadena Star-News*, Nov. 23, 1965, p. 1.
[18] Author interview with Lucy Harvey Wagner, Feb. 3, 1986.
[19] Rob Leicester Wagner, *Red Ink, White Lies: The Rise and Fall of Los Angeles Newspapers, 1920—1962*, (Upland, CA: Dragonflyer Press, 2000).
[20] Joyce Milton, *Tramp: The Life of Charlie Chaplin*, (Boston, MA: Da Capo Press, 1998).
[21] Les Wagner, *Script*, March 4, 1944.
[22] Charles Chaplin, "Gives Us More Bombs Over Berlin," *Script*, 1942.
[23] Les Wagner, *Script*, March 4, 1944.
[24] Joyce Milton, *Tramp: The Life of Charlie Chaplin*, (Boston, MA: Da Capo Press, 1998).
[25] John Sbardellati and Tony Shaw, "Booting the Tramp: Charlie Chaplin, the FBI, and the Construction of the Subversive Image in Red Scare America," *The Pacific Historical Review*, Vol. 72, No. 4 (University of California Press), pp. 500-501.
[26] Yori Wada, "A Soldier's Report," *Rob Wagner's Script*, April 11, 1942, p. 8.
[27] Alfred Cohn, "Santa Anita – Sukiyaki Style," *Rob Wagner's Script*, April 25, 1942.
[28] Les Wagner, "Neighborliness ... Begins at Home," *Script*, Jan. 9, 1943.
[29] Les Wagner "Presenting the Dies Committee," *Script*, July 10 1943.
[30] Dean Sherry, "Captain Uemura, Japanese," *Script*, July 1947, p. 11.
[31] "Judge Dean Sherry," *The Quan*, September 1987, p. 9.
[32] Les Wagner, "American-Japanese Heroes," *Script*, Jan. 5, 1946, p. 1.
[33] Leonard Pitt and Dale Pitt, *Los Angeles A to Z: An Encyclopedia of the City and County*, (Oakland, CA: University of California Press, 1997), 571.
[34] Les Wagner, "Our Chickens Come Home," *Script*, June 26, 1943, p. 2.

[35] "Honorable in All Things," Oral interview with Carey McWilliams by Joel Gardner, Oral History Program, University of California, Los Angeles, Tape Number IV, Side 1, July 13, 1978.

[36] *The Appeal News* (Sleepy Lagoon Defense Committee newsletter), Vol. 1, No. 12, Oct. 18, 1943.

[37] Les Wagner, "Who Greeted the Mayflower?" *Script*, March 1, 1947, p. 4.

[38] M.J. King, "The Hooded Brethren Ride Again," *Script*, June 8, 1946, p. 1.

[39] Anthony Slide, *Hollywood Unknowns: A History of Extras, Bit Players, and Stand-Ins* (Jackson, MS: University of Press Mississippi, 2012), 187.

[40] Karen J. Leong, *The China Mystique: Pearl S. Buck, Anna May Wong, Mayling Soong, and the Transformation of American Orientalism* (Oakland, CA: University of California Press, 2005), 60.

[41] Graham Russell Gao Hodges, *Anna May Wong: From Laundryman's Daughter to Hollywood Legend* (Hong Kong University Press, 2012), 13.

[42] Anna May Wong, "Manchuria," *Rob Wagner's Script*, Jan. 16, 1932, p. 6.

[43] Karen J. Leong, *The China Mystique: Pearl S. Buck, Anna May Wong, Mayling Soong, and the Transformation of American Orientalism*, 60.

[44] Rob Wagner, "A Chinese Girl Goes 'Home,' " *Rob Wagner's Script*, Jan. 10, 1936.

[45] Karen J. Leong, *The China Mystique: Pearl S. Buck, Anna May Wong, Mayling Soong, and the Transformation of American Orientalism*; Graham Russell Gao Hodges, *Anna May Wong: From Laundryman's Daughter to Hollywood Legend*.

[46] Les Wagner, "Tin Cup Advertising," *Script*, Jan. 18, 1947.

[47] Rob Wagner letter to Will Hays, Producer's Association, Feb. 15, 1940 (Rob Wagner Papers, 1925-1942).

[48] Membership enrollment card for Leicester Wagner, National Association for the Advancement of Colored People, "expires Sept. 1949" (Author's collection).

[49] Lawrence DeGraaf, Kevin Mulroy and Quintard Talor, eds., "Seeking El Dorado: African Americans in California," (Seattle, WA: University of Washington Press, 2001).

[50] Florence Wagner, "Here's to Script," *Script*, March 1947, pp. 14-15.

[51] Rob Leicester Wagner, *Red Ink, White Lies: The Rise and Fall of Los Angeles Newspapers, 1920—1962*.

AFTERWORD

[1] Old FBI Case Files. Batch of miscellaneous reports totaling 74 pages from the Department of Justice, Bureau of Investigation, War Department and the Military Intelligence Branch on "Rob Wagner, suspected German spy" and "suspect in pro-German activities" dated April 1, 1918 through July 30, 1918. (https://www.fold3.com/search/#query=robert+wagner&offset=1&preview=1&t=74) Accessed April 25, 2016.

[2] Ibid.

[3] Paul Gerard Smith, "An Open Letter to Boys of Military Age," *Rob Wagner's Script*, Sept, 24, 1938, p. 6.

INDEX

Académie Delecluse 45, 47
Académie Julian 41, 46, 47
Academy of Motion Picture Arts and Sciences 5, 146-147
Actors' Equity 135
Addams, Jane 103
Adventurer, The 93
African Americans 106, 166, 168, 172, 175
Arkham House 157
Alaska-Yukon-Pacific Exhibition 55
Allen, Alfred 55
All Quiet on the Western Front (film) 120, 133, 135
America Tropical (mural) 158
American Civil Liberties Union 80, 91, 103
American Defender Press 136
American Federation of Labor 56
American Humane Association 148
American News Co. 37
American (magazine) 95
American Tobacco Co. 28
Andrus, Ethel Percy 62
Arbuckle, Rosoe "Fatty" 61, 88, 90, 115, 116-118
Artist's Sons, The 60-61, 66
Ashleigh, Charles 102-103, 106
Associated Press, The 141
Atta Boy 66
Author's League 150
Ayers, Sidney 61

Baker, Josephine 173
Ballin, Hugo 112
Bangs, John Kendrick 30
Barrett, Wilson 111
Barr, Robert 38
Barry, Joan 164
Bataan Death March 168
Battle of Fort Blakeley 21-22
Battle of Harpers Ferry 39
Battle of Hastings 13
Battle of Lookout Mountain 12
Battle of Nashville 12
Battle of Shiloh 12
Battle of Perryville 12
Battleship Potemkin 114, 133
Beattie, Elia W. 30
Becky Sharp (film) 147
Belsaigne, Jean 14
Belsaigne, Mary Jane 13, 14
Belsaigne, Mathieu 14
Bellman, The 65
Benchley, Robert 150
Bergman, Ingrid 175
Bern, Paul 112-113
Berkeley Lyceum Theater 34
Berkman, Alexander 57
Beverly Theater 132
Biltmore Hotel 146
Binney, Constance 122
Bischoff, Franz 55
Block, Ralph 112
Blondin, Grace (Welch) 78, 79

Blondin, Joseph 79
Blue Book 30, 85
Boggs, Francis 60-61
Bolshevism 2, 47, 52, 90, 93, 100, 104, 105, 125, 133, 134, 140, 143-144, 179
Bolles, William Edward, 25
Bosworth, Hobart 60
Borzage, Frank 147
Bovingdon, John 91
Boyland 80-82, 96-97
Boys Republic of Chino, 82
Bradbury, Ray 4, 156-157
Breese, Lawrence 177
Brennan Building 131
British Labour Party 143
British Royal Navy 13
Browne, Lewis 151
Brodhead, Alexandrine 48
Brodhead, Archange 48
Brodhead, Eleanor 48
Brodhead, Jack 48, 83
Brodhead, Jessie Mary Willis 39-41, 49
Brodhead, John 39
Brodhead, John Thornton 39-40, 48
Brodhead, Katherine 48
Brodhead, Richard 48, 49
Brodhead, Thornton 48
Brodhead, Col. Thornton Fleming 39-40
Brodhead, Willis 48, 83
Brooks, Louise 173
Buck, Pearl S. 174
Buell, Gen. Don Carlos 12
Bunker Hill 160
Burbank Hall 57-58
Burke, Frank 104
Burroughs, Edgar Rice 4, 150, 156

Cabinet of Dr. Caligari, The 112
Cable, George Washington 30
California Art Club 55
California Theatre Co. 119
California District Court of Appeal 170

Call of the Wild 70
Campau, Alexandrine Macomb Sheldon 39
Campau, Melancthon Woolsey 25
Canadian Jewish Review 141
Cantor, Eddie 155
Capote, Truman 25
Capra, Frank 6, 63-64, 126, 155
Cass School 40
Castalian, The 24
Catholic Church 115
Catholic Truth 39
Catholic World 39
Century Dogs 148
Century Films 148
Century Theater 34
Chambers, Robert W. 43
Champion, Kate 17
Chancey, Jack 131
Chap-Book 28
Chaplin, Charlie 6, 54, 55, 61, 76, 87-89, 90-105, 106, 110, 112, 116, 120, 122, 130, 137, 155, 161-162, 164-166, 180-181
Character Actors' Association 136
Charles Ray Productions 120
Charlot, Jean 157
Chase, William Merritt 47
Chattanooga Campaign 12
Chicago Daily World 71
China-Burma-India Theater 168
Chouinard School of Art 158
Christian Science Monitor, The 65
Citizen Publishing Co. 68-69 75
City Lights 138
Civil Air Patrol 178
Clack Book, The 26, 28-31
Clarke, Chauncey 91
Clarke, Marie Rankin 91
Cohn, Alfred 167
Collegians, The 127
Collier's 85, 127, 129, 132
Columbia Pictures 147
Columbia University 80
Committee on Public Information 1
Common Law, The 43

Communist Party of America 105,
   120, 143, 144, 179
Connell, S.A. 104
Cooper, Merian C. 147
Corbaley, Kate 109
Cork, Ireland 13, 14
Cornwall (Canada) 10
Cotten, Joseph 170
Covered Wagon, The 124
Crapo, Henry Howland 45
Creel, George 1, 149
Critchlow, Donald T. 136
Criterion Independent Theater
   Group, The 3, 34, 63
Criterion, The 3, 26, 31-34, 37
Crocker, Alicia 171
Crocker, Harry 171
Crocker, Isabel 171
Crocker, Jeanne 171
Crocker, Muriel 171
Cupid's Boots 126

Dakota Wars 1
Dali, Salvador 178
Daly, Augustin 35
Dare-Devil, The 66, 123
Dark Carnival 157
Darrow, Clarence 58, 68, 72
Daugherty, Frank 114
Dau's Blue Book 41
Davidson, Grace 31, 37
Davies, Ralph K. 178
Debs, Eugene V. 56
De Freedericksz, Baron Alexandre
   45-47, 48, 140
Delano, Fred M. 49
Delano, Teddy 49
Del Ruth, Hampton 125-126
Dell, Floyd 103
de Mille, Agnes 155
DeMille, Cecil B. 108, 111, 146
deMille, William C. 4, 6, 55, 61,
   105, 112
Democratic National Convention
   125
Detroit 3, 9, 10, 12, 16, 18-20, 21,
   27, 32, 33, 35, 38, 40-42, 45,
   46-47, 49, 50, 110
Detroit Comedy Club 38
Detroit Fine Arts Academy 28
Detroit Free-Press 26, 28, 38, 41,
   172
Detroit High School 40
Detroit Museum of Art 48-49, 50
Diaz, Jose 170
Dickinson's Landing (Canada) 10,
   12
Diggins, Eddie 118
Dodd, Fr. Neal 31
Dog's Life, A 94, 96
Donovan, John 45, 48-49
Doolittle, Jimmy 63
Doran, Ragge 113-114
Douglas, Helen Gahagan 150
Dreiser, Theodore 137
Dumay, Henry, 31-32
Duncareen, Ireland 13, 15
Dwan, Allan 66

Eastman, Max 6, 54, 89, 100, 102,
   103, 179, 181
Edwards, Anne 62, 140
Edwards, H.D. 27
Einstein, Albert 103
Eisenstein, Sergei 6, 114, 133-140
Eisenstein, Messenger from Hell
   134
Eldridge, Fred 115
El Encanto Hotel 161
Emanuel Presbyterian Church 117
Encyclopedia Britannica 38
End Poverty in California (EPIC)
   149, 151, 156, 181
Espionage Act 96
Essanay Film Manufacturing Co. 89
Exceptional Photoplays 111
Experimental Cinema 138
Experimental Film 114

Fairbanks, Douglas 54, 95, 98, 99,
   106, 112, 122, 135, 180
Fair Week 124

Famous Players-Lasky 109, 116, 122, 123
Fanny Fern (See Sarah Payson Willis)
Fatty, Mabel and the Law 61, 90, 123
Federal Art Project 159
Federal Petroleum Administration 178
Federated Press League 105
Federation for Women's Clubs for Southern California 112
Felton, James 178
Fidler, Jimmie 6
Filmarte Theater 113-114, 132, 134
Film Folk 85, 109
Film Spectator 114
First National Studios 93, 94, 95
Fish, Hamilton 137
Fiske, Bertha 91
Floorwalker, The 92
Ford, James L. 31
Ford, J.B. 50
Ford, John Anson 91
Foster, William Z. 105, 120
Four Horsemen of the Apocalypse, The 107
Fowler, Gene 150
Fox Studios, 66, 95
Fox West Coast Theaters 132
Frank Capra: The Catastrophe of Success 63
Frick, Henry Clay 57
Fricke, Charles W. 171
Friday Morning Club 112
From Dusk to Dawn 2, 69, 71-73

Gamble, John M. 53
Garbutt, Frank 116
Gartz, Kate Crane 90, 103-105, 130
Gee Whiz, Genevieve 126
Gerome, Jean-Leon 47
Gerson, Dr. T. Perceval 74, 91
Giesler, Jerry 164
Gill, Irving 91
Gillman, Tom 14

Glyn, Elinor 117
Going to Congress 125
Goldman, Emma 56-59, 96, 102, 105, 180
Good Earth, The 174
Gould, Gloria 112
Gould, Jay 112
Graham, Earl 53
Grand Trunk Railway 10, 12, 27
Grass: A Nation's Battle for Life 141
Gray Goose, The 65
Great Dictator, The 92, 164, 165
Greaves, George Hudson 13
Greaves, John Henry 13
Greaves, Leycester 13
Greek Review, The 18, 24
Greenfield, Alice 170
Grey, Zane 150
Griffith, D.W. 61, 64, 66, 95, 112
Grosse Ile, Michigan 40, 48, 49
Guitermann, Arthur 31

Haldeman-Julius, Emmanuel 69, 70-71, 75
Hallroom Boys, The 66
Hal Roach Studios 66, 123
Hamlet (film) 112
Hammond, Ruth 63
Hans, Bella 106
Harlow, Jean 162
Harlow's Cafe 90
Harriman, Job 2, 54-55, 56-57, 67-70, 72, 75-76, 91
Harriman Karl Edward 30, 85
Harrison, Marguerite 141, 144
Harrington, Tom 93
Harry Garson Productions 127
Hart, H.A. 56
Haver, Phyllis 63
Hayden, Florence 131
Hayes, Arthur 19
Hayes, Donn W. 138
Haynes, Dr. Randolph 68, 90, 103-105
Hays, Will H. 120, 148

Hayworth, Rita 170
Hearst, William Randolph 163
Hearts of the Wild 95
High Brow Stuff 125
Himm, Carl 138
His Forgotten Wife 110
Historians' History of the World, The 37
Hitler, Adolf 162, 164, 165
Hollywood Bowl Association 91
Hollywood Citizen 117
Hollywood Crescent Athletic Club 118
Hollywood Reporter 176
Hollywood Technical Directors Institute 120, 134, 136
Holman, George T. 105
Holmes, Ross 27
Hoover, Herbert 25, 120, 133
Hoover, J. Edgar 164
Hopkins, Prynce 62, 80-81, 82, 87-88, 96-97, 102, 106
Hopper, Hedda 6, 106, 165
Hornibrook, Charlotte (Greaves) 13, 15
Hornibrook, James Hudson 15, 17
Hornibrook, John "Jack" Henry 15, 17
Hornibrook, Matthew Belsaigne 13, 14, 15, 17
Hornibrook, Thomas 15
House on Un-American Activities Committee (HUAC) 6, 167
House Special Committee to Investigate Communist Activities and Propaganda 137
Howe, James Wong 156
Hughes, Rupert 4, 30-31, 35, 37, 49, 61, 112, 116
Huguenot Settlement Plan of 1751-1753 14
Hull House 62, 103
Human Comedy, The 156
Hunker, James Gibbons, 31
Hutchins, John 113

Ibsen, Henrik 31, 34
I'd Hate Myself in the Morning 143
Ince, Thomas 108
Indiana State Journal 29
Industrial Workers of the World (IWW) 59, 96, 101-104, 105
Ingram, Rex 66, 107, 110
Intercollegiate Socialist Society 54, 85
It's a Bear 66
Ives, Alice 40

Japanese Americans 6, 145, 166-168
Jazz Singer, The 167
Jesse James 148
Jewish Telegraphic Agency 136
Johnny Got His Gun 143
Johnson, Nunnally 150
Johnson, Sir John 11
Jones, Gregory 163
Jordan-Smith, Paul 1
Julian, Rodophe 41
Julius, Emmanuel (See Haldeman-Julius, Emanuel)
Jungle, The 90
Juvenile Protective League 112

Kai-shek, Chiang Madame 175
Karno's Vaudeville 94
Keaton, Buster 110
Kelly, Paul 118
Keena, Etta, 49
Keena, James T. 49
Kennedy, Edgar 126
Kenny, Robert 171
Keramic Studio (magazine) 53
Keyes, Asa 104-105
Keystone Studios 89, 90, 123
Kid Auto Races at Venice 89
Kimbrough, Hunter 138
King, M.J. 171-172
King of Comedy 123
King's Royal Regiment 11
KTM radio 132
Ku Klux Klan 6, 145, 171

Ladies' Home Journal 95
Laemmle, Carl 6, 137
Lakerim Athletic Club, The 30
L'Amour, Louis 156
Langdon, Harry 126
Lansbury, Angela 143
Lansbury, Edgar 144
Lansbury, George 143
Lapworth, Charles 96, 98, 181
Lardner, Ring Jr. 143
Lasky, Jesse 122, 132
Laurens, Jean-Paul 45
Leavenworth Federal Penitentiary 102
Lenin, Vladimir 140
Lesser, Sol 116, 138
Levee, Mike 147
Lewis, Arthur M. 55
Lewis, Charles Bertrand, 28, 172
Liberator, The 88, 100, 179
Liberty 85, 129, 132
Liberty Bond tour 95-99, 106, 180
Lidgerwood, Imogene (Wagner) 10, 79
Lindsey, Estelle Lawson 43-44
Literary Digest 150, 151
Little Blue Book series 69
Little Cinema 111-112, 114
Little Theater 111
Little Theater Film Movement 111
Little Theater Films Inc. 112-113, 147
Llano del Rio 2, 67-70, 71, 73, 74-76, 84
Llewellyn Iron Works 56
Loeffler, Gisella Lacher 159
London Daily Herald 143
London, Jack 54, 70-71
London University 80
Loos, Anita 150
Los Angeles Citizen 71
Los Angeles City Council 69, 119
Los Angeles County District Attorney's office 103-104
Los Angeles County Grand Jury 1, 2, 4, 76, 85, 90-91, 103-105, 130, 181
Los Angeles County Museum of Art 55
Los Angeles Daily News 162, 163-164, 169-170, 175, 176, 177-178
Los Angeles Evening Express 115
Los Angeles Evening Herald 115
Los Angeles Examiner 115-116, 163, 166, 169
Los Angeles Graphic 58
Los Angeles Herald 69
Los Angeles Herald-Express 163, 169, 177
Los Angeles Mirror 177
Los Angeles Opera House 100
Los Angeles Police Department 170
Los Angeles Record 44
Los Angeles School Board 62
Los Angeles Teachers' Union 68
Los Angeles Times 2, 55, 56, 91, 114, 149, 157, 163, 165, 169, 177
Lovett, Robert Morss 105
Lubitsch, Ernst 110, 112
Lubyanka Prison 141, 144
Ludwig, Emile 170
Lumbard, A.L. 151
Lynds, Benjamin M. 131
Lynds Co. (See Wagner-Lynds Co.)

MacCameron, Robert Lee 47-48
Macdonald-Wright, Stanton 145, 158, 159
Macgowan, Kenneth 112
MacGurrin, Buckley 158, 159
Mack Sennett Comedies 66, 90
Madison Square Theater 34
Making a Living 89
Mankato, Minnesota 10, 17
Mann Act 164, 165, 166
Man's Castle 147
Manual Arts High School 62, 64, 80, 98, 126, 140
Marion, Frances 107
Marooned in Moscow: The Story of

an American Woman Imprisoned in Russia 141
Martin Dies Committee 167, 168
Martinez, Alfredo Ramos 157, 158
Martyr to His Cause, A 73
Marx, Samuel 109
Masses, The 88, 100, 103, 179
Mayer, Louis B. 137, 146, 149
Maynard, Mila Tupper 56, 62, 69, 76
Maynard, Rezin A. 69
McAdoo, William G. 98
McBride, Joseph 63
McGowan, Robert F. 126
McNamara, James 2, 56, 73
McNamara, John 2, 56, 73
McWilliams, Carey 170
Melancholiac, The 122
Melnitz, Curtis 112-113
Merriam, Frank 150, 153
Merrill's Marauders 168
Merry Widow, The 112
Mescal Water and Land Co. 69, 75
Metro-Goldwyn-Mayer studios 109, 113, 148, 149, 174, 175
Mexican Americans 6, 65, 81, 145, 157, 159, 166, 168-170, 172
Michigan Exchange Hotel 27
Milestone, Lewis 66, 120, 135
Military Intelligence Branch (War Department) 106
Millier, Arthur 114, 157
Milwaukee Leader 71
Minter, Mary Miles 116
Mix, Tom 155
Modern Times 92
Montessori school 75, 80, 81
Morgan, Jack Ainsworth 131
Morgan, J.P. 101
Mortal Clay 113
Moss, Carlton 156
Motion Pictures Producers and Distributors Association 116, 117, 120
Mozart Theater 72
Muir, Florabel 164

Murder, a Collection of Short Murder Mystery Puzzles 156
Musical Times, The 39
Mutual Studios 92, 93, 95

Nagel, Conrad 146
Name the Man 113
National Association for the Advancement of Colored People (NAACP) 177
National Board of Review of Motion Pictures 111
National Citizens Political Action Committee 144
National League of Mineral Painters 53
National Police Gazette 19
Native Americans 6
New Theater, 3
New York Call 68, 70
New York Commercial 50
New Yorker 88, 178
New York Globe 112
New York Life 31
New York Seventh Regiment Infantry, 32
Niblo, Fred 146
Nicholas II, Czar of Russia 47

Nielson, Asta 112
Nixon, Richard 144, 150
No Greater Glory 147
Normand, Mabel 61, 90, 116
Northwest Mounted Police (film) 148

Occidental Motion Picture Co. 72
O'Conner Electroplating plant 177
Office of Economic Warfare 91
Office of War Information (OWI) 168
Old and New 140
Olvera Street 157, 158-159, 160
O'Neill, Eugene 111
Orena, Acacia 53
Orozco, Jose Clemente 157

Otis, Harrison Gray 55, 60
Our Congressman 125
Our Gang comedies 1266
Our Wonderful Schools 64, 66, 109

Palladium, The 23-25
Palmer, Alexander Mitchell 101
Palmer, Frederick 108
Palmer Photoplay Corp. 108-110, 121
Panama-Pacific International Exhibition 64, 66, 84
Paramount Studios 95, 116, 124, 132, 158
Paris Art Exposition of 1900 53
Paris Society of American Painters 47
Parker, Dorothy 150
Parker, Dr. Delos L. 33
Parnassus cooperative 73-74, 84
Parsons, Louella 6
Pasadena Playhouse 103
Pasadena Tournament of Roses Association 50
Pease, Frank 120, 133-139
Pease, Mabel 135
Philadelphia Daily 71
Photodramatist 108
Photoplay 109
Piccadilly (film) 173
Pickford, Mary 96, 98, 99, 112, 134, 173
Pinkerton detectives 57
Plant, Richmond, 74
PM 144-145
Pole to Panama 136
Politi, Leo 145, 157-161, 175
Pollard, Percival 30, 31
Polytechnic High School 80
Pope Pius IX 39
Pope Pius X 39
Portrait of Present Day Mexico (mural) 158
Princeton University 131
Purviance, Edna 93, 95

Quad, M. (See Charles Bertrand Lewis)

Ralph, Elsie (Reasoner) 42, 48-49
Ralph, Julian 42
Ralph, Lester 42, 48, 49
Rappe, Virginia 88, 115
Ray, Charles 55, 61, 108, 120-121, 122
Raymond, Ray 118
Red Book 85, 122
Red Cross 181
Red Scare 88, 181
Reinhardt, Max 112
Reitman, Ben 59
Reliance-Majestic Studios 64, 66
Republican National Committee 120
Republican National Convention 120, 125
Revolutionary War 11
Reynolds, W.J. 116
Rich, Dr. Herbert 49
Rich, Irene 124
Rink, The 92
Rivera, Diego 142
Roach, Hal 62, 66, 123-125
Robeson, Paul 173
Robinson, Carlyle 96, 98
Robinson, Edward G. 142
Robinson, Gladys Lloyd 142
Rob Wagner's Beverly Hills Script (See *Rob Wagner's Script*)
Rob Wagner's Script 4-7, 26, 47, 57, 62, 79, 86, 88-89, 98, 106, 118, 120, 122, 127, 129-135, 138, 139-153, 155-179, 180, 181
Rockefeller, John D. 101
Rogers, Betty 124
Rogers, Bruce 105
Rogers, Ginger 175
Rogers, Will 116, 124-126, 150
Roosevelt, Franklin D. 144, 166
Roosevelt, Theodore, 32, 33-34
Rose Bowl 5
Rosebud Charitable Society 38

R.S.V.P. 121
Russia 46, 93, 143
Russian cinema 113-114, 133, 134, 137
Russian education 5, 62, 91, 100, 140
Russian revolution 2, 91, 134, 140
Ryskind, Morrie 151

Sacred Heart Academy Catholic School 38
Sacred Heart Review 39
San Jose Mercury News 135
San Quentin prison 170
Santa Barbara News Press 162
Santa Barbara Realty Co. 50
Santschi, Tom 61
Saroyan, William 4, 156
Saturday Evening Post 2, 85, 89, 109
Schayer, Richard 148
Schmidt, Ruben S. 171
Schulberg, Bud 136, 137
Scranton Tribune 29
Screenland 85, 89, 132
Screen Writers Guild 145
Scully, Frank 150-151
Seastrom, Victor (Sjöström, Victor) 113
Second Battle of Bull Run 39
Sedition Act of 1918 1, 101
Selig Polyscope Co. 60
Selig, William 60, 61
Selznick, David O. 175
Sennett, Mack 61, 66, 89-90, 123, 126, 127
Severance, Caroline 54
Severance Club 54, 68, 74, 85, 90, 99, 103
Shaw, George Bernard 31
Sherman, Fr. Thomas 53
Sherman, Gen. William T. 53
Sherry, Dean 168
Sherwood, Robert E. 112
Shoulder Arms 95
Sibley, Col. Henry 21

Sigma Phi 18, 22, 23
Sinclair, Mary Craig 90, 137-138
Sinclair, Upton 5, 6, 54, 90, 91-92, 96, 99, 102, 130, 137-138, 149-153, 155, 181
Singer Sewing Machine Co. 80
Siqueiros, David Alfaro 145, 157-158
Sixth Minnesota Volunteers 1, 21-22
Sixty-Ninth New York Infantry 32
Sleepy Lagoon Defense Committee 170
Sleepy Lagoon murder case 168, 171
Smart Set, The 65
Smith, Bertha Cristy 45, 48
Smith, Hal Horace 25
Smith, Herbert Booth (Dr.) 117
Smith, Martin 46
Smith, Robert L. 177
Smudge 121
Socialist Party 2, 6, 33, 54, 56-57, 85, 93, 96, 101, 149, 152, 180
Sons of Italy 158
Spanish-American War 1, 32, 33, 42
S.S. Deutschland 37
S.S. Kroonland 48
S.S. Mauna Kea 93
S.S. Minnetonka 41
Stalin, Joseph 5, 47, 134, 140, 142, 143, 161, 179
Stanford University 50
Stanwyck, Barbara 175
Stearns, Frederick S. 49
Steckel, George 51
Sterling, Christine 158
Stern, Seymour 138
Sterry, Nora J. 106, 180
Sterry, Ruth 106, 180
St. Francis Hotel 115, 118
St. Louis Life 31
Street Meeting (mural) 158
Sts. Peter and Paul Jesuit Church 38, 39, 41

Sudermann, Herman 34
Sutter's Gold 137
Swanson, Gloria 132

Taylor, Capt. Harry A. 106
Taylor, William Desmond 115-116, 118
Ten Days That Shook the World 114, 133, 134
Tessie Moves Along 122
Theater Arts Monthly 113
Theater Guild 147
Thompson, Hunter S. 25
Thompson, Vance 31
Thunder Over Mexico 137-139
Tibbett, Lawrence 63
Tinning, Bessie Jane (Hornibrook) 14, 15, 19, 20, 42,
Tinning, Jack 49
Tinning, Richard 19
Tojo, Hideki 161
Topeka Daily Herald 78
Topeka Daily Capital 78, 84, 131
Trader Horn 148
Treaty of Nantes 14
Trotsky, Leon 5, 142
Trumbo, Dalton 4, 143, 144, 156
Truthful Liar, A 126
Tully, Jim 151, 155
Turner, Frank 97, 181-182
Tweed, William "Boss" 39
Twentieth Century-Fox 162, 175
Two Wagons, Both Covered 124, 126

Uemura, Kazuhiro 168
Union Labor News Publishing 75
Union Labor Party 55
Union Reform League 103
United China Relief 174, 175
United Press 161
United States Department of Justice 1, 26, 76, 91, 96, 99,
United States Military Telegraph 10, 12
Universal Studios 95, 109, 127

University of Michigan 18, 22-25, 28, 50, 85
U.S. Bureau of Investigation 96-98, 100-106
U.S. Grant Hotel 59
U.S.S. Yosemite 32-33

Van Dyke, W.S. 148
Van Wirt, Edwin 97, 182
Van Ettisch, Raymond 115
Variety 110, 130, 176
Vernon Parish, La. 75
Vitagraph Studios 95
Volstead Act 18
von Stroheim, Erich 112
Voorhis, Jerry 144

Wachtel, Elmer 55, 106, 180-182
Wada, Yori 166-167
Waggoner, Jacob 11
Waggoner Jr., Jacob 11
Wagner, Ann Frances (Brown) 22
Wagner, Arietta 10, 17, 21, 53, 55, 65
Wagner, Arline 50, 79
Wagner, Benjamin 11
Wagner, Blake 1, 64-66, 107, 123
Wagner, Carol 83
Wagner, Charlotte 15, 16, 17, 27, 28, 50, 79
Wagner, Clarence Rangley 16, 17, 28, 32-33, 51
Wagner, Daniel 10, 11, 12
Wagner, Edith (Gilfillan) 64
Wagner, Eliza (Hawley) 10, 21
Wagner, Florence (Welch) 5, 18, 78-79, 80-86, 90, 122, 124, 127,129, 131, 139-140, 142-145, 156, 161-163, 170, 171, 176-179, 181
Wagner, Georgia 162
Wagner, Harriet 50, 72, 79, 82, 163
Wagner, Howard 162
Wagner, Jack 1, 64-66, 107, 118
Wagner, James Richard Hawley 16, 17-18, 22, 26, 50, 77-78, 83-84,

97, 119
Wagner, Jessie Willis (Brodhead) 18, 38-42, 45, 48, 49, 50-51, 53, 130
Wagner, John Henry 10, 12, 21
Wagner, Leicester 41, 49, 50-51, 53, 61, 79, 80-84, 87, 130-132, 144, 145, 161-163
Wagner, Lucy (Howard) 83, 161
Wagner-Lynds Co. 131
Wagner, Mabel (Monahan) 50
Wagner, Mary Leicester (Hornibook) 15, 16, 17, 18, 22, 26-27, 32, 42, 48, 50, 53, 55, 79, 82, 119
Wagner, Max 64-66, 118
Wagner, Rhoda Juliet (Hawley) 10
Wagner, Rob 1, 12, 16, 18, 19-20, 22, 28-32
  and animal cruelty 148
  and attitude toward ethnic minorities 25, 172-173
  and attitude toward models 43-44
  and attitude toward religion 45
  and attitude toward Germany, 106, 180-181
  and attitude toward Russia 46-47
  and Bureau of Investigation 96-98, 100, 102, 106, 180-182
  and Emma Goldman 57-59, 102, 180
  and EPIC 149-153, 181
  and Figureoa Street studio 52-53
  and ghostwriting for Chaplin 93
  and government censorship 118-120, 181
  and Llano del Rio 67-70
  and marriage to Florence Welch 77-78, 79
  and marriage to Jessie Brodhead 18, 38, 40-43, 45
  and publishing *Script* 129
  and relationship with mother-in-law 40-41
  and *The Criterion* 3, 26, 31, 32, 34
  and Theodore Roosevelt 33-34
  and *The Western Comrade* 68-71, 74, 80, 84
  death 161
  under federal surveillance 106, 180-182
Wagner, Robert 10, 12, 16-17, 18, 26-27, 64
Wagner, Robert H. "Bob" 64-66
Wagner, Sarah (Coberly) 83
Wagner, Thornton 50, 51, 53, 61, 79, 80-84, 161-162
Wagner, William Wallace 10, 21, 64
Walker, Harley M. 125
Walsh, Raoul 107
War Department 106
War of the Worlds 137
War Relocation Authority 167-168
Welch, James Miller 78
Welch, Ruth 78
Wells, Frank G. 29
Wells, H.G. 137
Wendt, William 90
Wentworth, Eleanor 69, 75-76
West, Mae 162
Western Comrade, The 3, 68-71, 74-76, 80, 84
Weston, Edward 54, 91
What I Learned in Nazi Germany 136
Wheeler, Frederick C. 56, 69, 72
Whistler, James McNeill 47
White, Stewart Edward 51, 53
White, Pearl 173
Wilde, Oscar 31
William R. Staats Co. 50
Willis, Nathaniel Parker 39
Willis, Richard Storrs 39, 49
Willis, Sarah Payson 39
Wilson, Dr. J.E. 74
Wilson, Stanley B. 68, 72
Wilson, Woodrow 1
Wolfe, Frank E. 2, 56, 69, 71-73, 76
Woman's Home Companion 85
Women's Christian Temperance Union 115

Wong, Ana May 145, 173-175
Woodhouse, John T. 26-27
Woods, Frank A. 116
Woods, Frank E. 109
Woolwine, Thomas L. 103-104
World War I 1, 6, 32, 55, 66, 80, 88, 91, 110, 158, 177
Wright, Chester M. 68-69, 75
Wrinkle, The 23, 25-30
Writers' Club 116, 117

Yale University 80
Yellow Book 28, 31
Yoke of Gold 109
Young, Loretta 175

Zeitlin, Jacob 91
Ziegfeld, Florenz 63
Zoot-Suit riots 6, 145, 168-169

ABOUT THE AUTHOR

———•◆•———

Rob Leicester Wagner is the great-grandson of Rob Wagner and the grandson of Leicester Wagner. As a teenager he worked on the Robert Kennedy and Eugene McCarthy presidential campaigns. In 1970 he was on Mrs. Medgar (Myrlie) Evers' campaign staff during her bid for the 24th Congressional District seat in Arcadia, CA. He began his journalism career in 1974 at his hometown newspaper in Sierra Madre, CA. He worked for suburban daily newspapers in Southern California, rising through the ranks from police reporter to managing editor. Outside of his general circulation newspaper reporting he wrote on a wide range of topics. He contributed crime stories for *True Detective,* automotive articles for classic car magazines and covered legal affairs for the *Los Angeles Daily Journal.* He has authored more than 20 books on automotive and architectural subjects, as well as journalism and Southern California history. His books include *Red Ink, White Lies: The Rise and Fall of Los Angeles Newspapers, 1920-1960, Witness to a Century* and *Sleeping Giant: A Pictorial History of the Inland Empire.* Since 2004 he has been working as a journalist in Saudi Arabia covering politics and religion. He was the managing editor of the Jeddah-based English-language daily newspapers *Saudi Gazette* and *Arab News.* He now works as an independent journalist in Jeddah, where he lives with his wife, Sabria, and youngest daughter, Emily.

www.ingramcontent.com/pod-product-compliance
Lightning Source LLC
Chambersburg PA
CBHW030134240426
43672CB00005B/126